RE-THINKING
CHRISTIANITY

This book is based on lectures given at Gresham College, London, in 2006.

RE-THINKING
CHRISTIANITY

KEITH WARD

ONEWORLD

OXFORD

RE-THINKING CHRISTIANITY

A Oneworld Book
Published by Oneworld Publications 2007
Copyright © Keith Ward 2007

ISBN-13: 978–1–85168–506–6
ISBN-10: 1–85168–506–5

Typeset by Jayvee, Trivandrum, India
Cover design by Transmission
Printed and bound by TJ International Ltd, Padstow, Cornwall

Oneworld Publications
185 Banbury Road
Oxford OX2 7AR
England
www.oneworld-publications.com

Contents

Introduction		vii
1.	Strange Messiah	1
2.	Embodied Wisdom	18
3.	The Cosmic Christ	33
4.	Time and Eternity	50
5.	The Triune God	71
6.	Purifying Fire	82
7.	By Faith Alone	101
8.	Critical Faith	114
9.	Eternal Life in the Midst of Time	125
10.	Apprehending the Infinite	149
11.	Christianity in a Global Context	169
12.	From Liberalism to Liberation	187
13.	A Truth that Lies Ahead	206
Notes		225
Index of Names		229
Subject Index		227

Introduction

This book is a sequel to *Pascal's Fire*, a book that expounded a specific doctrine of God, but without specific reference to Christianity. Incidentally, that makes the point that it is perfectly possible to talk of God without reference to Jesus or to Christianity, and indeed that Christianity can only be rightly understood against the background of an initial idea of God. We might expect that Christian revelation would modify that idea of God, perhaps to a great degree. But Christian revelation can hardly exist without some initial idea of God.

In this book I address the issue of Christian faith specifically. I seek to articulate and defend a view of Christianity that is coherent and plausible and integrates well with modern scientific and historical knowledge.

The main question is: 'What is Christian faith?' The main argument is that Christian faith has re-invented itself many times. I select six major slices of history to show how this is so:

- The revolution in the first generation from a Jewish Messianic sect to a gentile universal church (chapters 1–3).
- The fourth- to eighth-century development of doctrines of incarnation and Trinity by the adoption of Greek philosophical terminology. This largely occurred in what is now Turkey, and the approach is still characteristic of the Eastern Orthodox churches (chapter 4).
- The twelfth- to fourteenth-century development of doctrines of atonement, Purgatory and papal supremacy by the Roman Catholic Church. These can still be found in very traditional forms of Roman Catholicism (chapters 5 and 6).
- The sixteenth-century Protestant Reformation, rejecting the hierarchical teaching authority of the church, and re-interpreting faith as personal trust in God rather than acceptance of authoritative dogma (chapter 7). This is characteristic of many mainstream Protestant churches.

- The eighteenth- and nineteenth-century liberal response to the European Enlightenment, stressing the importance of informed critical enquiry, and the acceptance of scientific and historical study of the Bible (chapters 8–10). Liberal views exist within most Christian churches, to varying degrees.
- The twentieth-century re-thinking of Christianity in a global context, as one faith among many, with a specific vocation in history (chapters 11 and 12).

These case studies show that Christianity is essentially a diverse and developing faith. There is no one unchanging 'correct' teaching handed down from Jesus himself and preserved by some group. Different Christian groups find themselves comfortable with different 'stages' of this development. But all of them are different from what we can recover of the 'original' faith in Jesus, and all of them require modification at various points to take account of expanding human knowledge.

My argument is that Christian faith has developed throughout its history and that it must continue to do so. The general direction of development is clear – towards a more pluralistic and critical faith, committed to the cause of human flourishing and centred on liberating apprehensions of Transcendence.

In the course of the book, I develop a positive Christian theology that is both liberal and orthodox. So the book can be seen as a modern defence of liberal Christianity, and a systematic presentation of my own views as a Christian theologian.

Chapter 1

Strange Messiah

The foundation of the Christian faith is that in Jesus God personally encountered human beings. Jesus showed the nature of God's love as he healed, liberated, forgave and reconciled, as he mixed with social undesirables and was critical of religious status and hypocrisy. His disciples believed that he gave his life for them, that he was raised from death to live with God, and that through him God had acted to deliver them from evil and unite them to God for ever.

THE MANY VARIETIES OF CHRISTIANITY

I have begun with this positive statement to make it clear that I think the gospel of Jesus still has the power to speak to humans and to change their lives today. Christians now, two thousand years later, can share with the first generation of Christian disciples this faith that God encounters humans in and through Jesus, and unites them to the divine life.

In view of this, it may seem unnecessary and even presumptuous to speak of 're-thinking Christianity'. Is the Christian faith not something clear and unchangeable, which might need to be re-stated again and again, but which certainly does not need to be re-thought?

However, Christians have hardly ever been content to stay with the basic faith that I have just expressed. They cannot resist providing additional beliefs and interpretations. And these further beliefs turn out to differ from one another enormously. If you look around the world at the varieties of Christian faith that exist, from traditional Roman Catholicism to the Society of Friends (Quakers), from Coptic Christians swinging censors in Egypt to Pentecostalists speaking in tongues in Brazil, it soon becomes very obvious that there are many different sorts of Christian faith – hundreds of them, in fact.

It is a peculiar fact that many of these varieties think that theirs is the only real or true Christianity, and that all the others are mistaken in some way. But it is an evident fact that there exist hundreds of different varieties of Christian faith.

Not only that, but most of them have changed considerably over the years. The Roman Catholic Church, whose leader, the Pope, in the four-teenth century claimed absolute authority to crown and depose all earthly kings (in the Papal Bull *Unam Sanctam*, of 1302), would be much more likely now to insist on a separation of church and state. The Church of England, which forbade the wearing of vestments in the years after the Reformation, now has many ministers splendidly arrayed in full High Mass dress every Sunday. These are just two small examples, but it would be easy to find examples from almost any Christian church. Beliefs and practices change over time. It would be very odd if they did not.

So there are many forms of Christian faith, and they change in many ways. There is not just one Christian faith, which has remained unchanged ever since it started.

SEARCHING FOR JESUS

But is there perhaps an unchanging core underlying all these differences? That is one question that lies at the basis of these reflections. To answer it, I will need to go back to the beginning of Christian faith, and at least we know where and when that was. It was north of Galilee, near Caesarea Philippi, when Jesus of Nazareth was first explicitly said to be 'the Christ', the Greek word for the Messiah, by his disciples. The event is recorded in the Gospels, when Peter, in response to Jesus' question, 'Who do you say that I am?' is recorded to have said, 'The Messiah of God' (Matt. 16:16; Mark 8:29; Luke 9:20). Strangely, the Gospels record that Jesus then sternly commanded the disciples not to tell anyone. But there, surely, we have the origin of Christian faith, belief that Jesus is the Messiah, God's anointed.

That seems clear enough. Unfortunately, it is not clear at all. A critical historian, looking at these texts, might suspect that the writers, or their sources, had just made up this episode. There are plenty of critical historians who doubt whether Jesus made, or was aware of, any claim to be the Messiah. Since the Gospels were probably written at least forty years after the death of Jesus, though they no doubt depend on sources that are earlier, there was plenty of time for early Christians to have invented all sorts of stories about Jesus that were only loosely related to the facts. We know that the Gospel writers thought Jesus was the Messiah. But might this not have been a belief that grew up after the death of Jesus, or perhaps one with which Jesus was rather uncomfortable (thus his command to the disciples to keep quiet)?

And this is the problem. There have been at least three main 'quests for the historical Jesus', the first culminating in the work of Johannes Weiss and Albert Schweitzer. These were attempts to say what Jesus was really like, underneath what most historians would say were the probably embroidered and partly conflicting accounts in the Gospels. Albert Schweitzer thought that Jesus was a prophet who preached that the world would end very soon, within one generation. But Jesus was wrong, and so we certainly cannot today take Jesus' beliefs as a reliable guide to truth. The later 'quests', from Ernst Kasermann to Gezer Vermes and John Dominic Crossan, do not entirely accept Schweitzer's view, though they admit its importance. They focus on different aspects of the possible life and teaching of Jesus. Crossan, for instance, contends that Jesus was a cynic philosopher, teaching renunciation of possessions and family and living a peripatetic life, who was largely misunderstood by his later followers.[1]

The fact is that there are still as many different theories about what Jesus was really like as there are varieties of Christianity. Indeed, there are more, if you include all the non-Christian views. Of course all these theories agree that the Gospels – our only real source of information about Jesus – cannot be assumed to be completely accurate without a good deal of further argument. And we must agree that, if we are looking at the Gospels as historical documents, any historian would be justified in treating them with the critical suspicion that is appropriate for any ancient document.

FOUR GOSPEL ACCOUNTS COMPARED

The best way to approach the Gospels is to possess a 'synopsis' of the Gospels, a text that places different Gospel passages alongside one another. Then you can read all the Gospels in parallel, side by side, note similarities and differences between them and try to account for the sometimes quite large differences of emphasis and presentation between them.

I will take one quite important passage and compare the treatment of it in the four Gospels, in order to assess what historical value we can give the Gospels. I will take the account of the women visiting the tomb of Jesus. I will divide the accounts into sections, to make comparison easier. It will be seen that there are marked disagreements, which reflect in part the different interests of the Gospel editors. The conclusion will be that the differences are marked enough to render the exact original history uncertain. So the critical historian is justified in thinking that the historical Jesus might not be just like the Jesus of the Gospels. However, it will also become clear that the Gospels were not meant to be literally exact historical records. So I will argue that it is reasonable to take them as generally reliable records of a person who had a unique unity with God, and who understood his life as realising a Messianic vocation. And that, I suggest, is all that Christian faith requires of our knowledge of the historical Jesus.

The accounts go as follows:

- In Mark 16:1–8, A. Three women, Mary Magdalene, Mary the mother of James and Salome went to the tomb with spices, B. when the sun had risen. C. They saw that the stone had been rolled back. D. Then they saw a young man in white E. who told them to tell the disciples that he would go before them to Galilee. F. But they said nothing to anyone.
- In Matthew 28:1–8, A. Two women, Mary Magdalene and 'the other Mary' went to the tomb B. before dawn. C. They saw an earthquake and an angel rolling away the stone, and the guards trembled at the sight. D. The angel sat on the stone, and E. invited them into the tomb, and told them to tell the disciples he would be seen in Galilee. F. They ran and did so.

Matthew's account differs in almost every detail from Mark's, though both agree that some women visited the tomb and found it empty, and were told by someone to expect appearances of Jesus in Galilee. Matthew has heightened the miraculous elements in the story. The angel is definitely not just a young man, but descends from heaven with an earthquake. The women tell the disciples at once, and Matthew says that they are joyful as well as fearful. The story in his hands is less cryptic and puzzling than in Mark.

- Luke 24:1–12 records that A. A number of women, including Mary Magdalene and the mother of James, went with spices to the tomb B. at dawn. C. They saw the stone had been rolled back (as in Mark). D. They entered the tomb, and two men in white appeared. E. They do not say that Jesus will appear in Galilee (in Luke's Gospel Jesus appears only in or near Jerusalem). F. The women told this to the disciples, who did not believe them.

Luke agrees with Matthew and Mark that Mary Magdalene and James's mother were there, that the tomb was empty and that there was some sort of apparition, communicating that Jesus had been raised from death. But Luke puts a longer speech into the mouths of the 'two men', and does not speak of Jesus appearing in Galilee. This reflects his general tendency to write poetic literary pieces (it is Luke who gives us the songs of Mary, Zechariah and Simeon). He also makes Jerusalem a more important focal point in his telling of the story of Jesus.

- John 20:1–13 has A. Mary Magdalene come to the tomb alone B. while it was still dark. C. The stone was already rolled away. F. There is no angelic appearance at that point, but she ran back to tell Peter and the 'beloved disciple'. Later, back at the tomb, D. she saw two angels in white, and then she saw Jesus, whom she took to be a gardener.

John has Mary Magdalene, an empty tomb and angelic appearances. Otherwise, his account is quite different from that of the other three Gospels. It concentrates on an appearance of Jesus himself to Mary Magdalene, not recorded elsewhere.

The main point here is to see that the Gospel accounts of the same event are different. So they are not all literally accurate in detail, but more like different memories collected from different sources, and worked into a larger narrative, the shape of which partly dictates the account that is given. Mark is abrupt and puzzling (Mark's original Gospel, or the original text we have of it, ends here). Matthew is concerned with supernatural wonders. Luke gives a literary flourish, and does not hesitate to omit mention of Galilee, though presumably he had heard of such appearances. John comes from a quite different angle, and is mainly interested in Mary Magdalene as the first person to see the risen Lord.

This short example shows how the Gospels present differing perspectives on a core of events, accounts of which have been passed on in different oral traditions. The events as we have them have already been interpreted twice, first by oral re-telling, and then by the Gospel writers. So what we have is not how things actually happened, but how different people interpreted the disclosure of God that came to them, or their teachers, through events of Jesus' life, accounts of which had been passed on orally for a number of years.

The emphasis is on diversity (there are four different accounts), interpretation (each account is from a distinctive perspective) and disclosure (each is meant to evoke a disclosure of the presence and purpose of God). There is no concern for unanimity, matter-of-fact dispassionate recounting and strict literal historical accuracy. This is enormously important for considering the character of Christian revelation in the Gospels. It is not one coherent literal account of the life of Jesus. Gospel revelation lies in a number of different interpretations of or reflective responses to disclosures of God that occurred in and through Jesus' life and teachings, accounts of which were treasured because they continued to evoke such disclosures.

JESUS AS MESSIAH

Recognising that we are really investigating what the different Gospel writers thought Jesus was like, or how they wanted to present Jesus to others, what then can we say about the historical Jesus? To help in this task, we need to analyse the Gospel records in detail, noting the differences and similarities between them. This has, of course, been done by many biblical commentaries, and there is no point in doing again here what has been done so often. So what I shall do is to take one standard commentary on the Bible – the *Oxford Bible Commentary* (ed. John Barton and John Muddiman, Oxford University Press, 2001) – as a reliable guide to what most contemporary biblical scholars would say about the biblical writings.

The contributors to this commentary include Baptists, Anglicans, Eastern Orthodox and Roman Catholics, so they are not biased in one direction. The wide degree of consensus among them is testimony to the real gains that have been made in biblical scholarship over the last 150 years, despite the many divergent interpretations that remain possible.

This reflects the great amount of historical and literary analysis and research that has been carried out, bringing out much more clearly the original contexts and complex layers of meaning in the biblical texts. No theological assessment of Christian faith can be made intelligently without taking the findings of this biblical scholarship into account. I would go so far as to say that any exposition of biblical teaching that fails to refer to and use the conclusions of the scholarly community cannot be taken seriously as an account of the 'true meaning' of the texts.

Bearing that in mind, and given that the Gospels are the only evidence we have for the life and teachings of Jesus, what sort of picture of Jesus might we come up with? That is, what picture of Jesus is presented by the synoptic Gospels, the Gospels of Matthew, Mark and Luke?

I am sure there is more than one picture that we might have. But we would certainly have to say that Jesus was believed to be the Messiah, so that is a relief! But what does that mean? There might be a dozen different meanings of the term 'Messiah', and in modern Judaism there are.

One place to begin is to look at the infancy narratives of Matthew and Luke (there are none in Mark and John), to see what they say about Jesus. He is said to be the 'Son of God' (Luke 1:35), to save people from sin (Matt. 1:21), to be King of the Jews (Matt. 2:2), to be the glory of Israel and light of the gentiles (Luke 2:32).

His job, according to the Song of Zechariah, is to deliver Israel from her enemies (Luke 1:78, 79). People are depicted as looking for the liberation of Jerusalem (Luke 2:38) and Israel from their enemies, for a King of the royal house of David, who will be the ruler of a free Israel, a righteous and peaceful people, with a Temple to which all the people of the earth will go.

So the Messiah is King, or ruler, of Israel, able to forgive sin, to punish the enemies of Israel and to bring peace and freedom to the nation. But there is something odd about his rule. He will 'rule over the house of Jacob for ever' (Luke 1:33), and his rule will never end. This is to be more than a political revolution. It will transform the conditions of human existence.

GOSPEL CONCEPTIONS OF THE KINGDOM OF GOD

Other parts of the synoptic Gospels spell this out in more detail. In the transformation of existence that the Messiah brings, all wickedness and evil will be destroyed – 'unless you repent, you will all perish' (Luke 12:40). On a cataclysmic day of divine judgment, the righteous will shine like the sun, but the wicked will be cast into a furnace of fire (Matt. 13:40–43). The Son of man will come in glory with his angels, and the twelve apostles will rule over the twelve tribes of Israel (Matt. 19:28). When will this be? Jesus, according to Matthew, says that some of those who hear him speak will 'see the Son of man coming with power in the Kingdom' (Matt. 16:28).

It is important to note that when these words were written down Jesus had been dead for some years. What was expected was that he would return in glory with angels, punish the wicked and call the righteous into his kingdom, centred on a new Jerusalem Temple. Abraham, Isaac and Jacob and the prophets will return to earth, and under the rule of the twelve apostles Israel will be the ruler of a new world. Its members will be the righteous and those who have repented and been forgiven by God.

The picture is very much centred on Israel, and it seems to be much more concerned with moral righteousness than with faith in Jesus. Not much is said about gentiles, and the main emphasis is on the liberation and cleansing of Israel, though it seems that righteous and penitent gentiles will be admitted to the renewed Jewish community, and the wicked expelled, because of their good or bad deeds, however much faith or belief they claim to have (Matt. 25).

The good news that Jesus proclaimed was that God is coming soon to establish the liberation of Israel and to execute judgment on all hypocrites and oppressors. Now, before that 'day of wrath', he offers forgiveness to all who repent, and he promises a restoration of a renewed and purified Jewish faith, when Torah will be kept to the letter (Matt. 5:18, 19) and in its deepest spiritual sense.

Jesus heals, liberates (exorcises demons) and forgives sins. By these acts, and by his amazing and total power over material nature, the wind and the waves, he shows that the kingdom is already near ('If it is by the finger of God that I cast out demons, then the kingdom of God has come upon you': Luke 11:20).

The kingdom comes near in the person of Jesus. It will grow rapidly until the harvest, when good and bad will be separated for ever. For Jesus did not come to bring peace, but to bring 'division' (Luke 12:51), to divide good from bad, the penitent, humble, poor observers of Torah from the hypocritical legalists and the rich. Jesus' concern is not primarily with the righteous, for the righteous will enter the kingdom in any case. Jesus' vocation is to call sinners to repent (Luke 5:31), and his mission is only to Israel (Matt. 15:24).

It is hard to miss the note of urgency in this message. 'The time is fulfilled' (Mark 1:15). 'The kingdom is among you' (Luke 17:21). 'Even now the axe is laid to the root of the trees' (Matt. 3:10). So the writers of the synoptic Gospels wait for the coming of the Son of man in glory very soon – the day or hour is not known (Matt. 25:13), and he will come unexpectedly (Matt. 24:50), but it will be in their own generation ('This generation will not pass away before all these things take place': Mark 13:30). They expect a restoration of Jerusalem, a kingdom of those who are righteous and of the penitent who are forgiven, and the expulsion and torment of all the unjust (the vast majority, it seems – 'the gate is narrow and the way is hard, that leads to life, and those who find it are few': Matt. 7:14). In the new Jerusalem, the twelve apostles will rule the twelve tribes, the prophets and patriarchs will be raised to eat and drink in the kingdom, and, though many gentiles will be present, it will basically be a Jewish monarchy under the rule of a transfigured and glorified Jesus, who is the 'Son of man'.

THE FIRST REVOLUTION – REVISIONS TO
EARLY IDEAS OF THE KINGDOM

This seems to be the faith, or one form of the faith, that is expressed in the synoptic Gospels. I do not think it is possible for anyone to hold this faith today in the exact form in which it is written. To put it bluntly, in that generation Jerusalem was destroyed and the Jews scattered throughout the earth. These Messianic hopes were confounded by history.

The extraordinary thing is that this did not destroy Christian faith, faith in Jesus as Messiah. But – and here is the vital point – it did change the nature of that faith in major ways. At the very start of Christian history, there was a radical change in Christian beliefs and expectations. Far from being a changeless faith – 'once delivered to the saints' – it changed sharply and unexpectedly in its earliest years, in the very first generation.

There may have been changes in faith before the Gospels were written. Some biblical scholars think there were, and that the synoptic Gospels are themselves re-writings of earlier beliefs, which may have been both more varied and quite different in their Messianic views. The non-canonical writings give some hints of this, but we are limited to guesswork, since there is no hard evidence of earlier beliefs. But we are on firm ground in saying that the Messianic beliefs of the synoptic writers – an immanent restoration of the twelve tribes and of true Torah in Jerusalem, under the kingship of Jesus – were rapidly adjusted in quite basic ways, as generations came and went, and Israel was wiped off the political map.

There are five main ways in which this strand of belief in the synoptic Gospels was adjusted. First, when the first generation of disciples had all died, it was clear that the return of the Son of man in glory was not something that was going to happen before the apostles had died. The apostles all died, and that belief had to be revised.

Second, the kingdom would not be the return of the twelve tribes to Jerusalem under the rule of the twelve apostles, and the liberation of Jerusalem from Roman occupation. The Romans destroyed Jerusalem and the Temple, and the Jews were scattered throughout the world.

Third, the kingdom would not consist in the restoration of Torah in all its fullness for all those who were truly righteous or at least truly penitent. In fact quite soon (mostly owing to the arguments of Paul), Torah was abandoned by Christians, and emphasis came to be placed on faith in Jesus rather than in rigorous moral commitment to justice and the love of God.

Fourth, Jesus was probably not going to return to earth with angels and be a political ruler to whom the whole world would pay homage. History was going to continue perhaps for a few thousand years, or even longer.

And fifth, there was probably not going to be a sudden cataclysmic ending of history, an actual day when the dead would be raised and judgment would be executed on living and dead. There would hardly be room on earth for all the dead.

Christians now, two thousand years later as I write, have no option but to give up the first of these beliefs, that Jesus would come before all his hearers died. Some Christians claim to believe that the coming in glory may still happen at any moment. But in doing so they are giving up the whole synoptic stress that the time of Jesus was virtually the end of historical time. They are revising the synoptic belief in a major way. They are certainly not preserving unchanged the synoptic belief that Jesus would return before the death of the last disciple. They do not believe what the apostles believed.

The second belief, about the rule of the apostles in Jerusalem, is also historically obsolete, and Christianity has long since abandoned any thought of being a movement for the renewal of Judaism. It has become a totally separate religion, often regrettably and shamefully hostile to its parent faith.

The third belief, in the universal acceptance of Torah, was discarded as an almost wholly gentile church came into existence, based on faith in the redeeming death of Jesus and not primarily on moral renewal. It can be a shock to modern Christians to discover that the theme of moral renewal is more prominent in the synoptic Gospels than the theme of redemption through the death of Jesus – though of course the synoptic Gospels do stress that following Jesus by renouncing all possessions and family ties (not something that the modern churches usually emphasise) is of primary importance.

The fourth and fifth beliefs, in the return of Jesus to rule in Jerusalem and in a decisive Day of Judgment, have not been definitively rendered obsolete as the first three have been. But the churches have on the whole come to make a distinction between political and spiritual rule, and to accept that political life will continue in accordance with its own principles, while the task of the churches is to preach a 'spiritual kingdom' that will leave politics mostly untouched. They do not expect Jesus to be an actual king in Jerusalem.

The notion of Judgment Day has also been displaced from a precise time in history. Considering the vast number of the dead, who could not be accommodated on the earth, the Judgment is now normally taken by theologians not to describe a future historical event, but to symbolise some state beyond history in which humans will be faced with what they have made of their lives and with how they really stand before God.

A SPIRITUAL INTERPRETATION OF THE KINGDOM

What the churches have done to these fourth and fifth beliefs suggests a possibility for re-interpreting the teaching of the synoptic Gospels. Jesus is not a political king, it may be said. He is a spiritual king, the ruler of human hearts. His kingdom is not part of the world; it is a fellowship of the spirit. It is hidden from the world, growing secretly within human lives and bearing fruit in lives of active love. This spiritual reality is real, but it is not physical. The king is not a physical person in a physical court. Those are images for the subordination of the human spirit to the divine Spirit, as it was embodied in Jesus. The images are of physical things. But they symbolise realities of inner experience, of the relation of the soul to God, and of the actions of God in relation to the soul.

At the end of history, which will surely come, though perhaps in thousands or even millions of years, all human deeds will be made clear before God. Then, not on earth but in a spiritual realm, love will at last rule purely and solely in the community of those who have loved God truly. And those who have continued to reject God, if there are any, will be excluded from the divine life by their own choice. That is the great division, the 'harvest', of which Jesus speaks. But when it will be, what exactly it will be like, or who will be accepted in and who excluded from it, are things we cannot know.

Again, the images are of physical things. But what they symbolise is a reality that is not part of this physical universe. In that spiritual realm, there are real individuals, communities and relationships. It is not after all just a matter of what goes on in individual minds. But it is a realm beyond this physical spacetime, a world in which the presence of God is clear, and inner feelings and attitudes are made clear. It is a realm of clarity, of transparency, when 'the secrets of all hearts will be revealed'. On this account, Christian belief is about the reality of a spiritual world, beyond this physical cosmos, with different forms and structures, yet touching this world through personal experiences and responses.

Can we apply a similar process of spiritualisation to the first three beliefs I listed? We could say that the imminence of the kingdom will not be a temporal imminence, but a spiritual one. The return of Jesus in glory will not be at a specific time in this cosmos. Just as Jesus is not, and will not ever be, a physical king in Jerusalem, so Jesus will not return tomorrow or the next day. He comes to us imminent in every time, taking us into that glory which is the very life of God. The kingdom comes as Christ comes to the soul, taking each moment of time into the presence of the eternal God. It does not come externally and physically, for the kingdom is within.

It comes in every moment, with the promise of final glory and the life-giving, healing, liberating touch of the presence of Christ.

What of the return of the twelve tribes to Jerusalem and the rule of the apostles, and the liberation of Israel from her enemies? These too can be seen as images of things in the physical world that represent realities of the spiritual world. The return of the tribes represents the unity of God's people in 'the city of peace', the heavenly Jerusalem, a renewed community of the Spirit, living, as the apostles did, by the presence and power of Christ. The 'enemies' are not political powers, but spiritual forces from which we are liberated. We live, not necessarily in a historical time without wars, but in the peace of God, by which the heart is never separated from the source of its life.

Finally, the restoration of Torah and the triumph of justice is not something that will happen in history. The external rules of Torah represent the spiritual reality that was always the true heart of Torah, the rule of the Spirit. The churches have been right when they have made faith in Christ central. For faith is not just acceptance of a set of intellectual beliefs. It is the willing submission of the heart to the rule of the Spirit of Christ. And that is the only way to live justly, not out of obedience to rules, but from a life transformed by the power of love.

So the main beliefs of the synoptic Gospels can be given a spiritual interpretation as a set of symbols that speak overtly of physical things, but speak more deeply of the realities of the spiritual world in which God interacts with human souls, and calls them into union with the divine life.

Spiritual interpretation is familiar to Christians in other contexts. The notoriously difficult final verse of Psalm 137 reads like this: 'Happy shall they be who take your little ones and dash them against the rock.' The reference is to the children of the Babylonians, in whose cruel deaths the Psalmist apparently rejoices. Those who pray the Psalms today would not associate themselves with such vengeful feelings. When they say that verse they often identify the 'little ones', the Babylonian children, with their sins, and identify 'the rock' with Christ. Thus they can honestly bless those who dash their sins against the rock of Christ, so that sins are destroyed and their power broken. That is almost certainly not what the original Psalm-writer had in mind, but it expresses a deeper insight into the universality of sin and the mercy of God. So it uses a wider reflection on the Bible as a whole and on Christian life to give a spiritual interpretation to the text.

Another obvious case from the New Testament is the hymn of Zechariah: 'He has raised up a mighty saviour for us ... that we would be saved from our enemies' (Luke 1:69–71). Israel was not physically saved from her enemies. It was destroyed completely by Rome. Again, the enemies must be regarded as spiritual enemies, and salvation must be regarded, not as political liberation, but as spiritual fulfilment and liberation from sin. So we see that spiritualisation is not foreign to Christian interpretation. It is central to it.

The 'spiritualisation' of the synoptic symbols is indeed already carried out in a radical transformation of the idea of Messiah. Jesus is not an earthly king, liberating Israel by armed insurrection. He is the suffering servant of God who redeems his people by the self-sacrifice of love. That much is clear in the Gospels. But did they not, nevertheless, hope for an imminent return of the Messiah in glory with the angels of God, who would liberate Israel politically and nationally? It seems to me, and it seems to most scholarly readers of the synoptic Gospels, that they did. And that suggests that the writers had as yet an incomplete understanding of the relation of God to human history.

That is not surprising. They believed the earth was the centre of the universe and had only existed for four thousand years – they could count and name the generations of humans since the creation. They believed Israel was the centre of God's purposes for the earth, and that the 'whole world' had its boundaries not too far from Israel – the gospel of the kingdom could be proclaimed in all of it within a generation. They believed the world, their entire universe, would end fairly soon, and that there was very little human history lying ahead in the future. So, seeing Jesus as the fulfilment of the history of this small universe, they saw him also as its end and culminating point. They were living in 'the last days', and in their generation the whole of human history had reached its apogee, its culmination and climax. There was nothing still to come, no new knowledge, no discoveries to make or major social changes to occur, no new art or music or literature. For them, God's historical purpose for the earth was ended, and the divine creative Spirit had little left to do, except to bring the news of the kingdom to the hearing of the remaining, rather small population of earth, before the whole created universe – basically, the earth – was brought to an end.

THE NECESSITY FOR RE-THINKING BELIEFS

For most modern people who accept a scientific view of the universe, all these beliefs have to change. We know that we live on a small planet circling around a rather small star, in a galaxy of a hundred thousand million stars. We know that there are a hundred thousand million galaxies in the known universe, and that there may be other universes, other spacetimes, beyond this one.

So when the Gospels say that 'the stars will fall from heaven' (Matt. 24:29) just before the Son of man returns, we know that we cannot take that literally. The destruction of this planet would have negligible effects on most of the universe, and would certainly not bring it to an end. The apostles may have taken the statement literally, because they thought the stars were just lights in the sky.

So we only have two choices. Either they were simply wrong. Or, though they were mistaken about the physical facts, there was a truth that was symbolised by talking of stars falling from the sky. As a matter of fact, that truth is spelled out for us in the Old Testament passage that is quoted – Isaiah 13:10, which is part of a prophecy of the destruction of Babylon by the Persians. The symbol of falling stars is a symbol of the destruction of politically oppressive powers at a particular time in history, not of the end of the world.

So we might plausibly think that what the Gospel symbols are referring to is the destruction of the politically oppressive power of Rome. Such a historical interpretation makes good sense of many of the symbols of the 'end of the age' in the synoptic Gospels, and enables us to say, without dissimulation, that these prophecies were realised within a generation.

Yet most biblical scholars agree that such an interpretation, which is basically that of the British theologian C.H. Dodd, and is often called 'realised eschatology', does not give the full spiritual sense of the text.[2] The writers were still looking for the coming of the Son of man with glory in the future, and still thought that it would be soon. Our vastly expanded view of the cosmos renders that belief obsolete, in a literal sense. Yet it can still have a future, if symbolic, content. It can be saying two main things. First, that history will not end with complete extinction and emptiness. At the end of history, whenever it comes, humans will be raised to the presence of God, the God who was seen in the person of Jesus, and reap the rewards of their lives. Second, this is not just an event that can be ignored in practice because it will happen only in the far future. On the contrary, it confronts each one of us as an imminent possibility. Each moment of our lives is under God's judgment, and we cannot tell when our earthly lives will end. We will be wise, then, to be ready for 'the coming of the Son of man', the fully manifest presence of Christ, as though it might occur at any time. I think that is an intelligible interpretation of Jesus' teaching about the Day of the Lord that comes 'like a thief in the night'.

Moreover, within the synoptic Gospels, we can discern important strands that imply that the judgment will not literally come soon. Though Jesus' mission was only to Israel, he does speak of many people entering the kingdom from east and west, from the corners of the earth. He does pronounce judgment on Jerusalem and the Temple, prophesying that the kingdom will be taken away from them and given to others. He does say that the kingdom is to be preached throughout the world. He does institute a 'new covenant', for what is presumably a new community. And he does, in Mark, speak of a people whom he will ransom by giving up his life (Mark 10:45). All these things seem to point to a future in which a new covenant will be worked out over a fairly long history and expand throughout the known world. As we now know, the extent of the known universe is vastly greater than the disciples could have imagined, and that will force a re-interpretation of the symbols of the kingdom in a more spiritual and a less physical or literal direction.

What seems to follow from all this is that there are many beliefs in the synoptic Gospels which we cannot share – where the kingdom would be, what it would do for Israel, when and how it would arrive. Christian faith has changed in important ways since the days of the apostles. But that does not mean such beliefs are no more than mistakes. We must try to see what the spiritual reality was to which such beliefs may have pointed, and ask how they might be rephrased in the light of new knowledge or in the new contexts of our own day. That is why it is important to re-think Christianity. Christian faith needs to be re-thought in each new place and generation. That is something that may become apparent as a result of a reflective and informed study of the synoptic Gospels and the form of their beliefs about the nature and coming of the kingdom of God. It is part of the essential nature of Christian faith that it should be open to constant change and creative exploration. The history of Christianity is the history of such change, and I have suggested that a fairly radical change was necessary even in the first generation of Christians, as they had to revise their beliefs about the nature of the Messiah and the kingdom of God. It should be no surprise if we find that we have to undertake a similar task in our own day. It can be an encouragement to realise how very radical the change of beliefs was at the very inception of Christian faith.

Chapter 2

Embodied Wisdom

The eternal Wisdom of God is the pattern on which the universe is formed. It directs the universe towards the emergence of intelligent and responsible forms of life. John's Gospel teaches that this divine Wisdom can itself take finite form. It has done so on earth in Jesus, providing an ideal of human life in relation to God, and mediating through that human life the purpose of God to unite human lives to the divine life. Thus the Wisdom of God, manifest in the person of Jesus, is the way to eternal life with God.

THE GOSPEL OF JOHN

The Gospels of Matthew, Mark and Luke have different ways of approaching Jesus and of seeing his work. But they are recognisably similar in seeing Jesus primarily as the Davidic King of Israel, the fulfilment of the ancient Hebrew prophecies, bringing the kingdom of God near in his own person, having absolute authority over nature and over the powers of evil, teaching mysteriously in parables, healing, exorcising and forgiving sins, living in the last times, shamefully put to death, but triumphant over death, seen by the disciples, and soon to return in glory with the angels to usher in God's full rule on earth.

Many things remain unclear in the synoptic Gospels. Was Jesus, as Mark implies, very liberal in his attitude to Torah (Mark 7:19), or was he, as Matthew says, wholly orthodox in teaching that Torah must be kept to the smallest detail (Matt. 5:18)? Was his mission solely to Israel, or did he have an interest in the wider gentile world also? Did he foresee the existence of a 'church', a continuing sacramental organisation, or was he wholly focused on the imminent coming of the kingdom, in which his inner group of twelve would rule the re-united twelve tribes?

Those are tantalising questions to which there is no clear answer in the Gospels. The absolute authority and divine commission of Jesus to be King of a renewed Israel and the one who brings God's rule near to those who meet him is undoubted. But there is much we would like to know about Jesus that we can never know. And that problem, of what Jesus was really like, is magnified enormously when we turn from the synoptic Gospels to the Gospel of John.

Here we seem to be in a completely different world of thought. The prologue to John's Gospel begins in a way that contrasts strongly with anything in the synoptic Gospels. It does not start with the beginning of Jesus' public ministry, as in Mark. It does not even start with his birth, as in Matthew and Luke. It begins in eternity, with the eternal Word of God, existing before all time.

All the Gospels, of course, were written for groups of believers who already accepted the resurrection faith that Jesus lives, and so their accounts are meant to inspire their present faith, not simply or even primarily to give a factually correct account of Jesus' daily diary. As has often been said, the Gospel accounts of Jesus are written in the light of faith in the resurrection. They are meant to be catalysts to evoke and inspire faith in the risen Lord of the church. They are not the sort of records a neutral historian would write.

Furthermore, each Gospel is written in a way that expresses the main interests and character of the final editor of the text. Mark presents Jesus as a supremely powerful and authoritative, yet strangely secret, Messianic King. Matthew is interested in Jesus as the new Moses – one even greater than Moses, but teaching the inner meaning of Torah, the divine Law. For him, Jesus is the supreme teacher and ruler of the Jews. Luke writes a poetic account of Jesus as the universal Saviour (he is the only synoptic writer to use that term of Jesus), who is especially concerned with the poor and who reaches out to gentiles as well as Jews.

The Gospel of John is quite different from the three synoptic Gospels. In it, Jesus is not presented as a secret Messiah who speaks cryptically in parables about the kingdom of God. Jesus is presented from the first as the eternal Word made flesh, taking human form. He speaks openly about his identity with God, about being the bread of life, the light of the world and the true vine. He calls for belief in him as the Son of God, not for belief in the coming kingdom (the term 'kingdom' appears only in two passages, John 3:3–5 and 18:36). He speaks, not in parables designed to conceal the truth, but in long discourses that make the truth quite plain, if shocking to his hearers. He speaks, not of the kingdom of God, but of the gift of eternal life, which he himself gives. John's Gospel begins with the eternal Word, and as it comes to an end the apostle Thomas kneels before the risen Jesus and says, 'My Lord and my God', the only explicit confession of the divinity of Jesus in the Gospels.

THE DISTINCTIVENESS OF JOHN

John is not writing about a different Jesus, though he puts many of the events in a different order and context than the synoptic Gospels – for instance, he states that the Last Supper was not a Passover meal, as the synoptic Gospels thought it was. But John is giving a very different picture of Jesus, and it is the one that has become most influential in the Christian churches. Many Christians have even tried to combine the accounts of John and the synoptics into one seamless story. But that cannot be done very convincingly, and it is very important to see the theological implications of this.

The reason it cannot be done is this: the synoptic writers simply did not have the concepts (of *Logos* or Word, for instance) that John used. The idea of Jesus 'coming down from heaven' does not occur to them. For them, Jesus is a human being who is raised up to supreme authority by God, who is indeed designated King in the kingdom of God, and who may therefore be seen as having divine authority. Perhaps the idea of incarnation is implicit in these views. But it never becomes explicit, as it does in John – 'the Word became flesh and lived among us' (1:14).

That is the distinctiveness of John's Gospel. It makes explicit what is only implicit in the synoptics – the divinity of Jesus, and the fact that the kingdom of God is the person of Jesus, or the eternal life that he gives. This is connected with two other distinctive features of John's Gospel. John has begun to speak of those who oppose Jesus as 'the Jews', and so to distance the new Christian church from what was to become Rabbinic Judaism. And

John speaks explicitly of the Holy Spirit, the Paraclete or Advocate, as one who is sent by Jesus to continue the work of Jesus in the world. The idea of a Trinitarian God, Father, Son and Spirit, is much more explicit in John than it is in the synoptic Gospels, where, if it is even present, it does not play a major role.

You could easily read the synoptic Gospels and never think of the idea of the Trinity – the relation of Jesus, the Father and the Spirit is never defined clearly at all. After all, the concepts of God the Father, the Son of God (applied to Solomon, David or the people of Israel) and the Spirit of God are all found in the Old Testament, but never give rise to a doctrine of the Trinity. But in John the mysterious diversity-in-unity of Father, eternal Word of Son, and Spirit whom Jesus 'sends' lays the groundwork for the long debates about the Trinity that were to characterise the Christian church of the third and fourth centuries.

These three distinctive emphases of John – the divinity of Jesus, the parting of the ways from the Jews, and the idea of God as Trinity – have been a very ambiguous blessing to the church. The idea of Jesus' divinity has been used to support the idea that all who reject Jesus are damned, since they are thereby rejecting God. John's insistence that 'the Jews' killed Jesus has encouraged persecution of the Jews in much European history. And arguments about the Trinity have led to mutual accusations of heresy and an orthodox insistence on abstruse points of philosophy that are hardly comprehensible to anyone.

In some ways, we might wish that the churches could have stayed content with the simpler gospel of the synoptics, a message of the lordship of Jesus as the one who mediates the presence and liberating power of God to the community founded in his name. Yet that was not possible, as the churches passed beyond the boundaries of Judaism, where the hope for the Messiah was generally understood, if not always accepted. In the gentile world, unfamiliar with and largely uninterested in Jewish hopes for the coming of a renewed kingdom of David, things had to be put differently. In the Greek-influenced culture of the eastern Mediterranean there was available the concept of the *Logos* or Wisdom of God, on which the known universe was patterned. The idea is found particularly in the *Timaeus* of Plato, for which the visible world is patterned on the invisible archetypes used as a template by the World Architect.[3] It was effectively used by the Jewish thinker Philo of Alexandria. John was able to appeal to this concept of the world archetype, the archetype that contained that of humanity as the culmination of the known world, and state that it had taken visible form in the human life of Jesus. The very word 'Messiah', translated into Greek as *Christos*, lost its Jewish connotations, and 'the Christ' was henceforth understood as the eternal archetypal Wisdom of God, embodied in the person of Jesus.

JOHN'S GOSPEL AS A THEOLOGICAL REFLECTION ON JESUS

This was a brilliant imaginative move, but was it true to the historical Jesus? The vital and essential theological insight here is not the answer you give to that question, but the perception that it is a real question. It is not easy simply to fuse the Jesus of John and of the synoptics into one figure, as though there was no problem. John's Jesus knows he is the eternal Word, he publicly teaches that he is and he goes to his earthly death knowing that it cannot touch his essentially divine being. The synoptic Jesus knows indeed that he has supreme authority and power over nature and forces of suffering and evil, but he does not publicly teach that he is Messiah. He knows he will die, and looks for his return with the angels of God in a glorious Davidic kingdom. But, at least in Matthew and Mark, his life ends with those tragic words from the cross, 'My God, my God, why have you forsaken me?' followed only by a loud cry (Matt. 27:46; Mark 15:34; significantly omitted by Luke, for whom Jesus is more in command of the situation).

How are we to deal with these facts? Once you see there is a problem here, you are bound to accept that there is room for legitimate disagreement. The foundation of Christianity in the person of Jesus is clear – Jesus was seen as the source of the new life of liberation from sin and unity with God through the Spirit that the first Christians experienced. What is not clear, however, is exactly what Jesus himself taught and how he taught it.

Most biblical scholars agree that John's Gospel was the last to be written, and that it reads more like a series of prayerful reflections on the person of Jesus than like a set of verbatim records of what he actually said. In other words, it is the synoptic Jesus who speaks in cryptic parables who is likely to be nearer the real historical figure.

If you agree with that majority view – and I do – it will follow that Jesus did not speak the actual words he speaks in John's Gospel. They are literary constructions of great sophistication that put into the mouth of Jesus perceptions of the person of Jesus that in fact belong to one group of early believers. So, for instance, Jesus never said, 'I am the bread of life.' This arises out of reflection on the Eucharistic practice of the early church. It may be a God-inspired reflection. But Jesus never said it. It must be seen as a meditation on the person of the risen Christ that arose in the early church.

In other words, Christian faith changed between the teaching of Jesus, which was more like that recorded in the synoptic Gospels, and the writing of John's Gospel. Jesus did not teach these things explicitly to the apostles, who remembered them and saw them written down. Early Christians made them up as they reflected on their own experience of the risen Christ, and on the oral memories that still existed of Jesus' actual life and teachings.

It is important to say two things here. First, John's Gospel is the teaching of some of the earliest Christian believers, not of Jesus himself. Second, that does not mean it is a betrayal of what Jesus actually said, or a misunderstanding of Jesus. It just means that things moved on, even in the first Christian century, so that things got stated in new ways, and implications were seen in the faith which had not been explicit, or even thought of, at an earlier time. Again we see that change is a central feature of Christian faith from the very first. So it is a complete misunderstanding to think of the faith as passed down from Jesus to the church unchanged and perfectly formed, to be protected against all innovation for ever.

But if Jesus never said things like 'I am the bread of life', how can they be accurate insights into the person of Jesus? The simplest way to understand this is just to put all these statements into the third person. Where the text says, 'I am the bread of life', read that as 'Jesus is the bread of life.' And do the same with all Jesus' reported remarks about himself in John's Gospel. Then you will see more clearly that these are expressions of beliefs about Jesus. The beliefs may well be correct, even though Jesus did not utter them.

What Jesus actually said is probably like the statements recorded in the synoptic Gospels. Then John comes along and says, 'Given these statements, and our experience of the presence and power of the risen Christ in the church, we believe the following things about Jesus: he is the bread of life, the true vine, the good shepherd, and the eternal Word of God.' In writing his Gospel, John puts these beliefs into the mouth of the character 'Jesus'. And that is how you can have an accurate insight into the person of Jesus, using terms that Jesus himself would probably never have used. The problem disappears, unless you insist that the historical Jesus must have said whatever John's Gospel attributes to him. Then, and only then, you do have a major problem. For John's Jesus speaks in a different way, and says quite different things, from the synoptic Jesus.

By the time John's Gospel was written, three beliefs had begun to develop in the Christian community, or at least in parts of it. Jesus was regarded, not so much as a Jewish Messianic King, but as the embodiment of the eternal Word of God. The church saw itself not as a Jewish Messianic movement, but as a distinct Eucharistic community, separate from Judaism. And Jewish monotheism ('Hear, O Israel: The Lord our God, the Lord is one,' quoted by Jesus from Deuteronomy 6:4, in Mark 12:29; perhaps it is significant that Matthew and Luke omit this phrase) was beginning to be complicated by the thought that there were eternal relationships between the Father, from whom all things come, the Son who says, 'I am in the Father and the Father in me' (John 14:11), and the Spirit 'who proceeds from the Father' (John 15:26).

These relationships were by no means clearly worked out. In John it looks as though the Son and the Spirit are subordinate to the Father ('the Father is greater than I': John 14:28), and it is not obvious that the Spirit (the Paraclete or Advocate) is fully divine, as opposed to being some sort of emanation from God. It took the church hundreds of years to develop what we now think of as the doctrine of the Trinity. But in John the idea of God's relationship to the world is already more complex than that of Messianic Judaism.

THE MINIMAL CONDITIONS FOR JESUS' AUTHENTICITY

Most scholars think that Mark's was the earliest Gospel (possibly written just after 70 CE), and John's the latest (possibly about 90–100 CE in Ephesus). This is not a huge gap, and given that some of Paul's letters are earlier than any of the Gospels, and are more similar to John than the synoptics in many ways, it is not certain that we can speak of a linear development between the synoptics and John. The sort of thinking found in John could be as early as anything we have in the New Testament. It was probably not, as some scholars used to claim, a late and alien import into Christianity.

Nevertheless, the consensus of opinion is that Mark is more likely to represent something nearer the historical Jesus than John and Paul (Paul probably never knew Jesus historically). So it seems likely that Jesus was a Jewish Messianic teacher and healer, whose words and acts reflected the Jewish context of an urgent expectation of the kingdom of God, fulfilling Hebrew prophecy and bringing Jewish history to a significant climax.

It is perfectly in accord with such a view to believe that Jesus was a teacher and healer of extraordinary charisma who brought the stern judgment and the unlimited loving-kindness of God near to those who met him. He had a power of releasing people from disease and the power of sin. He communicated the presence of God in his own person. He taught that Israel was at a point of crisis, and had to choose life or destruction within his generation. He went to his unjust death to give his life so that God's rule, God's kingdom, might be realised. Then, amazingly, he appeared after death to many disciples, assuring them that he was alive with God. Soon afterwards, the Spirit of God fell on the disciples with power, transforming them from disappointed nationalists into fervent evangelists for the liberating, self-giving, death-defying love of God, which they had seen in Jesus.

Jesus might not have thought of himself as the eternal *Logos*. If he had, it is almost incomprehensible that the synoptic writers should not have mentioned it. Jesus might not have thought of the church as a largely gentile community with a millennial history ahead of it. If he had, the synoptic writers would not have included teaching about the return of the Son of man in glory within their generation. Jesus might not have thought of God as Trinity. If he had, the synoptic writers would surely have had some record of such teaching, which is in such stark contrast with Jewish orthodoxy.

But the synoptic Jesus could have thought of himself as the Messianic King, destined to rule in the kingdom of God, and thus as having divine authority and power. He could have thought of himself as the ruler of a people of a new and inward covenant with God, primarily for Jews but open to the whole world. And he could have known that his knowledge of and feeling for God was far beyond that of his contemporaries, and that he had a unique power to forgive sin and give the divine Spirit to those who followed him.

In fact these are, in my view, the minimal conditions that Jesus would have to fulfil in order to be thought of, as Christians do think of him, as the Lord and Saviour of the world. If he had not thought of himself as having absolutely supreme power, under God, I do not think he could plausibly be seen as the human agent of God's act of supreme revelation and liberation. If he had not thought of himself as originating a new and deeper covenant with God through his own self-sacrifice, he could not reasonably be thought of as the Lord of the universal church. And if he had not had a sense of a unique intimacy with the divine, he would not be worthy of the worship that the Christian churches have subsequently accorded him.

There are scholars who disagree with this, and who think it is possible to delve beneath the synoptic testimony, to discern a rather different Jesus – perhaps a cynic philosopher, or perhaps a prophet of imminent divine judgment to be mediated by a coming Son of man, different from himself (Albert Schweitzer's view). We have to accept that such things are possible.

We have seen that John's Gospel is not an actual record of what Jesus said, but the construction of a drama in which Jesus, the main character, expresses an early churches' theological understanding of the historical Jesus. So it is overwhelmingly probable that the other Gospels do the same sort of thing. They do not preserve an exact record of Jesus' teaching. For a start, they are in Greek, not the Aramaic that Jesus probably used for his teaching. The exact wording differs in different Gospels. So, while in my view they probably record memories of Jesus' teaching which are likely to be accurate in many respects, they are placed in the context of a story told to present a particular perspective on Jesus, that of the editor of each Gospel.

That means the historical Jesus could have been different from the figure presented in the synoptic Gospels, as he is different from the figure presented in John. It is almost impossible to say with any certainty in what ways he would be different. Did he call himself the 'Son of man', and think of himself as Messiah? Did he really heal and exorcise quite as effectively as the Gospels record? Did he talk with Satan in the desert, walk on water and turn water into wine? Personal answers to these questions will depend on your view of what you think is likely, in general.

If you do not think Satan and the demons exist, you will regard such episodes as legendary accretions, based on pre-scientific diagnoses of mental illness, perhaps. If you think that lives of holy people usually get exaggerated very quickly, so that miracles are multiplied and magnified over the years, you may think that Jesus' healing ministry may have been real, but not quite as dramatic as depicted in the Gospels. If you doubt whether miracles occur, you will be sceptical about Jesus walking on water, multiplying loaves and fishes and turning water into wine.

What you will not be able to say is that these things must have happened just because the Gospels say they did, and for no other reason. If the Gospels are typical of religious writing in general, they are quite likely to contain hyperbole and a good deal of projection of present beliefs back onto the hero figure of the narrative. So maybe you should just say that Jesus must have been the sort of figure who could unsurprisingly give rise to these accounts, within a few years or decades of his death, and within the lifetimes of many who knew him personally, especially some of his closest disciples.

He was, it seems reasonable to say, a person whose personality and teaching attracted the total loyalty of his disciples. He was a Galilean Jew, teaching with immense wisdom, healing the sick and mentally distressed, calling disciples to give up everything to follow him, choosing an inner group of twelve and going freely to his death with a strong expectation of the coming of God's kingdom. He was a man with a sense of divine calling, and his disciples continued to feel that he had commissioned them to continue that calling, of preaching the coming of the kingdom, the forgiveness of sins and union with God.

But it is not unreasonable to say more than that. The most important point of all is that the Gospels only came to be written because his disciples thought Jesus was the Messiah, the King in the coming kingdom. There is nothing absurd in the thought that he might have accepted such a role, even if in a non-traditional sense. The apostles believed Jesus had appeared to them after his death, confirming their mission. If we take their testimony seriously, those resurrection appearances greatly increase the probability that Jesus' life also manifested the power and wisdom of God in extraordinary ways. While certainty is unobtainable, the element of the miraculous in the Gospels need not be regarded with total scepticism.

However, it is clear that the Gospel editors recorded the life of Jesus in the light of their belief in his resurrection, and depicted the divine glory already shining through the events of his life. That is how the Gospels were written, and that is the sense in which they should be read.

JOHN'S INCARNATIONAL PERSPECTIVE

If Jesus did think of himself as having a Messianic role, as the synoptic Gospels say that he had, then the path to John's wider cosmic vision of the role of Jesus can be seen as a development of themes implicit in Jesus' actual teaching, though not explicitly spelled out there.

What that would imply is that Jesus was a fully human person, with the cognitive limitations that are proper to human beings. Brought up in a rural Galilean setting, his forms of thought would be those of his society. His ideas of God, of the Messiah and of God's kingdom would have originated there. If he had a deep and intimate sense of unity with God, that would shape those ideas in original and unique ways. But it would not place completely new ideas – that of *Logos* for instance – in his mind.

It is intelligible to suppose that he could have come to believe that he was the prophesied Messianic King, and that he could have re-shaped the idea of Messiah in a new way, as a Suffering Servant rather than as a conquering king. That was, after all, part of the tradition, though it had not quite been interpreted in that way before. But it is hardly intelligible to suppose that he could have thought of himself as the eternal Wisdom of God, incarnate in the flesh.

The latter idea, developed in John, can be seen as interpreting Jesus' life as if from the divine point of view. If Jesus was King in the kingdom of God, if God's power was channelled through him to heal and forgive, if he had authority to call people to commit themselves totally to him, and thereby forge a renewed Israel, a new community of the Spirit, then Jesus had a unity with and a transparency to God that was wholly unique in his society. It could be said that the Wisdom of God was working in and through him, or that the divine love was being expressed in him in a paradigmatic way. The anointed King of Israel and the divine Wisdom expressed in a human life are, in Jesus, one and the same.

Thus, though Jesus in all probability never said the things ascribed to him in John's Gospel, that Gospel gives a deep insight into the nature and role of Jesus in the history of God's relations with humanity. It puts Jesus' ministry into a wider context, and permits us to see it in a perspective that is not yet fully global but extends beyond the boundaries of Hebrew prophecy and tradition.

Jesus lived within those boundaries. John writes for a church that has moved beyond them, that regrettably has even separated itself from them, and shows how the kingship of Christ not only brings Hebrew faith to a point of crisis and fulfilment, but discloses the nature of God to the whole known world. That nature is one of compassionate wisdom, unlimited love, and concern for the welfare of all who are oppressed and enslaved by desire, hatred and indifference. It is embodied, incarnated, in the person of Jesus, now seen not as the king of a small tribal nation, but as a person in human history in whom the eternal love of God is embodied in time.

As John's Gospel inaugurates an incarnational theology, it moves towards stressing the importance of history as the arena of God's embodiment, and thus as having an importance and a potential too great for it to be peremptorily ended by divine fiat. This move is not fully made by John, for in his Gospel 'the world' is still opposed to 'the spirit', as something to be hated and eschewed. It would take further theological reflection before a truly sacramental theology, one that sees matter in general as at least potentially capable of manifesting the divine life, became established.

THE DIVERSE PERSPECTIVES OF THE GOSPELS

There is immense theological importance in the fact that Christian faith has, not one detailed historical account of the life of Jesus, but four different perspectives on his life, all seen through the lens of the resurrection and stamped with the interests and characters of their editors and the different groups for which they wrote. There have been many attempts throughout history to 'harmonise' the Gospels, to make them provide one coherent account of Jesus' life. But this seems to miss the importance of the fact that the Gospels all present Jesus' life in different ways and from different points of view. Perhaps the most helpful way to approach the Gospels is to use a synopsis, and try to find the spiritually important reason for the differences that you will then find in the different Gospel accounts of the same incidents or teachings.

This fact could be used in a negative way, as if to say, 'There, I told you so. The Gospels are not accurate. Christian faith is a fiction.' But the fact of the diversity of the Gospels has a wholly positive message to give. It is a message about the very nature of Christian revelation. The message is this: Christian revelation is not divinely dictated words in a book. It is found in human, partial, historically conditioned and diverse perceptions of Jesus as the person in whom God acted to disclose the divine nature and purpose, to liberate humans from sin and unite them to the divine life by the gift of divine love.

The perceptions are subjective, in the sense that they are governed, as all perceptions are, by the cognitive and psychological limitations of the observers. Yet they are perceptions of an objective act of God, an act of self-disclosure and human liberation. If these perceptions be genuine, they really do apprehend an act of God in Jesus, though the perception is coloured by the nature of the observers.

The person of Jesus, for his disciples, genuinely shows what God is, and it is intended by God to do that. God, through Jesus, genuinely liberates humans from sin and unites them to the divine. God is present and active in Jesus in a historically unique way – unique because of his place in history as a plausible claimant to Messianic status.

A neutral historian, who may be agnostic about divine acts of disclosure and liberation, can only record that Jesus was believed to be Messiah at least within a few years of his death, and that Jesus' life was recorded to express that belief, using materials collected in oral traditions springing from those who had known Jesus personally.

If a historian is sceptical about God, that historian will naturally be sceptical about any claims that someone is God's Messiah. Jesus will be seen as a deluded prophet. But a historian who is open to seeing divine acts in history may well be persuaded that in Jesus there is a distinctive disclosure of God as forgiving, suffering love, and the origin of a distinctive way of achieving unity with God through the inner working of the Spirit that was in Jesus.

What no historian, sceptical or Christian, can say is that we know *for certain* exactly what Jesus said and did. It is not open to us to appeal to the words ascribed to Jesus in the Gospels in order to settle some point of doctrine or church practice now. For those words have already been interpreted by some church group, and perhaps – as in almost all of John's Gospel – changed quite radically from anything that Jesus would have said. The appropriate thing to say, then, is not, 'Jesus said this; so that is binding for all time.' It is, rather, something like, 'John puts these words into the mouth of Jesus, and that shows John's understanding of and response to Jesus. We might revere or admire John. But he is not God. What we must do is make our own response to the living Christ, taking into account John's response, but not making it binding on everyone for all time.'

The Gospels may then be seen as collections of oral traditions about Jesus, presented in the light of subsequent experiences of God's continuing activity among the disciples, and intended to evoke new disclosures of God through Jesus in those who hear or read them.

THE NATURE OF CHRISTIAN REVELATION

I have suggested that within the synoptic Gospels we can see changes already being made to what seems to be the original form of the expectation of the imminent arrival of God's rule primarily among the Jews in Jerusalem. These changes enabled the early disciples to come to see God's rule in a wider and also more inward perspective, as the rule of the divine within all people. John's Gospel takes this process a step further, changing the perspective again to that of an eternal divine decree for all the earth. But the focus of these diverse perspectives is the same, the life of Jesus as the place where Hebrew prophecies are fulfilled and God ordains a new covenant for a new Israel, through the self-giving passion of a man who was filled with the Spirit of God, and was able to give that Spirit, at least in some way and to some extent, to his disciples.

The common message of the Gospels is this: in Jesus God acts to disclose the divine nature and unite humans to that nature in a new and distinctive way. God really and objectively acts. But that act must be discerned by observers whose own reactions will strongly influence what is seen and recorded. The four Gospels present diverse discernments of God's act in Jesus. Difference is not contradiction. But the lesson to learn is that there is no interpretation-free revelation. The revelation of God in Jesus is from the first both perceived and interpreted by its observers. We have the records of their discernments, and the main point of those records is to evoke further discernments in us, discernments that will express the diversity of our own characters and cultural–historical contexts. In that way, Christian revelation calls for continual re-thinking.

The point can be made quite sharply by contrasting Christian with Muslim revelation. In Islam, the Qur'an is believed to be the actual words of God. Of course, they need to be understood and interpreted, so there is much room for diversity there too. Nevertheless, the words themselves are not interpretations. They are divine speech. In the Gospels, we do not have the actual speech of God – even though some Christians talk as though we do. What we have are four rather different interpretations of what all the

Gospel writers believed to be divine actions in Jesus. What Christians have in writing, therefore, are interpretations of, testimonies to, divine action. But that divine action is believed to be in a living human person who wrote no books and recorded no exact words for posterity.

When Christians respond to divine revelation, what they hear are the interpretations of revelation given by others. There is not a very firm foundation here for any doctrine of verbal inerrancy or for one final closed and absolute interpretation. There is, rather, an invitation to enter into a community of diverse and continuing interpretations.

Any claim to absolute, unrevisable truth in the Gospels is undermined by the foundational and unquestionable fact that we have no means of direct access to the life and teachings of Jesus. We know only what the Gospel writers thought. We know that they did not entirely agree with one another, and that they were themselves probably developing and changing in understanding even as they collected and edited what came to be the Gospels we now have.

Thus it is that the sources of Christian revelation tell us that such revelation, by its foundational nature, is dynamic, personal and pluralist. It is dynamic, for it expresses and calls for changing understandings and perspectives. It is personal, for it is rooted in the life of a person who always retains his otherness and hiddenness, since that person is always described for us at second and third hand. It is pluralist, for it encourages a diversity of interpretations, a diversity that is required if anything like an adequate understanding of the personal mystery of Jesus Christ is to be attained.

Christian revelation is, therefore, never entirely bound by the words of a written text. The written Christian texts are interpretations, perspectives, personal testimonies. They encourage and inspire us. We may believe that they themselves are inspired by the creative Spirit of God. But what they do for us is not ask us just to agree with them, as though that was the end of the matter. They ask us to be creative, to interpret for ourselves, to uncover our own perspectives, to respond to the God who was in Jesus (and who still is in the risen Lord) in our own way and from our own vantage points, while acknowledging all the limitations of those vantage points.

This view of revelation seems to be present in the very form the New Testament takes, and it may have important implications for the way we, in our own age, approach and interpret Christian revelation in the Bible.

Chapter 3

The Cosmic Christ

C hristian faith began with visions of the risen Christ, inspiring the disciples with a vital and joyful sense of new life. The Spirit of God came to them with power, confirming their belief that Christ somehow continued to live in and through them. They were called to be the body of Christ, the physical presence and vehicle of the risen Lord. So today Christians are baptised into the death of Christ, renouncing selfish desire. They rise to live with Christ, as the Spirit of Christ lives in them, liberates them from desire and unites them with the life of God. They look for the final victory of the love of God and the abolition of evil, when the eternal Christ, who was known on earth in the person of Jesus, will be seen as he truly is, in the glory and beauty of God. All this is encapsulated in the Church's shortest liturgical creed: 'Christ has died; Christ is risen; Christ will come again.'

PAUL AND THE APOSTOLIC SUCCESSION

It is generally agreed that Paul's first letter to the Christians at Thessalonica is the earliest writing in the New Testament, predating the Gospels as we now have them. Being an occasional letter, it does not give a full account of what Paul taught the converts he made in his journeys around the Mediterranean Sea. But it is clear that he taught that Jesus 'died and rose again' (1 Thess. 4:14), and that Jesus will return in judgment, when all who believe in him will rise to live with him for ever (4:17). The message of the first Thessalonian letter is of deliverance from 'the wrath that is coming' (1:10), for those who live with Christ.

It seems that Paul has changed a message of Jewish renewal into a message of salvation from coming universal judgment by faith in Christ, which is to be preached to all people. Jesus is not proclaimed as the Jewish Messiah, but as the universal Saviour from the judgment of God. There is a theological problem left to be resolved here, since the Judge and the Saviour are in fact the same God. It has yet to be worked out just what the relationship between divine judgment and salvation is. Nevertheless, in Paul's earliest extant letter, the kingdom of God is not regarded as the restoration of the Temple and of the true Torah in Jerusalem, but as life with Christ when the earth has been purged of evil.

Since this letter predates the Gospels, this is not a change from an early gospel teaching to a later Mediterranean salvation cult. Nevertheless Paul's teaching seems to have been from the first significantly different from that of the apostles appointed by Jesus. The difference is not disguised by the New Testament. Indeed, it is emphasised.

When Paul writes his own account of his conversion from Pharisaic Judaism to faith in Jesus, he makes a point of saying that he was an apostle not 'by human commission' or human authorities, but directly from God (Gal. 1:1). The historical Jesus did not appoint him. Neither did the other apostles. He thrust himself upon them, claiming direct revelation from the risen Jesus. He says that he did not confer with any human being, or consult with the apostles. Only after three years did he visit Peter in Jerusalem for a fortnight, seeing in addition only 'James the Lord's brother' (Gal. 1:16–19).

Acts 9:26–31 gives a different account of when Paul visited Jerusalem and whom he met there, but, if Paul did indeed write the letter to the Galations, presumably the account in the book of Acts is less accurate. Fourteen years later, Paul writes in Galatians, he went back to Jerusalem and saw the leaders of the Jerusalem church, whom he names, in this order, as 'James and Cephas (Peter) and John', arguing the case for the legitimacy of his mission to the gentiles. 'But', he writes, 'those leaders contributed nothing to me' (Gal. 2:6). They offered him the right hand of fellowship, but apparently they did not lay hands on him or ordain or consecrate him in any sense. The 'apostolic succession' was evidently pretty weak, if it existed at all, in the first-generation church.

There is therefore a precedent in the New Testament for becoming an apostle by direct private revelation from God. It seems likely that most of the leaders of the early gentile church, being in line from those first appointed by Paul and his colleagues, would have had little or no contact with the original twelve apostles.

That original twelve, as we have seen, were to have been rulers over the twelve re-united tribes in Jerusalem. When Judas hanged himself, a 'twelfth man' was appointed on the grounds that he was one who had followed Jesus from the earliest times and was a witness to the resurrection (Acts 1:22). This function must have died out with the death of the last witness, so the idea of 'apostle' must have changed a second time. It then became, in Paul's sense, 'one sent by God to proclaim the kingdom', a leader of mission. Paul calls Peter the apostle to the Jews, and sees himself as the apostle to the gentiles. Paul does not seem to see himself as under the authority of Peter or of the other apostles at all. So the idea of a succession of bishops, or leading ministers of the church, their authority passed on from one to another, looks as if it grew up naturally enough as a way of organising a rapidly growing group of churches. It was an innovation – a natural and perhaps even an inevitable one – in and by the early church. Yet again, change seems to be of the essence of the new faith, change virtually forced by rapidly changing circumstances.

THE FIRST COUNCIL OF THE CHURCH

Paul was largely responsible for an even bigger change than this. The change is recorded in Acts 15, at what is sometimes called the 'first council of the church' at Jerusalem. The problem was whether gentile converts to faith in Christ should keep Torah, including being circumcised, or not. Many passages in the New Testament show that this was an ongoing dispute between Paul and the Jerusalem apostles. In Galatians (2:4), Paul writes of 'false brethren', sent to spy on the freedom from Torah that Paul's converts enjoyed. James, 'the Lord's brother', sent delegations to try to make converts keep Torah. Peter was reluctant even to eat with gentiles until he had a threefold vision from God encouraging him to do so.

In short, all those who had actually known Jesus were in favour of keeping Torah. This fits with Matthew's insistence on keeping Torah, put into the mouth of Jesus (5:16–19). But it was Paul who won the argument. The Council of Jerusalem came to a compromise decision, giving up circumcision, but insisting that the kosher food laws should still be kept. As we know, those laws too were given up quite soon after that.

So the early church moved rapidly from being a Jewish Torah-observing sect to being a gentile movement without any written law. It seems likely that the Jerusalem apostles and their followers continued to observe Torah until they became extinct, vanishing from history with the destruction of Jerusalem in 132 CE.

There are one or two peculiarities about the account of the Jerusalem Council. Peter describes himself as the one chosen to preach to the gentiles, whereas Paul had called Peter the apostle to the Jews. Then it is James, not Peter, who says, 'I have reached a decision ...' All we can say is that there is unclarity about who is leading the Jerusalem church, and about Peter's role in the church. There is also unclarity about just what Jesus' own attitude to keeping Torah was. In view of these unclarities, it is not fitting to be too dogmatic about exactly what the situation was. But it does look as though those who had known Jesus expected Torah to be kept, and that this did not prevent them agreeing that it need not be kept, in a new situation in which many gentiles were becoming disciples.

The first-generation church did not hesitate to change what many thought to be the literal teaching of Jesus, in view of new circumstances. In other words, they tried to be true to the spirit of Jesus' teaching, rather than be tied to the letter of what Jesus might have said.

THE RENUNCIATION OF TORAH

That is absolutely central to Paul's teaching. 'The letter kills, but the Spirit gives life,' he writes (2 Cor. 3:6). I have commented on Paul's attitude to the law in my book, *What the Bible Really Teaches* (SPCK, 2004), and I will not repeat that here. The bottom line is that Paul in effect replaces the whole Torah for gentile Christians, so far as it concerns other human beings, with the command 'Love your neighbour as yourself.'

Paul has plenty of strong moral views, and he insists that Christians are called to the highest moral code they know. But he abandons the idea of a revealed religious law, a Torah or Shariah. In its place he puts the person of Christ, the life of service and self-sacrifice Jesus exhibited, and the 'law of the Spirit', working inwardly in each human person.

It would undermine the whole tenor of Paul's teaching to take his expressed moral views as a new religious law. His moral exhortations are responses to the disclosure of God he has found in the risen Lord, not laws binding on other disciples for all time. New disclosures are possible and even invited – he approves of 'prophecy', of speaking in the Spirit, and of new revelations of the will of God.

He changed the apostolic teaching of obedience to Torah because of what he believed were new promptings of the Spirit. So it seems that we follow his teaching best if we feel we may, and often should, change his moral teachings, if and insofar as we find them restricted by social context, lack of knowledge, or unreflective acceptance of the conventions of his day. This, it seems to me, is true of what Paul says about slavery, about the place of women and about some issues of sexuality. If we follow Paul's teaching and example, we should not answer a moral question by saying, 'The Bible says ...' We need to ask, 'What makes for true love of neighbour, in the light of Jesus' self-giving love and unity with the Spirit of God?'

That may lead us, as it led Paul, into conflict with the views of other Christians. The point is that, if our knowledge grows and our social contexts change, then we must be prepared to change our beliefs appropriately. That is the teaching of Paul, and it renders impossible any insistence on strict obedience to whatever beliefs he happened to have when he wrote his letters, in very different contexts and historical situations.

Paul and Peter, after their respective visions, were responsible for a huge shift in belief, involving a renunciation of the very basis of Messianic Judaism, obedience to Torah. This shift was not due to the teaching of Jesus, though it was obviously not felt to be out of line with the spirit of Jesus. If that is what characterised the first generation of Christian belief, we might expect that Christian beliefs might change again in major ways in subsequent generations.

The New Testament thus seems to say that Christian beliefs were not given by Jesus to the twelve apostles to be guarded and protected without change for ever. They were developed within the church as disciples reflected on the disclosure of God that came to them both through the historically remembered Jesus (in the Gospels) and through their new experiences of the risen Lord (in the letters).

What the Christian church in subsequent generations might therefore look for is not an insistent repetition of ancient doctrines, but a re-evocation of the primal disclosures that had led to the formation of the church, in quite different contexts that will naturally lead such disclosures to be formed and expressed in changing ways.

Christian faith is a continually renewed encounter with the God who was disclosed in a paradigmatic way in Jesus Christ, and who continues to be disclosed in new ways in the church, the community or set of communities that seeks to make the spirit of Christ present in every age.

EARLY TEACHING ABOUT JUDGMENT

As in the Gospels, so in the New Testament letters there are rather different understandings of just how people are to be united to God through Jesus. Unlike the Gospels, the letters are not very interested in the life and teachings of Jesus, except in a general way. It is assumed that Jesus must have lived a sinless life of total obedience to the divine Father. But what matters is that Jesus died to liberate people from sin, that he was raised to life by God and that human history will culminate in a judgment in which he will play a central role, giving eternal life to all who are united to him.

Specific Jewish concerns about the Messiah and the restoration of a Davidic kingdom are quietly replaced by universal human concerns about divine judgment on evil and the possibility of liberation from evil and deeper unity with God. In the first letter to the Thessalonians, Paul sees the world as estranged from God, imprisoned by evil, greed, pride and hatred. This is the world that killed Jesus, and each person must share in the sacrifice of the cross, being crucified to the world as he was crucified by it.

Paul sees Jesus as conquering evil and death, raised to the immediate presence of God, and living an incorruptible and imperishable life in God. God raised Jesus from death, and each person can share in the resurrection life, being raised with Christ to glory.

Paul sees human history as culminating in a final destruction of all evil and in the *parousia* of Jesus. That is perhaps best thought of as the full manifestation of the beauty of Jesus' humanity, transfigured by the unimpeded presence of God, a beauty in which all can share as the cosmos itself is transformed into a new and more glorious form of being.

That is a picture that captivated many of Paul's hearers, and gave rise to many communities who saw themselves as salvaged from a world of cruelty and despair, and raised with Christ to new life in God. It is a picture that still has the power to speak to a world that remains largely corrupted by greed and violence, and that desperately needs the new life that Christ can give. But in the letters we can see this picture taking a number of different forms.

We can only speak with caution about a development in Paul's own thought, since scholars do not agree about which letters were actually written by Paul. If 1 Thessalonians and Romans were both written by Paul, the former early and the latter late in his life, we can trace a definite development of view. The later view can also be found in the letters to Ephesians and Colossians, but some scholars think those letters may have been written by someone else, maybe a later follower of Paul. Again it is necessary to read a good commentary, and again I recommend the *Oxford Bible Commentary* as an excellent place to start.

Whatever your views on authorship, it remains true that there are different perspectives on the crucifixion, resurrection and return of Christ in different letters. This emphasises the point that diversity of perspective is an integral part of Christian revelation. It is not something to be regretted, but rather something to encourage us to form our own perspectives, in the light of our reading of the Bible and our experience of the Spirit in the contemporary church.

The perspective of 1 Thessalonians, and even more of 2 Thessalonians (probably not by Paul), strikes me as rather harsh and severely judgmental (that is, of course, from my perspective!). Paul in the first letter to the Thessalonians sees Jesus as returning within his generation. He writes, 'We who are alive, who are left until the coming of the Lord, will by no means precede those who have died' (1 Thess. 4:15). This seems to me very short-sighted, if only because it allows no time for the message of salvation to be proclaimed throughout the whole world.

It has moved beyond the symbolic thought-world of Jewish thought, which presented political events in the guise of cosmic catastrophes, and which seems most clearly evinced in Mark 13. It has moved into a statement about the end of the world and the resurrection of the dead within a generation. If that had happened, we would never have been born and would never have had the chance of eternal life with God.

In 2 Thessalonians the return of Christ becomes harshly judgmental, for 'he will come with his mighty angels in flaming fire, inflicting vengeance' (1:7, 8). Such thoughts of vengeance are deeply rooted in biblical thought, and in the underlying thought that terrible evil cannot go unpunished. The unjust will be subject to 'everlasting destruction' and exclusion from the glory of God.

That perspective of harsh and purely retributive justice is present in the New Testament. The unjust will be punished, apparently with no hope of remission, and excluded from God's presence for ever. But this is a very odd perspective on the disclosure of God in the person of Jesus Christ, who came to seek and to save the lost, not to condemn them. When, in Luke's Gospel, James and John wanted to call down fire on a Samaritan village, Jesus (in some manuscripts) said, 'You do not know what manner of spirit you are of; for the Son of man came not to destroy men's lives but to save them' (Luke 9:55).

Just as James and John misunderstood Jesus' message, so it seems that the writer of 2 Thessalonians did not fully understand the love of God shown in Jesus. That misunderstanding has endured through the centuries, and there are still Christians today who think that God will send the unjust into torment for ever. Somehow they fail to see the contradiction between supposing that there is a God of unlimited love and supposing that God will torment sentient beings for ever, without hope of release.

JUDGMENT AND GOD'S LOVE

The question is: what will a God of unlimited love do to those who have chosen the path of evil? Some notion of retribution and punishment does seem appropriate. Even a God of unlimited love could not simply grant eternal life to those who continue to choose evil. Eternal life implies a unity with the divine life, and in that life there can be no evil, selfishness or hatred. So the evil are excluded from the glory of God by their own acts.

Moreover, some form of retribution seems appropriate and just. If by your actions you cause great suffering or deprivation to others, it seems just that you should come to realise this, and to feel what such suffering is like. That does not merit a literally everlasting punishment, but it does merit some form of disadvantage or form of life that will bring you to feel the harm you have caused. This will not, however, be nothing more than the infliction of pain because you have done wrong. A truly just retribution would be some form of life that might bring you to a true understanding of the nature of your own evil acts. Perhaps it would most appropriately be immersion in a world of the sort of greed and hatred that you have helped to create. True retribution could be your being forced to experience the consequences of the evil you yourself have caused. The damned create their own Hell, and imprison themselves in it.

True retribution is not simply the infliction of pain by another agent, even by God. There must be an internal connection between the pain and the evil acts that have brought it about. The punishment should be thought of as the experiencing of the world your evil has helped to create, without the possibility – a possibility that the unjust exploit on earth – of evading its worst consequences. You will get what you deserve, because you will get the worst that you yourself have created, and you will not be able to evade it. Such a state can rightly be imaged as torment, torment by the flames of conflicting and frustrated desire, by exclusion from all that is life-giving and beautiful, and by hatred of everything, including eventually even yourself.

It is this state that Christian imagery of Hell – of Gehenna, the rubbish heap, the outer darkness and the lake of sulphurous fire – seems to depict. This state will be everlasting, and from it there will be no escape, so long as your mind remains fixed in hatred, greed and selfish desire. But may your mind not change, as it experiences the desolation of loveless existence? And is the grace of God not sufficient to embrace any who come, by whatever tortuous path, to repentance?

Early Christian reflection on these subjects must have been influenced by knowledge of Jesus' death on the cross. The glory of Israel and the light of the world, bringing God's rule near in his own person, had been tortured and killed by his own people, and especially by the religious and political leaders of the day. A major perversion of Christian history has been to blame 'the Jews' for this terrible act – a perversion sadly helped by careless phrases in John's Gospel. But it was human religious hypocrisy, political collusion, hatred, bigotry and ignorance that killed Christ. It might be convenient to blame someone else, but it is the hatred in our own hearts that kills Christ anew in every generation.

So early Christians could not see the world as innately good. They saw a world ready to follow a political revolutionary, but equally ready to reject him when he called not for violence but for forgiveness and patient love. They saw a world that had turned against God. In such a world, the return of Jesus in glory might well appear to be an act of divine vengeance for the blood of the saints and martyrs.

Yet it is a fundamental misunderstanding of the gospel to suppose that, though violence is prohibited in this age, it will be perfectly acceptable in the age to come. The German writer Friedrich Nietzsche called this *resentisse-ment*, the desire for delayed revenge, the belief that we might have to suffer persecution now, but God will take revenge in the end.[4] The true Christian perception is that the cross of Christ is God's last word on violence. The divine love will never turn into divine hatred. It will go as far as possible to bring people to divine life, and it will always seek the welfare of every sentient being. And that is the last word.

So those, even in the New Testament, who still seem to long for a day of divine vengeance and hatred have not yet seen the true message of the cross. The desire for vengeance must be exposed for what it is, a failure to take to heart the disclosure of the suffering and redeeming love of God in the face of Jesus Christ.

The God disclosed in Jesus is not a punitive avenger. But it is possible for rational creatures to exclude themselves from love, and therefore from the divine life. In that state, they will be tormented by their desires and by the desires of those who are like them. They will set themselves on a path that leads to final destruction.

A God of love cannot leave them in that state. A God of unlimited love would go to any lengths to persuade them to return to the path of eternal life, and to help them on that path. So Jesus says, 'I came not to call the righteous, but sinners, to repentance' (Luke 5:32). And his death on the cross is, John says, to take away the sins of the world.

THE UNIVERSALITY OF DIVINE GRACE

There is a deepening perception of God in the Old Testament, as it moves from the command to exterminate the Amalekites (Deut. 25:19) and the destruction of whole families because of the sin of one member (Achan – Josh. 8:24, 25), to acknowledgment that foreigners should be loved (Lev. 19:34) and that persons should be punished only for their own sins (Ezek. 18:4). So in the New Testament there is a move from seeing Jesus as returning in fiery vengeance and slaying his enemies (2 Thess. 1:7, 8), to acknowledgment that Jesus gave his life for the sins of the whole world (John 1:29) and that God wills everyone to be saved from sin ('God ... not wishing that any should perish, but that all should reach repentance': 2 Peter 3:9).

God does not compel humans to repent, and repentance is required if people are to turn to the path of life. But if God wishes that all should reach repentance, God must make repentance and salvation possible for all, without exception. A God of love would always hold the door of repentance open. In that sense, Hell cannot be God's final word to any created being. It must be possible even in Hell to repent, and God, the God revealed in Christ, must be present and active to make that a real possibility.

That is the deepest meaning of the belief that 'Christ died for your sins'. He did not die for the sins of just a few selected believers. He died for the sins of everyone. He gave his life to seek to persuade everyone to repent of the evil that caused his death. And if you repent, he gives the assurance that you will have eternal life. The way to eternal life is never closed – not by your lack of knowledge of Jesus, and not even by your death.

In the letter to the Romans, probably written towards the end of Paul's life, Paul suggests precisely that. The argument of the letter is tortuous, and its reading is perhaps ambiguous. First, Paul speaks of the final judgment, and it seems that God will give the righteous eternal life, but condemn self-seekers to 'trouble and distress' (2:7–9). But before long Paul has decided that there are no righteous – 'All have sinned' (3:23). This is probably the deeper perception: we should not condemn others, while thinking that we are perfect. We all share in human weaknesses to some extent, and so we all fall under judgment. Yet ambiguity remains, and it would be possible to read the 'all' as hyperbole, and think that some may be righteous after all. Most commentators have read Paul, however, as holding that all fall short. It is from this thought that the later doctrine of 'original sin' developed, though Paul does not develop the doctrine himself, and it is a thought that is alien to Jewish tradition.

Second, Paul speaks of 'justification' – the fact that God accepts us despite our injustice. This acceptance is brought about, or exemplified by, the sacrifice of Christ on the cross. 'Just as the result of one trespass was condemnation for all men, so also the result of one act of righteousness was justification that brings life for all men' (5:18). It is unclear how far Paul is speaking symbolically here. He could be taking Adam as a symbolic figure representing humanity as such. But the parallel is between the first sin of Adam and the self-sacrifice of Jesus. The parallelism is that just as all are condemned in Adam, so all are justified in Christ. This parallelism is re-affirmed towards the end of Paul's argument, when he writes, 'God has bound all men over to disobedience so that he may have mercy on them all' (11:32).

This sounds like a gospel of universal grace – good news indeed! The impression can be strengthened by the long discussion of the place of Israel in the purpose of God, which concludes with Paul's astonishing statement, 'All Israel will be saved' (11:26). Paul suggests that the hearts of many Jews were hardened, but the hidden purpose of this was that the gentiles might hear the message of the kingdom. When that has happened, then the Jews will recognise the purpose of God in Christ, and all will enter eternal life in God. In a similar way, we might suppose that those gentiles who reject the gospel now may be part of a hidden divine plan, and all will eventually possess life in God.

However, it must be admitted that ambiguity remains, and Paul could be read as saying that eternal life is only given to those who have faith in Christ, and by 'all Israel' he only means that one day all *remaining* Jews will have faith in Christ. That has been the interpretation of large groups of Christians throughout history. The trouble with that interpretation is that it seems to be incompatible with belief in a just and loving God. It is bad enough that God might condemn the unjust to Hell for ever, without hope of repentance. It is much worse if God condemns people to Hell just because they have not heard the message of redemption in Christ.

The difficulty Paul is in is that God's grace surely cannot accept every-one, even if they do not repent. Put another way, those who will not turn from evil will simply not accept God's grace. Yet if they do not hear the call to repent and accept God's grace in Christ, they cannot really be expected to repent. So it is vitally important to hear the message of repentance and faith – and yet only a tiny minority of the world's population will do so. It seems as though, while divine grace is universal in extent, only a tiny minority of people will ever be able even to know about it, much less accept it.

Paul struggles with the dilemma, but cannot be said to resolve it in a sat-isfactory way. That is why Christian churches have sometimes found them-selves saying that God loves all people and wishes them to have eternal life, and yet that God will condemn most people to Hell, often because of an accident of birth (they were born where they never heard the gospel). I think we should bluntly say that this is both an intellectual contradiction and a moral abomination. Either God somehow makes repentance and eternal life possible for all, or God is an arbitrary and irrational monster.

It seems to me that we should follow Paul's better instincts, and insist that the sacrifice of Christ on the cross reveals God's love to be universal, and eternal life to be a real possibility for everyone without exception. 'As in Adam all die, so in Christ will all be made alive' (1 Cor. 15:22). From this it immediately follows that conscious knowledge of Christ's sacrifice during this earthly life cannot be a necessary condition of gaining eternal life. Trust in Jesus and conscious acceptance of his sacrifice, while we are on earth, are not necessary for salvation.

What is necessary for salvation is presumably some analogy of repentance and faith, a turning from selfish desire and hatred, and a trust in the reality and power of goodness as we see it in our situation.

When Paul speaks of faith in the letter to the Romans, he does not confine himself to Christian faith. He speaks above all of the faith of Abraham, who trusted in the promises of God, though he had never heard of Jesus. Christians must believe that God is at work everywhere, though often not recognised as the God of Jesus Christ. Since God is the reality and power of goodness, it is plausible to say that whatever, in any person's experience, reveals such reality and power is in fact God, though it may be called by many names. To turn from selfish desire and act for the sake of good alone is, we might think, the only necessary condition of release from the 'outer darkness' and torment of a world excluded from the life of God.

We might think this because it is what the disclosure of the divine love in Jesus, a disclosure of a love unlimited and universal, entails. But if that is so, what is the point of preaching the Christian gospel?

This is precisely the question Paul asked about the Jews. If gentiles could be saved, was there any point in being a Jew? Paul's answer is that there certainly is a point, for Jews were, are and always will be the people of God's first covenant. They are to remain the guardians of that covenant, of its demands and its promises. Similarly, we might say that Christians are the people of God's new covenant, called to life in Christ and to the hope 'that the creation itself will be liberated from its bondage to decay and brought into the glorious freedom of the children of God' (Rom. 8:21).

It is precisely the revelation of God in Christ that shows the divine love to be universally inclusive. That is a message that is not at all obvious and that is of vital importance to the whole world. Christ's death shows the depth of God's involvement in the suffering of the world. Christ's resurrection shows that there is new life in God. And the promise of Christ's future appearing in glory gives a hope for the final flourishing of goodness that can withstand the darkest times. This is a message the world badly needs, and its importance is not diminished by the fact that all people can come to God, even without knowing about Christ.

They can, but Christians believe that when they do finally come to God they will then recognise that God is indeed the God who was authentically seen in Jesus Christ. They will recognise that Christ died for them and that Christ is the Son of God. People do not have to recognise the God and Father of Jesus Christ in order to be set on the path to eternal life. But as they near the end of their journey, they will realise that it has always been that God, working unrecognised, who has touched their lives. Then they will recognise God. The unknown Christ will be fully known. That is the *parousia*, the full consciously recognised manifestation of who Christ truly is.

In this way God can place all humans under condemnation, yet also offer all the free gift of eternal life, and give to all the space for repentance and faith, whether in this life or beyond it, and in many different forms. Precisely because that is true, the gospel of Christ is that God does everything possible to redeem us from sin, to give us a share in the life of God and to liberate the whole creation from its bondage. He reveals this in the person of Jesus, at one particular time and place on earth, and at that time and place God acts in a decisive way to make it true.

In the letter to the Romans, Paul has often been read as claiming that only a few – the 'elect' – will be salvaged by grace from destruction. That, however, would be to make the gospel bad news for most people, which seems self-defeating. What Paul does is to emphasise the new quality of life that is offered if we place our faith in Christ. Faith is not just a matter of adopting the intellectual belief that Jesus died and was raised from death. It is much more personal – 'We were therefore buried with him through baptism into death in order that, just as Christ was raised from the dead through the glory of the Father, we too may live a new life' (Rom. 6:4).

We must die to our egoistic nature, and live by the power of Christ, 'controlled not by the sinful nature but by the Spirit' (8:9). The Spirit of Christ must live in us, and it is that life that unites us ever more closely to God. If the Spirit that was in Christ lives in us, that will evoke in us the opposite of the belief that we and our friends alone are saved out of all the people in the world. It will rather evoke the belief that we must serve the world in love, and not rest until all have been offered God's free gift of eternal life.

RE-THINKING CHRISTIAN FAITH IN PAUL

Paul's thought in Romans is by no means crystal clear. He is wrestling with ultimate problems of divine justice and mercy, of human freedom and divine grace. This short letter has in Christian history given rise to millions of words of exposition and reflection. And that is exactly the point. There are no clear doctrines here, doctrines that put an end to speculation and dis- agreement. These are the complex and exploratory thoughts of a man whose religious perceptions have been transformed by a vision of the risen Christ, but who is still trying to work out just what that vision implies. In his early ministry, it seems that he stressed the severity of divine judgment and the return of Christ to end world history. Later in his life, that emphasis has diminished. He emphasises more the nature of new life in Christ, and he begins to develop the thought that the whole creation is to be transformed by the Spirit. Belief that Christ will come in glory has not disappeared, but it is being transmuted into a non-dateable hope for the triumph of goodness and the apotheosis of the cosmos.

Letters that may not be by Paul himself, but are probably by someone who knew him well, continue this development. In the first chapter of Ephesians the purpose of God is said to be 'to gather up all things in him [Christ], things in heaven and things on earth' (Eph. 1:10). Of course the universe (things in heaven and earth) was then thought to be much smaller than we now know it to be, but it still contained everything created. The whole of creation is to be united in Christ. Moreover, until that time the church is the body of Christ, continuing in a sense the task of bringing God's kingdom into the world.

The first chapter of Colossians, the authorship of which is disputed, but could be Paul's, develops similar thoughts, and speaks of all created things being reconciled to God, while the task of the church is to bring eternal life into the things of time, to begin the apotheosis of creation (Col. 1:15–20). I have discussed these passages in *What the Bible Really Teaches*, especially in chapter 4. I mention them now to show how New Testament thought was developing from an assumption that the eastern Mediterranean was the centre of creation, towards a truly cosmic vision. The church, as the body of Christ, the community of the new covenant, and the society of the divine Spirit, has the role of embodying and mediating the Spirit in history. The whole of creation is to be reconciled to God and united 'in Christ'.

These thoughts contrast with any idea that history will end within one generation, and suggest a positive and creative role for the church over a long period of time. This is beginning to be realised in the second letter of Peter, where the writer notes that 'with the Lord one day is like a thousand years' (1 Peter 3:8). Now that we realise the vastness of the created universe, our horizon needs to expand much further still. Our perspective, within which the earth itself is a tiny speck in the history of a hundred thousand million galaxies, requires a re-thinking of Christian faith in a major way. But this re-thinking is authorised by the structure of the New Testament letters, which already begin the process of re-contextualisation, yet also make clear that they have not completed the task.

Paul still struggles with the questions of the destiny of the Jews, of how the grace of God in Christ can extend to the millions who have never heard of him, and of how human freedom can be made consistent with the realisation of God's final purpose for the salvation of all people. His suggestions are sometimes still limited by the perspectives of his day – for instance, by his conception of the universe as very small, with the earth at its centre, and by his adoption of the conventions of his day, especially about slavery and gender and political obedience, as morally binding.

What we have, in the New Testament letters, are explorations of what is implied by faith in Jesus as the one who brings God near and establishes a new community of the Spirit of God. These explorations are sometimes tentative, limited by the conventions of their time, and in need of further development. There is no systematic or complete doctrinal system, no systematic theology or set of clear, definitive doctrines. The exact relation of the Lord Jesus Christ to God the Father remains obscure, and certainly leaves open the possibility that Jesus is something less than the Father, though given divine authority by the Father. (In John's Gospel Jesus says, 'the Father is greater than I': John 14:28. And in the letter to the Colossians, Christ is said to be 'the firstborn of all creation': Colossians 1:15, which implies that Christ is created.) A number of different metaphors are used for the way in which Jesus' death is 'for' the sin of the world. And there is unclarity about the relation between the risen Christ, who 'lives in you', the Spirit of God, and the Spirit of Christ. They could easily be seen as different ways of speaking of the same reality, or as pointing to different realities.

The letters, in other words, call out for further reflection. They form the starting point of such a process of reflection, not the termination of further creative thought.

What should be clear, from a study of the New Testament, is that the church has the task of continually re-thinking Christian faith, as human knowledge grows. The changes evident within the New Testament itself are breathtaking. The recorded teachings of Jesus about the kingdom, about Torah and about the coming of the Son of man in glory are radically revised by the first-generation church. The kingdom is thrown open to gentiles, the Torah is abandoned, Jesus' life is seen as the incarnation of the divine Wisdom, and the church begins to be seen as a continuing community, or set of communities, in history, as the body of Christ and the vanguard of the reconciliation of all creation to God.

It is highly improbable, on the evidence of the synoptic Gospels, that the historic Jesus said, or could have said, any of these things. They are the creative responses of leaders of the early church to the disclosure of God they had seen in Jesus, and to their own experience of the risen Christ and of the Spirit moving among them. The task of the church in the modern world is to continue making such creative responses in its own new and diverse contexts. Re-thinking Christianity is not a betrayal of unchanging Christian truth. It is a demand rooted in the very nature of the New Testament, and in an accurate perception of what New Testament revelation is – not dictated words from God, but a diverse set of testimonies to the acts of God in the person of Jesus the Christ.

Chapter 4

Time and Eternity

God, the unbounded and everlasting Lord, creates the cosmos as a place in which finite persons can come to knowledge and love of the Good. Within this cosmos the Lord takes finite form in the person of Jesus, assuming a human body and soul into the divine life. In Jesus, divine and human are indissolubly united in one. By this act of condescension the estrangement of the cosmos from God is overcome, and the ills of the world are healed, as humanity itself is taken into God. That is the goal and end of our earthly pilgrimage, that we might share in the life of God, and that through us the whole cosmos can ultimately be united to the divine. The core of Christian faith is that the Eternal enters into time, in order that time should participate in eternity and, purged of its negativity, be taken into the life of the Eternal.

THE BIBLE AND INTERPRETATIONS OF JESUS

The Bible is the book of the church. The New Testament Gospels and letters were compiled by members of the church, and they were selected for inclusion in the New Testament by the church. The New Testament was not dictated by God nor did it issue from the mouth of Jesus. It is written in various styles, by different authors who had differing perspectives on their faith in Jesus. It expresses beliefs that were still in the course of development in the early church, and that do not provide systematic doctrines such as those that were later formulated by the church. It is a set of responses to and reflections on the events surrounding the life of Jesus that had given rise to the church. It is a set of diverse and creative meditations on Jesus Christ as the source of the church's life.

The church has always held that the New Testament writers were inspired by God, and that the selection of their works for inclusion in the Bible was also inspired by God. Inspiration is not a process that began and ended with the writing of the New Testament documents. It is the guidance of the divine Spirit as the church begins to define and reflect on the basis of its own life.

The New Testament has a unique significance because of its nearness in time to the life of Jesus. In it the originative events of the faith are set out. But the character of the documents in my view precludes belief in exact verbal inerrancy, or in the finality and exhaustiveness of revelation either in the life of Jesus or in the New Testament itself.

I have argued that verbal inerrancy is ruled out by comparison of the Gospel records of the life of Jesus, such as the one I outlined in the first chapter. Since some (in fact, most) of these accounts must be inaccurate in detail, it is not possible to say there are no inaccuracies in the Bible.

That does not mean that the Bible is totally unreliable, or that it is all inaccurate. I agree with scholars who say that, if the disciples had not believed they saw Jesus alive after death, the Christian faith would never have got started. If they had not seen Jesus die on the cross, they would never have conceived the startling idea that 'God sent his only Son into the world so that we might live through him' (1 John 4:9) (and it is important to stress that 'His only Son' came to be seen in later theology not as someone other than God, but as God in person, so this is the sacrifice of God).

There are central facts about the life of Jesus that form a firm foundation for Christian faith. They fall into three main categories. First, Jesus was believed to be a man wholly surrendered to God, filled with the Spirit of God. He had a wisdom and authority that derived from his close sense of unity with the Father. That sense made it possible for him to claim to forgive sins, and to interpret the Law of God with authority. He had, or was believed to have, unique access to the mind of God.

Second, Jesus was believed to mediate the power of God, both in his freedom from ego, his absolute sinlessness, and in his healing power, by which he made God's power real for those who came to him for help. He was a unique channel of the liberating power of God.

Third, he was believed to have a unique vocation to be the promised King of Israel. This was not a political kingdom, but a new community of the

Spirit, under a new covenant that brought God near and united people inwardly to God in a new way. He was the one who founded a new society of the divine Spirit. He was the founder of a society that prefigures the fullness of God's rule over all creation (though this was conceived at first as a renewed Israel centred on Jerusalem).

So the New Testament does not give the exact words of Jesus without error. But it does record a variety of human responses to a life lived in complete unity with the divine, by a man who had a distinctive vocation to renew God's covenant with Israel in a new way.

The strictly neutral historian can say no more than that these things were believed of Jesus by some in his own generation. Most present-day Christians will also believe that these things really were true of Jesus. Christian revelation is then objective, in that it is founded on the life of an extraordinary human being who had a unique unity with the divine and whose historical vocation was to found a new way of divine–human union. Yet revelation remains objectively uncertain, in that it is possible for a historian to read the records of this life and decline to believe that the historical Jesus was as he is represented in the texts.

A decision about this will, I think, largely depend upon whether or not you have some belief in or experience of God as a personal and morally demanding reality, and some experience of what is believed to be the presence of the living Christ in the church. In other words, it will be reasonable to accept that Jesus is in general as he is represented to be in the synoptic Gospels if the church now conveys to you a life-enhancing experience of the living Christ. For such experience will confirm and give authority to the apostolic testimony to the words and acts of Jesus, who is the historical origin and pattern of present experience of Christ in glory.

Even if you accept that the texts give an accurate account of Jesus, it remains importantly true that they do not give just one account without any error or disagreement. They give rather different accounts, from different perspectives, of a life that demands constant re-thinking from further and wider perspectives if it is to be adequately understood.

It is in this sense that the New Testament does not give a final or exhaustive presentation of the truth about Jesus.

Early Christian thought developed by placing these claims about the person of Jesus into a new conceptual context that provided a set of central truths for the understanding of Christian faith. These central truths include the following: God is unlimited love. Human destiny, and the destiny of all creation, is liberation from sin and unity with God. The way to unity is sharing in the Spirit of Christ. Jesus is the matrix (the origin, mould and pattern) of the new community whose role it is to mediate the Spirit. It is especially in his proclamation of the kingdom of God, his sacrificial death and his resurrection to life in God that Jesus is such a matrix. Belief in the *parousia* (literally, the 'personal presence', but sometimes called the 'second coming') of Christ is belief that the final unity of all things in God will also be the full disclosure of the nature of the eternal Word who was incarnate in Jesus.

This understanding of Christian faith is common to the early Greek and Roman writers who are celebrated as the 'Church Fathers'. But it should be noted that when writers proceed to more detailed expositions of these beliefs they always have differed, and they probably always will. God is unlimited love; but the way this has been understood in detail has varied a great deal in Christian history. For many it has been understood to be compatible with the existence of an unending Hell, whereas for others (including me) that would seem to be a rank contradiction. For some, the *parousia* of Christ is a sort of literal return to earth, whereas for others (including me) it symbolises an event beyond, and at the end of, cosmic history.

The New Testament does not preclude such a variety of interpretations. Indeed, it includes such a variety itself, from the Messianic Judaism of Matthew to the incarnational theology of John and the largely gentile death-and-resurrection drama of the later Paul. Variety and creativity of response are licensed by the very nature of New Testament revelation, and we should expect them to characterise the church wherever it is truly alive.

THE BEGINNINGS OF CHRISTIAN DOCTRINE

So, after the writing of the New Testament documents, we see the church continuing to develop its thinking about Jesus and the revelation of God in and through Jesus. It did so with the aid of concepts that were not found in the New Testament, and that were drawn from Greek philosophy. Some of the more traditional bishops tended to oppose such new-fangled ideas, on the grounds that they were not part of the original revelation. They were right to think that these were new ideas, with which Jesus or the apostles were not familiar. They were certainly not part of the teaching of Jesus. But the traditionalists were wrong in failing to see that by the time the New Testament was written the church's teachings had already changed dramatically from the original teaching of Jesus. The new concepts simply illustrated the creative drive of the church towards wider and deeper understandings of the revelation of God in Jesus. Greek philosophy enabled the church to find a new perspective on those originating events, which would illuminate their significance for world history and the human understanding of the divine. Such a drive to fuller understanding is inevitable, and the church may fairly claim that the inspiration of the Holy Spirit will not totally fail to guide its thinking on such matters.

Unfortunately, the church also began to develop the view that there was just one 'orthodox', right-thinking interpretation on disputed matters, and to seek to eliminate competing views. Church leaders did not see that if you allow creativity you necessarily also encourage diversity. There is nothing wrong with coming to a majority view or with seeking to establish a consensus on certain matters. But everything is wrong with seeking to censor and destroy views that differ from such a consensus.

One reason we do not have a very clear or full account of Christian thought in the first few centuries is that many writings have been destroyed. Many of the accounts we have of 'heretical' writings are just from the mouths of their oppressors, so they are hardly likely to be unbiased. And many such 'heretical' writings have simply vanished.

On the whole, we get an impression of quite a wide range of creative interpretations of the Christian faith from the writings that do remain and are accessible to us. There are many good books on the development of Christian doctrine. A standard work is *Early Christian Doctrines*, by J.N.D. Kelly (A & C Black, 1958). *From Nicaea to Chalcedon*, by Frances Young (SCM, 1983) is an excellent guide. For something shorter and very readable, I would recommend *The History of Christian Thought*, by Jonathan Hill (Lion, 2003). What I want to do is to pick out a few representative figures from the first Christian centuries, to show how what came to be called Christian orthodoxy developed in an understandable yet highly imaginative and creative way from the forms of faith in Jesus that had preceded it.

The first of the group of writers known as the 'Church Fathers' was Justin Martyr, born in about 100 CE. He explicitly used the works of Greek philosophers to develop the *Logos* theology of John's Gospel. He depicted the *Logos* as the wisdom, intellect, thought or speech of God. It came to exist when God thought or spoke, as a sort of emanation of the divine being, rather as light emanates from the sun. How many emanations from the divine being there were, and exactly how they related to that being, is unclear, though the Son and the Spirit are expressly named. The idea of the *Logos* as a sort of 'second God', or an emanation of God, was to be a major theme of Patristic thought.

Irenaeus, later in the second century, further develops the theme. He sees the *Logos* as becoming corruptible and mortal in the person of Jesus, in order that humans can be 'joined to incorruptibility and immortality'. The incarnation begins the process of human divinisation, by which humans, made in the divine image, pass into God in an unending journey towards the divine likeness.

What is most striking in these writings is the way interest has moved from the historical Jesus to the nature of the eternal God, and to the general relation of God to creation through the mediation of the *Logos*. Messianic Judaism has been left behind, and Jesus becomes the bearer of the eternal Word for the world, leading humanity from the fading world of time to unity with the eternal divine.

All this belongs to the same thought world as Gnosticism, which developed elaborate theories of emanations from the divine 'Fulness', and of salvation as the return of the sparks of the divine that had become trapped in human bodies out of the darkness of matter to the pure light of the Fulness of God. Gnostic thought was related to what became Christian orthodoxy in a complex way, but it did affect many Christian formulations of doctrine.

Christians rejected the general Gnostic belief that matter was intrinsically evil, something to be liberated from, not celebrated, a view that reflected Plato's statement that the body (*soma*) is the tomb (*sema*) of the soul. Yet the growing Christian faith was not untouched by such thoughts. There were those who taught that Jesus never really suffered, and never even ate or drank. He just appeared to do so, whereas in fact he was totally liberated from material existence. He was not truly a man.

For most early Christians, however, such a belief misses the point of the incarnation, which is that God sanctifies matter by taking material form. Any true liberation must be a liberation of matter as well as spirit, and the risen Lord continues to have some sort of material form and is not pure disembodied Spirit.

JESUS AS A UNION OF DIVINITY AND HUMANITY

The Neoplatonic interest in the processions and emanations of the divine being into the world of time, and the return of the temporal into God, exerted a great influence on the churches. John's Gospel, which especially in its prologue expresses an embryonic form of such an interest, began to be taken as an authentic record of the historical Jesus. Jesus began in some circles to be understood as one who knew himself to be the incarnation of the *Logos*, the omnipotent and omniscient heavenly Son of God. He was fully conscious of his own pre-existence with the Father, able to raise himself from death by his own power (as opposed to being raised, as a man, from death by God). His miracles were no longer wonders performed by God in response to the prayers of a faithful prophet. They were proofs that God in person was at work in the world.

The church did not, however, accept that Jesus was the omnipotent and omniscient God who only appeared to be a man. In what became a definitive statement, the Council of Chalcedon in 451 CE promulgated the view that Jesus was 'fully man' as well as 'fully God', without claiming to explain how this could be. It is important to note that most Christians insisted that Jesus was a real man, not some sort of illusion or apparition of a man.

Much Christian thinking has not seriously explored the implications of the statement that Jesus was really a member of the species *Homo sapiens*. It means that the knowledge and power of Jesus was that possible for and proper to human beings in general. Omniscience is not possible for a human being. We must come to know things through the senses, and by learning them from others. Our knowledge will be bounded by the limitations of our culture. For instance, no Palestinian Jew could possibly have known the theory of relativity or the solution of Fermat's last theorem. Jesus would in general have believed what people of his culture believed, and that would have included many mistaken views – for example, about the nature and age of the earth.

We might expect that, because of his unique closeness to God, Jesus would have had a capacity of insight and wisdom far beyond that of most humans, but it would not have been inhuman. It would rather have been the moral and spiritual perfection of humanity – what human beings would know and believe if they were interpenetrated in indissoluble union by the divine. We cannot be sure what this would be like, but it is highly likely that such union would not remove all errors of fact or culturally limited opinion, though it might well ensure that Jesus was preserved from error in any matters that concerned God's will to reveal and realise the divine purpose of human redemption in him. We might say that he was omniscient in all things concerning human salvation (the fulfilment of human personality in unity with God). But he was not omniscient about, for instance, the structure of DNA.

Similarly, no human being can be omnipotent. Human powers are governed by our genetic inheritance (the virgin birth is irrelevant to this, since Jesus inherited a full genome from Mary even if he had no human father). No human can fly or lift a mountain or rise from death by his own power. God can work through a human being, and God could protect such a being miraculously or raise him from the dead if God so willed. But Jesus, as human, would not be or believe that he was omnipotent. He might well, however, feel himself to be wholly dependent upon the omnipotent God, with whom he was united in the most intimate possible way – and the synoptic Gospels depict him in that way.

It is important to be clear that, on an orthodox view, Jesus had a human consciousness, human powers and human knowledge. These could be perfected, but not obliterated, by his union with the divine.

JESUS AS 'TWO NATURES IN ONE PERSON'

In what, then, did such a union of divine and human consist? It was Tertullian, writing in Latin in the second century CE, who invented the terms that have since become standard in Christian theology. He said that Jesus was two substances (*substantia*) in one person (*persona*). Jesus is both God and man, having a divine nature and a human nature united in one person (the word 'nature' was adopted by the Council of Chalcedon as a clearer term than 'substance', so that Jesus was said to be a union of two natures in one person).

Tertullian was also the first writer to use the term 'Trinity' of God, saying that God was three persons – Father, Son and Spirit – in one substance. From this it follows that the one person of Christ is identical with the second person of the Trinity. It is easy then to conclude that Christ is a divine person who adds a human nature to his properly divine nature, or 'assumes' a human nature to the divine person, without really being a human person.

In other words, Jesus has a human nature, but is not strictly speaking a human person. He is a divine person with a human nature. And that divine person is one of three who together constitute the substance, the being, of God.

This is a major change from the Jesus of the synoptic Gospels, who is presented as a human person with unique and divinely given authority and powers, but who is (at least in Mark) expressly said to be limited in knowledge and power ('Of that day or that hour no one knows, not even the angels in heaven, nor the Son, but only the Father': Mark 13:32; 'He could do no mighty work there': Mark 6:5), and who insists, with orthodox Judaism, that 'the Lord your God is one Lord'.

The emerging orthodox doctrine is not a change in the sense of renouncing or contradicting what Mark's Gospel says. But what it says about God and Jesus would have been quite unknown to Mark – and, if Mark is right, to Jesus also.

Tertullian was therefore mistaken when he said that 'all doctrine which agrees with the apostolic churches ... must be considered true, as undoubtedly containing what those churches received from the Apostles, the Apostles from Christ, Christ from God' (*Against the Heretics* 21). Tertullian's own doctrine of the Trinity and of the person of Jesus originated with him and was not derived from the apostles or from Jesus.

That does not mean Tertullian's doctrine is false. It just means Jesus never thought of it and neither did the apostles. Tertullian is taking John's Gospel as historically accurate, whereas it was in fact a later interpretation of the person of Jesus.

The question Tertullian is asking, and that any reflective Christian must ask, is, 'Given that the Gospel records are in general accurate in portraying Jesus' ministry, death and resurrection, what must we say that Jesus was and now is, in relation to God?'

The question is quite proper. But what Tertullian did not see is that John's Gospel is not a literal record of what Jesus actually said. It is already an early attempt to answer that question, and even the synoptic Gospels provide not literal records but reflective interpretations of the person of Jesus. So what we should really be asking is, 'Given that the gospels are interpretations of Jesus, and we cannot with any objective certainty get back beyond them, what should we now say about Jesus in relation to the disclosure of God we have received through him?'

Could we today agree with Tertullian? My own view is that we could nearly agree with him, but not quite. One reason for not quite agreeing with him is that we now believe, with good reason, that Mark is closest to the historical Jesus, and John is quite far away. So it looks as though we should say that Jesus is a human person who has a unique closeness to God, a unique authority to mediate God's power and wisdom and a unique vocation to bring God close to those who are prepared to encounter him in and through Jesus. We can say that he is a human person uniquely united to, and in that sense one with, the divine. The point about stressing this is that he will be seen as a finite personality with his own autonomy, his own form of knowing and willing and experiencing. He will not be imagined as the infinite God, somehow squashed up into a human mind and body, or adding such a mind and body to his already omniscient power.

Yet what of John's Gospel, and Thomas's reported exclamation, 'My Lord and my God'? Jesus was worshipped in the early church, and calling him 'Lord' is equivalent to calling him 'God'. I would suggest that Christians believe that Jesus mediates God in such a perfect way, even if that mediation is limited to what is possible for a human person, that he can properly be worshipped as the personal medium of God's action. We might admire and revere a perfect person, as we do a saint. But if that person not only realises a perfect human life, but also – and in accordance with God's intention for his life – perfectly exemplifies and mediates God's power and wisdom, then it may be proper to go further, and *treat him as* God. What Jesus does is what God wills to do in the human world, for Jesus' human will is completely devoted and transparent to the divine will. Moreover, God wills that Jesus should be the image and model of the divine for the human world.

It is rather as if an ambassador were treated as the ruler he or she represents. But it is much more even than that, for in Jesus' case he really is the medium through whom God directly acts, and acts in such a way as to disclose the divine nature and open a new way of relating to God for human beings.

So the Gospels refer to Jesus, not as 'God' per se, but as 'Son of God', the human person who mediates God's decisive act of self-revelation and human liberation. And Jesus calls himself 'Son of man', the paradigm human being, made perfect by his complete union with the divine. In my view, these insights are well preserved by saying that Jesus is a human person perfected by the divine presence and power and designated by God as the image and mediator of that presence and power to human beings. Human and divine are united uniquely in Jesus, but it can be misleading to say that human nature is 'possessed' by a divine person. It misleads if it leads people to think that Jesus is really omnipotent and omniscient, for example, but somehow conceals the fact while walking around Galilee. But it does not have to mislead, and we need to remember that the terms 'substance' and 'person' have changed their meaning quite a lot since early Christian times, so we must not use them in their modern sense. As long as we are aware of the dangers, the language of substances and persons can still properly be used in thinking about the divine–human union in Jesus.

AN INTERPRETATION OF THE INCARNATION

The philosophy used by the Church Fathers claimed that properties, a set of which can be said to constitute a 'nature', are possessed by something, a substance. It seems logically possible for a substance to possess two such sets of properties, as long as they are not incompatible. They will not be incompatible as long as they are possessed under different conditions, or in different respects. For example, a person can be unconscious while asleep, and conscious while awake, yet be the same person. So the divine substance could be infinite and yet be manifested in, or take the form of, a finite substance, for specific purposes. God can coherently be said to be omniscient, in the divine nature, and yet limited in knowledge, in a human nature that God assumes. He can be immortal as divine, and yet killed as a human being. God can have human properties (have a human nature), as long as God retains all the properly divine properties, and as long as the human awareness (one of the human properties) retains its essential characteristics.

That does not seem too problematic. Yet a crucial problem for this view is that human beings seem to be, not only sets of properties, but themselves 'subjects' that possess those properties (persons). It is I who think, feel and act, not God. It may be possible for a set of finite properties to be possessed by an infinite God, but is it possible for one (finite) subject to be 'possessed by' another (infinite) subject? This is a difficult problem to resolve, and many early Christians thought that there was no human subject (no soul or human will) in Jesus, but that God's mind replaced his human mind. This, however, was seen to imperil the true humanity of Jesus, and so the Third Council of Constantinople, in 680, insisted that Jesus had a human soul – in my terms, he was a truly human subject.

In what sense, then, can a human subject be possessed by a divine subject? Since a subject is the knower of experiences and agent of actions, it would seem that one subject can possess another if it has the experiences and feelings the other has (and other experiences too), and if it is the intentional agent of the others' thoughts and acts (and of other acts too).

Yet the human subject, if it is to be fully and authentically human, cannot be a purely passive vehicle for the divine subject, the two subjects simply collapsing into one. There must be some sense of co-experiencing and co-acting, and the human subject must have some feelings and perform some actions in its own right.

This can perhaps be achieved because the infinite subject does not know in the way that finite subjects do. Divine knowledge is not limited or from a particular perspective. Divine knowledge may include the experience of what all finite subjects experience. But it cannot experience things exactly as they do. For instance, if Jesus experiences a sense of abandonment on the cross, the divine subject cannot experience that in the same way, because it will also know without doubt that Jesus is never really abandoned by the divine Father. So the experiences of finite subjects, though they may be known exactly and intensely by God, will nevertheless be known as the experiences of subjects who are in an important sense other than God.

Suppose, however, that there is an 'other', a human subject, who is completely obedient to God, who knows what God wills and who wills only what God wills. In such a case, its experiences would not be affected by sin and estrangement from God. To the extent that such a subject carried out the intentions of God in the world, its feelings and thoughts and experiences might be 'owned' by God in a way that would not be true of any other finite subject. The thoughts and acts of such a finite subject could be owned by the divine subject if they are just what God intends for that finite subject.

It might be the case, also, that God intends that life to manifest a human form of the divine love and to mediate the divine life to others. Then, by the divine will, a finite subject who knew and loved God fully would always do what God willed for it. It could be said to be performing the acts of God, and its experiences could be said to be the experiences of God in human form. The human subject with limited knowledge and experience would exist as well as the divine omniscient subject. But God could accept the human experiences as those of the divine, insofar as the divine can act and know in human form. This relation between human subject and divine subject is one of uniquely complete and indissoluble unity, not just of absorption of the human by the divine.

Such a relation would not deprive the human subject of all creativity and spontaneity. Jesus could make his own creative decisions on many matters, precisely because thereby he would be doing what God wills. Creative individuality is not removed from the soul of Jesus by total obedience to God. There can be a causal priority of the human will of Jesus, but only so far as that is consistent with the intentions of God.

So we might think of God, knowing everything, as specifically willing Jesus to do some things, and willing Jesus to be freely creative in other things. When Jesus feels and experiences, God regards these as feelings and experiences of the divine subject, in finite form. They are the feelings and experiences of a perfected human mind, and of a mind called to manifest the divine nature and enact the divine intentions in a unique and specific way. God can acknowledge them in a way that God could never acknowledge feelings of hatred, inordinate desire or rage. Jesus always knows in a limited, sense-bound way, but we may reasonably think that he is also aware of what God wills, and always obeys that will.

The uniqueness of Jesus' person lies in the fact that there is a necessary, unbreakable, unity of divine and human willing, and a form of human experiencing that is always necessarily compatible with the divine nature, being without hatred, prejudice or selfish attachment. Such unity and compatibility is not, for traditional Christian thought, to be envisaged as something that is achieved or grows gradually. It is an original endowment of Jesus' nature. The necessary and permanent unity of divine and human experiencing, feeling, thinking and acting in Jesus is a reasonable way of construing what is meant by 'incarnation'. Christians may hope that they, too, will achieve a state in which their experiences are all compatible with the divine experience and in which their acts are all in accordance with the divine will. But that union will never have been necessary and permanent. It will be achieved only through a gradual growth into Christ. Such persons will be 'sons and daughters of God by adoption', and not by birth (Gal. 4:4, 5).

These matters are exceedingly difficult to formulate precisely, and in the first five centuries the church argued repeatedly over whether Jesus had a human soul or will, whether he was of the same substance as God or not, whether he was less than or equal to the Father, and how his human properties related to the divine properties of the eternal Word that 'became flesh', according to John's Gospel.

The striking thing about these arguments is that, while they constantly refer to the Gospels, usually taken as literal accounts of the life of Jesus, they are really about highly abstract philosophical themes of the nature of God and the eternal Word or Son of God – something quite foreign to the synoptic Gospels.

There is no question, for the Gospels, that Jesus exemplifies a union of human and divine, and that he does so in a unique way, since he is designated as Messiah, the self-disclosure of God and the one who opens up a new way of union with God for all human beings. So there is a sense in which the church is not issuing a new doctrine, not previously thought of. Nevertheless, the way it is formulated, as a union of two natures in one person, is new and expresses a development in Christian thinking about Jesus. As I have implied, there may need to be further reformulations of our understanding of Jesus' relation to God, if our philosophical framework and understanding changes. My own suggestion, which undoubtedly needs refinement in many ways, is that we could think of incarnation as an original and indissoluble union of divine and human willing and experiencing, which is brought about by a particular act of God in human history, but which leaves the human subject creatively free as well as necessarily united in will to God.

Even for the most traditional Christian, the process of developing a doctrine of incarnation by no means ends with Tertullian. Whereas Tertullian clearly taught that Christ was less than the Father, the Council of Chalcedon insisted that Christ was co-equal with the Father. Tertullian speaks of the persons of the Trinity as differing in 'degree, form and appearance', and that terminology too was to be quarrelled over and redefined in the fourth and fifth centuries.

The point is that in the first five centuries of its existence, the church sought to develop a new terminology that would help it to understand more fully what it believed, that God had revealed the divine nature and acted for human liberation in the person of Jesus. This new terminology was accepted only after many arguments, some of them regrettably vicious, and it is now found in the classical Christian creeds, especially the so-called Athanasian and Nicene Creeds.

I do not suppose for a minute that either Jesus or any of the apostles could ever have imagined the Nicene Creed, or the later more elaborate definition of Christ's nature at Chalcedon. That does not mean the creed is false. It means that it does not come from Jesus and the apostles – even though the Council of Chalcedon quaintly claimed that the doctrine that Christ was two natures in one person was as 'the Lord Jesus Christ himself taught us'.

If Jesus ever had taught that, it took the church over four hundred years to discover it, and even then many fervent disciples continued to dispute it. It is nowhere in the New Testament, pious reading of which produced as many different theories as it is possible to imagine, and possibly even more. It is the creation of the fifth-century church, concluding (or trying to conclude) centuries of disputation. It is to be judged now on how adequately it enables us to understand what God has done for humanity in the person of Jesus.

THE SEVEN GREAT ECUMENICAL COUNCILS OF THE CHURCH

Is there just one definitive account of such an understanding? It is undoubtedly the case that the developing church became concerned above all with 'orthodoxy', with correct belief about things that Jesus and the apostles had never even mentioned. Jesus did claim divine authority, and call people to follow him in waiting for the kingdom, in which he would rule. But he did not ask people to agree with him that he was an assumption by the eternal Word of a human body and soul, that he was two natures in one person (as the Council of Chalcedon asserted), not just one nature (as Apollinarius taught) or two persons (as Nestorius was alleged to have taught), not created (as Arius held) or subordinate to the Father (as Tertullian and Origen said) in his divine nature.

Nevertheless it is reasonable to say that these sophisticated and difficult philosophical assertions do spell out what is implicit in Jesus' own claim to divine authority, and in his role of inaugurating God's kingdom in his own person, as a community of the new covenant in the Spirit. They were formulated in order to rule out beliefs about the person of Christ that were thought to threaten what became the central principle of early Greek Christian thought, that 'the unassumed is the unhealed', as Gregory of Nazianzus put it.

This principle understands the work of God in Jesus as the establishment of a union of divine and human. All that is human, and that suffers by its human estrangement from God, is to be healed by being united with or taken into God. If anything human is not so divinised, it remains estranged from God, 'unsaved'. In the person of Jesus, God takes into the divine life all that is essentially human. Athanasius, following Irenaeus, famously said, 'He became man, that we might become God' (*De Incarnatione* 54).

The first seven ecumenical councils of the church can be seen as successive attempts to formulate and safeguard this principle against views that could undermine it.

- Nicea I, in 325, asserted that the Word was 'begotten, not made', and was of the same substance as the Father – against those who held that Christ was created.
- This doctrine was confirmed at Constantinople I in 381, and was enshrined in what came to be called the 'Nicene Creed'. That council also stated that the Holy Spirit was fully divine, against those who held the Spirit to be simply a power sent by and dependent upon God.
- Ephesus, 431, condemned the claim of Nestorius that Mary should not be called 'Mother of God'. Nestorius was taken to be separating the human nature of Jesus, of which Mary was the mother, from the divine nature, which has no mother. The council, however, taught that in Jesus divine and human were truly united in one personal reality.
- Chalcedon, 451, issued the classical definition of this divine–human unity by saying that Jesus Christ was two natures, divine and human, united in one person or substantial and indivisible union.
- Constantinople II, 553, added further condemnations of those who divided Christ into two persons, or separate substances.
- Constantinople III, 680, affirmed that Christ has a real human will and was a truly human subject of action, against those who held that Jesus only had a divine will and subjectivity.

This series of councils ended with

- Nicea II, 787, which asserted that icons could legitimately be reverenced, thus seeking to defend the principle that the infinite God was truly known in the finite and material form of Jesus.

These seven great councils are accepted by the Orthodox churches and at least the first six are accepted by most Anglicans as the definitive councils of the undivided church.

The conciliar definitions can be seen as defensive formulations, condemning what they felt to be inadequate views of the person of Jesus, and insisting that in Jesus there was a real divine–human unity. This unity came to be by pure divine initiative, and was the foundation of the hope that all human life, and perhaps all creation, could in time be similarly united to God by the Spirit of Christ.

Jesus' call to wait for the coming of the kingdom in Jerusalem was thus re-thought over the first few hundred years of Christian history as the church's call to be united to God through entering into the sacramental life of the church, through which the Spirit slowly transforms human lives into the divine likeness.

It seems to me reasonable to regard this as an authentic development of the Christian gospel, bringing out the spiritual depth and breadth of Jesus' message of God's redeeming and unitive love (love that liberates from evil and unites to the divine life), which was present in his own person. But it certainly marks a major conceptual shift from Messianic Judaism, through John's embryonic theology of the incarnate *Logos*, and Paul's early fervent expectation of the return of the Lord and his later death-and-resurrection spirituality, to a sacramental path of union with the divine through the inner transforming action of the Spirit of Christ.

This is not, as the great German liberal theologian Adolf Harnack thought, the loss of an early gospel of the fellowship of all people under God, and its replacement by a Hellenistic mystery cult of divine emanations into matter and the return of the material into a world of pure spirit. So far as we can tell, there was no such early gospel. The person of Jesus was central to the earliest Gospel records, and the seeds of a theology of divine incarnation and human apotheosis are present already in John and Paul and make sense of many of the cryptic teachings of Jesus about the kingdom in the synoptic Gospels.

DISPUTE AND DIVERSITY IN THE CHURCH

Along with that deepening of insight there were more unfortunate developments. Each church council seemed eager to condemn and exclude opposing views. Arguments, and even the torture and burning of opponents, were not unknown in the early churches. There was an increasing intolerance as what were in fact the developing teachings of the orthodox churches came to be seen as the defence of an original divinely given faith that had to be preserved intact at all costs against its enemies.

The church was not just a path to life in the Spirit and union with God, though it always was that. It was also an organisation that anathematised and demonised all opposition and sought to exterminate all thought and practice that did not accept the 'true faith'. And with every new conciliar definition a new church sprang up that could not accept the definition. Christianity split into a thousand disputatious sects, so that every possible variant of interpreting the life of Jesus and of Christian faith, from God just appearing to be human, to a human claiming some similarity of character to God, from matter as an evil to be renounced, to matter as the sacrament of divine beauty, from strict obedience to divine law, to the total freedom of life in the Spirit, existed somewhere. And all these sects seemed to regard themselves as the 'one true faith', and the others as deviant and perverse corruptions.

Christians need to be much more aware of the tendencies to sectarianism, intolerance and arrogance in their faith. Early Christian writers quickly got themselves entangled in almost impenetrable technical terminology concerning hypostases, substances, natures and persons. They often confused themselves as much as everyone else by trying to define these terms in increasingly arcane ways. Why is it not enough to say that in Jesus a unique union of divine and human was manifested and that there are many ways of understanding this? Probably none of them is wholly satisfactory, but a majority view has been reached that some of them are more adequate than others. In particular, the Chalcedonian definition of 'two natures in one person' has come to be widely accepted, as long as it in turn allows different interpretations.

The important thing is that human lives should be united to the divine life through the inner action of the Spirit, which derives from the divine–human unity in Jesus. Pluralism of understanding is inevitable, given the limitations of all human concepts and the variety of human philosophical standpoints. It is not the case that you must have all the correct beliefs in order to be saved. What matters is that you try to understand as well as you can, and admit your limitations. If possible, instructed Christians should have some knowledge of past theological deliberations on these issues, and see how and why the early church councils decided as they did, what the most widely agreed positions are, and where differences arise and for what reasons.

Looking at the often violent and intemperate behaviour of many early Christian writers, I think we can learn that it is not possible to arrive at one finally correct definition of the divine activity in Jesus, that all our philosophical theorisings are pretty inadequate and that the more precise and minute our philosophical distinctions are, the worse our grasp of Christian truth gets. We should learn to accept that there will always be diverse responses to the disclosure of God in Jesus, and that very few of them are inerrant or final, and then only in the most general terms.

The first Christian theologians did change the Christian perspective in an illuminating way by creating a theology of divine incarnation, a union of divinity and humanity, and a subsequent human apotheosis. But they also sometimes fell into three gross errors.

First, they thought that they could pin down the divine nature in precise and detailed philosophical terminology. In this they were mistaken, and ironically the claim they also often made that the divine nature is ineffable should have made them aware of that. Where God is ineffable, few if any doctrines about God can be infallible or fully adequate.

Second, they thought that all must accept such terminology in order to be saved, so that those who demurred could not be tolerated. Whereas what is necessary to salvation is a life transformed by the Spirit of divine love, and plurality of understanding has been part of Christian faith from the beginning.

Third, they used the Bible in a curiously selective and literalistic way, to support the view that Christian truth had been taught by Jesus to the apostles and needed to be defended against all change. They took John's Gospel to report the actual words of Jesus and to be the source of detailed and complex theoretical beliefs about the divine nature, thus changing evocative poetic symbolism into particularly obscure philosophical prose. And they overlooked the fact that they themselves were being highly innovative in seeking to portray in very original ways the exact relationship between the historical Jesus, the eternal Son and the creator God.

What we can learn from these errors of the Christian Patristic writers, errors that led to violence, torture, censorship and repression, is that we must speak cautiously and tentatively about the ineffable God. We must accept a plurality of Christian understandings and look for growth in love as our test of Christian discipleship. We must restore to the Bible its function as a set of inspired and diverse responses to a discernment of God's liberating love in Christ. And we must accept that creative change is necessary as Christian faith finds itself in new contexts of life and thought. In fact such change is part of the proper creativity of the church, as it responds dynamically to the promptings of the Spirit of God.

PLATONISM AND EARLY CHRISTIAN DOCTRINE

The major conceptual change of Patristic thought is to take the concepts of a basically Platonic philosophy and use them to interpret the act of God in Jesus. It is not, I think, true, as an earlier generation of liberal theologians held, that such Hellenism subjected primitive Christianity to an alien thought-world. On the contrary, it was Platonism that was modified radically by the Christian belief that the Supreme Good was not just an unchanging perfection imperfectly imitated by the world, and that it does not lead us to renounce the world entirely in our pursuit of it. Rather the Good (conceived by Christians as a personal reality who contemplates its own nature, the Good, rather than an impersonal Goodness) had entered dynamically into the world in the person of Jesus and in the Spirit to assume an estranged world into the divine life, and thereby make the material realm a sacrament of eternity.

Some traditional Christians take the definitions of the first six or seven ecumenical councils as inerrant and final definitions of Christian faith, and the thought of the theologians they ratified as sufficient for all future Christian history. It might, however, seem rather odd that the process of Christian thought should be so innovative for five or six hundred years and then all innovation should cease. And there is at least one major issue that might lead to the thought that innovation needs to continue.

One of the chief influences of Platonism was that God, the Supreme Good, was generally conceived as immutable and impassible. Being perfect, God could not change, and divine perfection could not be affected by the sufferings and imperfections of the world. This creates major difficulties for any doctrine of incarnation, and especially for a doctrine that holds the eternal Word to be the only true subject of Jesus' acts and experiences.

John's Gospel says that 'the Word became flesh' (John 1:14). The Orthodox theologians did not really accept this, despite their proclaimed faithfulness to Scripture, for they held that the Word, being changeless, did not and could not *become* anything. Rather, they said, the changeless Word assumed a human body and soul into union with itself. This union is not after all like a union of two subjects, such that an infinite subject acts and experiences in and through a finite subject (though that is the view of it I have defended). The Word cannot be affected by anything that happens in the world, so it cannot receive sensory experiences or act in response to them.

The union of divine and human in Jesus, for some Patristic writers, is a union between a totally changeless Word and an acting and suffering human agent. The Word cannot even 'add' finite experiences to its knowledge, since nothing can be added to a changeless being. What is meant by 'union' is now almost wholly mysterious. How can a changing human agent be one with a changeless infinite being?

This will have to be a unique and sui generis sort of union. It makes Chalcedonian orthodoxy an assertion of union between divine and human without giving any idea of what the union could consist in. Perhaps that meets my request for a cautious and rather agnostic theology rather well. On the other hand, it may suggest that the Platonic notion of God as immutable and impassible may need to be modified by the Christian belief that 'In Christ God was reconciling the world to himself' (1 Cor. 5:19).

We might well think that Christian faith calls for further re-thinking of the idea of God beyond the Patristic period if it is to be adequate to belief in an incarnate and suffering God. Nicea and Chalcedon produced statements about the person of Christ that most (not all) subsequent Christians have found to define the limits of an adequate idea of the incarnation of God in Jesus. But many more recent theologians have thought that the Platonic idea of a totally changeless God is not really adequate to the Christian perception of a God who becomes incarnate and who suffers for the sake of humanity. A process of further re-thinking about God is positively mandated by the puzzles the ecumenical councils leave unresolved.

Chapter 5

The Triune God

God is known to Christians in three forms of being, as the totally transcendent creator of all, as the archetype of creation, manifest in human form in the person of Jesus, and as the Spirit present within the lives of men and women, uniting them to the divine life. It is one and the same God who is known in these three forms, and the church is called to witness to and mediate the divine drama of incarnation and transfiguration to all the earth.

THE ORTHODOX CHURCHES

The first seven ecumenical councils of the church were held in Byzantium, the Eastern Roman Empire (they were all held in what is now Turkey). They were summoned by the emperors and mostly presided over by bishops of the Eastern church. Western bishops were absent altogether at the First Council of Constantinople, and there were probably only six of them at the Council of Nicea. The church of the Western Roman Empire was never represented by the Bishop of Rome in person, though the Pope usually sent two representatives. He was always accorded primacy of honour among the ancient patriarchates of the church, though one pope, Vigilius, was exiled by the Emperor for a while during the Second Council of Constantinople, and the Third Council of Constantinople actually anathematised (condemned) the views of a previous pope, Honorius (because of an official letter of his that carelessly spoke of 'one will' in Christ). So the first great councils of the church were neither convened by nor presided over by the

Pope or his representatives. The councils were subject to the authority of the emperors, and of the Patriarchs of Constantinople, Jerusalem, Antioch and Alexandria, who gave primacy of honour, but not supreme teaching Authority, to Rome.

This was all to change. The Byzantine Empire and the church in Turkey virtually ceased to exist with the capture of Constantinople by the Ottoman Turks in 1453. But the Byzantine church had long ceased to recognise the authority of the Western church, based in Rome. The Pope and the Eastern church mutually excommunicated each other in 1054, and the Crusaders ransacked Constantinople in 1204, leaving a legacy of hatred and suspicion that was to endure for centuries to come.

The remnant of the Orthodox churches, most prominently in Greece and later in Russia, have always claimed that they represent the mind of the ancient church, over against the innovations of Rome and the West. One might unkindly say that they have preferred ancient innovations to modern ones.

THE DEVELOPMENT OF PAPAL AUTHORITY IN THE WEST

As the Western Roman Empire also collapsed, the Pope, Patriarch of Rome, became increasingly important, both politically and religiously. In the East, the emperors summoned church councils and appointed and deposed bishops. But in the West matters were more complicated. In 800 CE, Charlemagne was crowned Holy Roman Emperor by Pope Leo III. Although the emperors did appoint bishops and occasionally imprison popes, gradually the popes gained political ascendancy. There was a development in ideas of papal authority beyond anything that had been possible previously. This process reached its apogee in the Bull *Unam Sanctam* of Pope Boniface VIII, issued in 1302. The Pope there declares that all temporal power is to be subject to spiritual power (that is, to the Pope), that it is necessary to salvation for every human creature to be subject to the Roman pontiff and that opposition to papal decrees is opposition to God himself.

Any decent historian will be quick to assert that we must judge these things in the light of political events of the time, and see how the Pope was a political figure locked in desperate conflict with other political figures. Yet it must be confessed that this doctrine of absolute papal supremacy seems quite a change from the assertions of Jesus that his kingdom was not 'of this world' (John 18:36) and that those who would lead must be the servants of all.

Unam Sanctam can scarcely be considered an official teaching of the Roman Catholic Church. But it is salutary to remember that a pope did once make such claims – indeed, Innocent III declared that he was 'less than God but more than man' – and that many things that popes have said and done must now be regarded with some embarrassment by faithful Catholics. What is unarguable is that Catholic understanding of the role of the Pope did develop considerably from the fourth century, when most Christians gave the Pope a primacy of honour, but no unilateral legislative authority, to the fourteenth century, when the Pope could claim to be the one head of the universal church, with sole powers to appoint bishops (and even to appoint rulers), and with the sole power to convene and preside over authentic councils of the church. That power was neither claimed nor conceded for the first seven ecumenical councils. The development would be regarded by many Roman Catholics as a legitimate and necessary one if the church was to maintain its unity and mission. But that it is a major development is indisputable. Such papal claims have always been rejected by the Orthodox churches, whose bishops regard them as unjustified innovations. It is impossible to find any assertion in the New Testament that states that the successors of Peter, and they alone, have a spiritual authority that outweighs all others, and that even outweighs all temporal authorities on earth. Modern Roman Catholic teaching would give a much more nuanced view of papal authority than anything to be found in *Unam Sanctam*. But that only reinforces the point that changes have often occurred in Christian teaching, and have often done so in response to specific historical and political contexts.

THE TRINITY IN EAST AND WEST

If the Orthodox are asked what constitutes the greatest change in Western Christian thought, they usually point to the addition to the Nicene Creed that was made by the Western church at the Third Council of Toledo, in 589 CE. This addition states that the Holy Spirit proceeds from the Father *and the Son*, not from the Father alone. Orthodox theologians have always maintained that this addition was at best a private opinion of theologians like Augustine, was not part of the earlier Nicene Creed and is an unjustified innovation. It is certainly true that it is an addition, and that many Patristic writers opposed the doctrine. The Roman church has stuck to it, however (as have most Protestant churches), and it has become a major bone of contention between Orthodox and Catholic Christians.

It is very hard for most people to see what all the fuss is about. Basically, the Orthodox insist that the Father is the sole generative principle of the Trinity, so the Son cannot be given generative equality with the Father. Catholics have argued that, since they believe the Father and Son share all properties except for paternity and sonship, the property of 'spirating' the Spirit must belong to both. This is rarified doctrine indeed, good for grinding logical distinctions ever more finely, but hardly a matter on which Jesus spent a great deal of time (Jesus, according to Mark, said, 'The Lord our God, the Lord is one': Mark 12:29).

The issue does, however, raise the tricky question of how we can distinguish Father, Son and Spirit in God if God is one. The Bible itself contains no systematic or theoretical account of the divine nature. Jewish commentators sometimes say that the Bible tells us what God commands, but does not tell us what God is. Deuteronomy 29:29 sets the tone: 'The secret things belong to the Lord our God, but the revealed things belong to us and to our children for ever.' This has been taken to say that Torah is revealed, but the nature of God remains secret. Despite this, however, the Christian church did not hesitate to develop a complex and detailed theoretical account of the divine nature, and used the concepts and thought-forms of Greek philosophy to do so.

In the Orthodox Greek account, standardised by the Cappadocian Fathers in the fourth century, God is said to be one *ousia*, one being. But God exists in three *hypostases*, three individual exemplifications. Basil of Caesarea used the analogy of three individual men sharing in the one substance of humanity. That suggests that there are three distinct centres of consciousness in God, three persons in something like the modern sense of distinct individuals. For this reason, the Orthodox have sometimes been said to believe in a 'social Trinity'. God is not just one individual, but three distinct persons indissolubly linked together. Modern theologians who have used such a model include Wolfhart Pannenberg, Jurgen Moltmann, David Brown, John Zizioulas and Richard Swinburne.[5]

This allocation of a 'social Trinity' to the Cappadocians is complicated, however, by the fact that at least one of Augustine's analogies for the

Trinity – that in God there is a lover, a beloved and the love between them – seems social in some sense. And Richard of St Victor in the twelfth century speaks explicitly of three 'persons' of the Trinity as bound together in mutual love. These are undoubtedly Western, Latin theologians, so perhaps it is better to say that a social model of the Trinity has existed in both Eastern and Western Christian traditions and that it has always been balanced by models that stress more clearly the unity of God.

Nevertheless, part of the continuing argument over the precise nature of the Trinity that divides East and West is due to the fact that the Eastern Orthodox tradition has emphasised the distinction of persons and consequently has been concerned to preserve the sole causal priority of the Father. This has not been of particular concern in the West, where another Augustinian analogy, represented in recent theology by Karl Barth, Karl Rahner and John Macquarrie, has been more influential.

This is the analogy of memory, intellect and will (*memoria, intelligentia* and *voluntas*), which are three different faculties of one mind. It suggests that God is primarily a unity, though one that exists in three different forms or modes of being. Augustine rejected the Greek view that the source of divinity is the Father, a fully personal reality. Instead he held that the Father is not the source of divinity, for divinity lies only in the three persons taken together. So there is no reason why the Spirit should not proceed from both Father and Son. Out of such choices of different analogies a gap of understanding opened up between the Greek and Latin churches, which has not been closed to this day.

This shows how arcane arguments, often framed in different languages, Latin and Greek, just to add to the confusion, can generate major divisions in the church, even when all concerned (the major theologians, anyway) agree that they are not sure what they are talking about – as Augustine said, 'human language labours altogether under great poverty of speech' (*De Trinitate* V, 9).[6]

THE TRINITY AND DIVINE LOVE

Even for those who hold a social model of the Trinity, it has usually been asserted that all three persons of the Trinity act indivisibly together, and nothing divides them except their relationships – of begetting, being begotten and proceeding (whether from the Father alone, or from the Father and the Son).

The problem here is that if nothing divides the hypostases except the ways in which they are related to each other, there does not seem much point in having three entities. They will all know and do exactly the same things. They will have nothing to learn from each other, and no distinctive qualities of their own to contribute. There does not seem much point in having three identical beings in such a relationship.

Some proponents of the social approach drop the doctrine that the hypostases are all essentially identical in quality. They think of each hypostasis as having different properties and roles from the others. Richard Swinburne, following Richard of St Victor, even argues that love requires three different persons, one to give love, one to receive it and one to be the fruit of shared and co-operative love. Two persons, apparently, are too few and four are too many. Three is just right. That is certainly an interesting argument in favour of one-child families. I would think, and most social psychologists would agree, that the best number of persons for a loving community would be between twelve and fourteen – that is the number of persons who can readily relate to one another in a group. But that would not produce very good support for the Trinity, since it would suggest that there would be fourteen persons in a fully satisfactory God.

In any case, it is hard to see what sort of love could exist between persons who are all parts of the same being. It is as if different parts of a human being with three different personalities could all be said to love one another. That would be a very peculiar, even pathological, sort of love.

These speculations, it must be said, have a very slim basis in biblical thought. Everything that Christians know of the love of God must derive from the revelation of that love in Jesus. The love that is manifest in his life is a forgiving, reconciling, healing, compassionate, self-sacrificing and invincible love. It is essentially related to other persons, persons who are capable of rejecting personal relationship, who are in need of compassion and healing and who have very different histories and characters.

If the love of Jesus is our model for the love of God, then God, as love, must go out to persons who are other than God, who are capable of rejecting God, but who can be healed by divine love and united to the divine life by compassion and co-operation. This is not a love of one hypostasis of God for another hypostasis of God. It is a love for what is other than God but can be united to the life of God in fellowship. It is a love that requires a created other, perhaps, but not a love that can be operative within the divine being itself, where there is no possible scope for rejection, compassion, healing or a real autonomy of the other.

I think it is right to say that *agapistic* love requires self-giving to others. It requires the acceptance of love from another. And it requires co-operation and sharing. But such love requires real otherness and freely chosen community. That cannot be provided by an 'inner Trinity', without sundering the unity of God unacceptably.

What such love requires is a source of life that gives the gift of otherness from the perfection of its own being. It requires a love that places itself in real reciprocal relation to others, so that it both accepts love when it is given and permits the possibility of rejection when love is withheld. And it requires a love that co-operates with the free acts of others to create new forms of beauty and friendship, and to form a free communion of persons in which love can be fulfilled.

There is a sort of threefoldness in such love. But it is not the threefoldness of three separate persons in one divine being, loving one another when there is no possibility of loss, dissension or sacrifice. It is the threefoldness of love given through creation, love received through its reciprocal relation to creation, and love active within creation to unite it consciously to the divine source of all love.

Genuine self-giving love must relate the lover to what is genuinely other, relatively autonomous, and capable of accepting or rejecting love. So the biblical statement that 'God is love' (1 John 4:8) is best construed as saying that Being essentially flows out to create other relatively autonomous persons, and embodies itself in the finite, in order to unite finite persons to God in a free community of love wherein otherness and freedom, unity and communion, can all co-exist.

It is rather odd to take the phrase 'God is love' from the first letter of John as referring to internal relationships within the being of God. In context, it most obviously refers to God going out into the world in love, so that the world might share in the life of God. The text continues, 'God's love was revealed among us in this way: God sent his only Son into the world so that we might live through him' (1 John 4:9). What this suggests is a threefold movement, from God as creator to God as incarnate in creation, and then to God as acting to include creatures in the divine life. It relates God essentially to creation, in a dynamic and self-giving way. It does not seem to speak of a timeless and complete activity within the divine being itself.

The triune nature of God is articulated in this way by the Scottish Anglican theologian John Macquarrie as primordial being, expressive being – being expressed in a particular way or ways in creation – and unitive being – being present in all creation to unite it to the divine. These are three forms of the divine being, three distinct ways in which the divine being exists.

THE ECONOMIC TRINITY

This may seem to be a very different approach from that of the Orthodox tradition, with its stress on charting the inner relations of the divine being, even apart from any relation to creation. But in fact there is good precedent for it in Orthodox theology. The fourteenth-century Orthodox theologian Gregory Palamas elaborated a distinction between the divine *ousia*, which is completely unknowable, and the divine *energeia*, the divine acts in relation to us, by which alone we know God.

Armed with this distinction, we could say that we know God through three distinct sorts of 'energy' or forms of being and action. These are all forms of one indivisible 'essence' or being. But, since we cannot comprehend that essence, we must think of God in the threefold form of ultimate origin, intelligible archetype of the cosmos and inner unifier of the cosmos to the divine.

On this interpretation, talk of the Trinity is talk of God in relation to the created cosmos, and little or nothing is said about the being of God in itself, out of all relation to creation. That seems to me to reflect the general biblical position that the being of God is hidden in a cloud of dazzling darkness and is so ineffable that no adequate image can be made or conceived by human minds. 'Truly, you are a God who hides himself' (Is. 45:15).

It is when we think of God in relation to the cosmos that we find ourselves, as Christians, compelled to think of God in a threefold form. There is the ungenerated abyss from which all things derive and upon which all created things depend at every moment of their being. There is the archetypal form of this (and of every possible) cosmos, held in the divine mind, but articulating the divine being precisely as a mind or intellect. In Christian understanding, the divine mind is expressed or manifested in the created cosmos, as all things participate in the archetypes subsisting in the divine mind ('All things have been created through him and for him': Colossians 1:16).

There are many kinds and degrees of manifestation, which reveal the nature of the creator with different degrees of adequacy. Christians find in the person of Jesus a full manifestation of the archetypal form of humanity and a prefiguring of the fulfilment of the cosmos by its final transfiguring union with God (Eph. 1:9, 10).

It is in this respect, and only, I think, in this respect, that God the creator becomes God the Father of Jesus Christ. In a sense, the ungenerated abyss becomes knowable as a personal Father, but only insofar as the ungenerated is personally related to the eternal Son, and so takes form as Father of that Son. In other words, it is with the eternal generation of the Son that God becomes Father. The formless takes form in a particular way, with the generation of first the idea and then the actuality of this cosmos.

Moreover, the Son does not remain an archetype. The Son becomes incarnate, embodied in the material cosmos, in which the archetype is incarnate as example and ideal. There may be many particular forms and ideals within the cosmos, but for us on this earth it is the person of Jesus who is, Christians believe, the embodied archetype of humanity.

This process of archetype and embodiment is still incomplete, however, unless and until the whole cosmos can in some way be united to the divine life, by its participation in the union that Jesus has definitively established. In the case of Jesus, God preveniently and unilaterally unites a human subject to the divine life. Jesus cannot sin and fall away from God, for he is one with God in the innermost core of his being.

Other humans, however, are born in estrangement from God, and they need to be refashioned in the divine likeness by their free co-operation with divine grace.

So from the person of Jesus there grows a community in which humans can freely turn from the world and be formed in the divine likeness by their acceptance of the Spirit of God. Unlike Jesus, they are united to God in a gradual and developing process of repeated repentance and endeavour, but one that is guaranteed to issue in final union. It is the Spirit of God, working within human lives, that brings about such union. Humans, in turn, have the vocation of helping to bring the whole creation, or at least this earthly part of it, into a more transparent unity with God. They are, in this sense, called to be the priests of the earth.

In the economy of redemption God is the transcendent creator and sustainer of all. God is the archetype who becomes embodied in finite being, perhaps in many forms, but definitively for humanity in Jesus. And God is the Spirit working within human lives to transform them into the divine likeness and incorporate them into the divine life, and working within all creation to make the material cosmos a sacrament of the divine.

This is how God is known in relation to us, as creator, redeemer and sanctifier. It is truly how God is in relation to us. God does not just pretend to be threefold in nature. God really is threefold in nature, insofar as God turns towards a created universe in love. But it does not seem to me justifiable to say, as Karl Rahner does, that the economic Trinity (God in relation to us) is identical with the immanent Trinity (God as God is in the divine essence). Certainly the economic Trinity does not falsify or conceal the nature of God. It is how God can be truly known by us. But it is still God in relation to us, and how God is apart from any relation to us is simply beyond human knowing. There is no higher divine nature that we somehow know about. There is only the divine mystery, of which we cannot speak.

THE INADEQUACY OF HUMAN SPEECH ABOUT THE TRINITY

I believe we are most true to the New Testament, and to subsequent reflection on experience of the risen Lord and of the Spirit, when we say that God turns to creation in threefold form. The Lord our God is one, but the forms of the divine being and activity, as we know and experience them, are threefold. It can therefore be misleading to speak of God as three persons in one substance, if this leads us to think of three persons, identical in almost all their characteristics, somehow united in a unique divine society. For to speak of the three persons in God as almost identical would undermine the real diversity of the forms in which God exists. The 'persons' of the Trinity are not all individuals with identical properties. They are quite different forms of the divine being. But it is also misleading to think of the Trinity as three persons who love each other as separate individuals, since that undermines the unity of God. The three hypostases of God are three quite different forms of the one indivisible divine being, as that one God turns towards the world in love.

The great positive virtue of this account is that it stays close to the New Testament witness to the activities of Father, Son and Spirit and does not stray too far into the ontological wilderness of hypostases, subsistent relations and processions.

Overall, what theological speculation about the Trinity shows is that it is unhelpful to turn metaphors and analogies – of person, substance, essence and mode of activity – into hard and fast statements of fact. The split between East and West on the Trinity is an example of tentative and abstract theological debates being turned into unalterable and improbably precise church slogans.

If you ask, 'Does the divinity of God derive from the Father?' or 'Does the Spirit proceed from the Father alone?' perhaps the wisest answer would be to confess that any answers to such questions will be tentative and inadequate attempts to understand the mystery of God, as God has been disclosed to us in creation, in Jesus Christ and in the inner activity of the Holy Spirit. A pluralism of beliefs, and a greater tentativeness in their profession, might in this area be a sign of religious maturity.

If I am right, some theologians of both the Greek and the Latin traditions have erred in thinking that they can define the inner nature of God by the deployment of a few biblical texts, treated too uncritically, and the use of a little Greek philosophy, treated too dogmatically. A greater feeling for metaphor and a greater awareness of the limitations of the human intellect is the antidote to such metaphysical pretensions.

As the church in the West developed new views of papal authority and philosophically complex doctrines of the Trinity, it was carrying out its proper task of creatively re-thinking Christian faith, in new political and cultural contexts. But it did not always see just how new and provisional its suggestions were. Fourteenth-century doctrines of the papacy have since been radically revised to dissociate religious beliefs more clearly from political claims to authority. Medieval doctrines of the Trinity can now be seen to pose a set of philosophical problems that need to be re-thought in terms of more recent philosophical discussions. What the churches need to do today is just what the Catholic Church did in medieval times, that is, creatively re-think Christian faith in new ways. But they should take care to be fully aware of what they are doing, and of the radical limitations of all human thought while they are doing it.

Chapter 6

Purifying Fire

God wills that all should be saved, and come to full knowledge and love of the divine. But if free persons reject love, and choose paths of egoism and greed, they lock themselves into a world of empty gloom, lit only by the fires of passion and hate. Christ enters that world to liberate all who turn to him, or who turn towards the Good as they know it. Atonement is the gradual but certain uniting of human and divine, as Christ shares the world of pain in order to enable humans to share the world of divine bliss.

ORIGINAL SIN

The greatest theological difference between the Greek and Latin churches is not about the Trinity, despite what some theologians say. It is the increasing importance in the Roman church of ideas of original sin, atonement and the penitential system.

The doctrine of original sin and original guilt was stated by Augustine, and was gradually elaborated in detail in the Latin church, until it received definitive formulation at the Council of Trent, in the sixteenth century. It involves a literal interpretation of the fall of Adam and Eve from a state of original innocence, and a Platonic thesis that somehow all of humanity (human nature itself) is involved in the guilt of Adam's sin. This guilt, for Augustine, is transmitted by the procreative act, and it involves both the loss of sanctifying grace and the punishment of suffering and death. In fact every newborn infant is fated for eternal damnation by reason of its guilt 'in Adam', even before it has actually done anything.

The doctrine is incompatible with the now generally accepted view of evolution and genetics that acquired characteristics (like committing some sin and suffering some defect of will as a result) cannot be inherited (cannot be passed on genetically or by natural procreation to offspring). It is also not now generally thought by anyone who accepts the findings of modern science that there was ever a historical state of innocence, or a literal Adam and Eve. So the doctrine has to be revised in some way if it is to be compatible with modern scientific thought – though of course such problems did not occur in the medieval church.

The idea that people are guilty before they have actually done anything is hard to maintain for any philosophical system that is non-Platonic, that does not regard 'humanity', with the property of guilt, as prior to the existence of free individual human beings. The fact that the notion of the solidarity of the human race in original guilt is based on such a Platonic premise makes it unlikely that it was a New Testament view, or Paul's view. A more plausible reading of Paul is that he saw the consequences of Adam's sin as consisting in suffering, death and estrangement from God for all Adam's descendants. That is a severe punishment, but it does not involve participation in a guilt that merits eternal punishment. If this is Paul's view, it is a fairly typical Jewish view. Paul had no recorded view that sin was transmitted by procreation, or that it involves the guilt, and therefore the death and irretrievable damnation, of all who are not baptised. Such a belief is very difficult to reconcile with any plausible belief that God is revealed in Jesus to be a God of supreme love. It is therefore both factually and morally questionable.

The doctrine of original sin will have to be re-thought in the light of modern knowledge of genetics, of the evolutionary development of humans from earlier species that suffered and died long before any human committed any sin, and of a general rejection of Platonic thought.

We could still speak of an estrangement of the world from God that is a consequence of the willed acts of our ancestors, and that needs to be countered by divine grace if humans are to attain their destiny of sharing in the divine life. But the developed doctrine of universal human solidarity in sinning, not just in the consequences of sin, of transmission by procreation, and of the penalty of eternal retribution, was itself a re-thinking and development of a Pauline insight that human beings are alienated from God and unable to love fully and truly, even though they remain morally free and under obligation. The medieval re-thinking seems to me a particularly unfortunate one, and to be a definite regression from earlier non-Augustinian views that, though the wages of sin is death, God offers life to all who will freely accept it. To put it bluntly, unbaptised babies are not, as Dante supposed, deprived of the vision of God for ever (as I write this, Pope Benedict XVI has just publicly affirmed that Dante was wrong). The divine will for all of us, without exception, remains that we should become sharers in the divine life (1 Peter 1:4), and a loving God will deprive none of that possibility.

HELL, JUDGMENT AND PUNISHMENT

In any case the idea that the punishment for sin will be everlasting torture is highly questionable, and probably unacceptable to anyone who believes that God is just, merciful and loving. The doctrine of eternal Hell seems to be a construction of the church, even though quite an early one. Any reasonably critical view of the New Testament would see the parables of Jesus – which speak of wheat and tares, throwing tares on a fiery rubbish heap, or consignment to 'outer darkness' – as vivid and picturesque warnings of the ultimate self-destructiveness of rejecting love, rather than as literal predictions of hard times to come for almost everybody (see *What the Bible Really Teaches*, ch. 9).

The Bible does speak of divine judgment, and of a division between the just and the unjust. It warns that injustice will bring sorrow, torment, death and ultimate estrangement from the divine life. It also speaks of an alienation of the human world from God. Paul, especially, writes that 'the scripture has imprisoned all things under the power of sin' (Gal. 3:22). Humans are born into a society estranged from God, under the power of greed, hatred and ignorance.

But Paul also writes, 'God has imprisoned all in disobedience, so that he may be merciful to all' (Rom. 11:32). All are called to repentance, and God's mercy is extended to all without exception. It is God's will and desire that all should turn from injustice and receive the mercy that is offered supremely and definitively in Christ. God wills the salvation of every human being

(1 Timothy 2:4: 'God our Saviour, who desires everyone to be saved'). Presumably if God wills this, God must make it possible. It follows (since most humans who have existed on earth have not heard of Jesus) that salvation cannot depend on explicit confession of belief in Jesus, made during this life. God's grace is given through Jesus, but it is not limited to those who have heard of Jesus (think of how human life depends on oxygen, even for people who have never heard of oxygen).

Salvation is a possibility for all people. It is what God wills, and the idea of Hell stands as a warning of the consequences of rejecting God, not as a prediction of what will happen to the majority of the human race. The New Testament hope is that all will heed the warning. God will certainly help them in every possible way to do so. And it seems reasonable to hope that God's power and patience will be sufficient to bring about what God wills, however long it takes.

In the early Hebrew Bible there was no clear belief in an afterlife. So God's judgment and salvation had to take place in history. Judgment was seen by the prophets primarily as judgment on military oppressors, but it was broadened to include those who broke God's Law and so separated themselves from union with God. Salvation similarly was freedom from oppression, but it was also life in full knowledge and love of God.

Jesus, like the Pharisees, believed in the resurrection of the dead. So judgment and salvation came to be taken to occur after earthly death.

No mature spiritual view would think of judgment as torture imposed simply for past disobedience. But nor would it be fair for those who have killed and hated to live happily for ever. If the universe is morally ordered, there must be something like a law of moral compensation or desert – you will be treated as you treat others.

This is present in Jesus' teaching. 'The Son of man is to come with his angels in the glory of his Father, and then he will repay every man for what he has done' (Matt. 16:27). 'With the judgment you pronounce you will be judged, and the measure you give will be the measure you get' (Matt. 7:2).

Yet in the Sermon on the Mount Jesus teaches that we should not resist evil, but turn the other cheek (Matt. 5:38), that we should love our enemies and those who hate us (Matt. 5:44) and that in this way we will be 'perfect as your heavenly Father is perfect' (Matt. 5:48). At the very least, this means that God is not vengeful or vindictive, and will never cease to love us, even though we hate God.

That explicitly rules out any punishment that is purely retributive ('an eye for an eye'), or any punishment that is a final cutting off of divine love and that does not express concern for our ultimate well-being. All divine 'punishment' must attend to what could correct our faults or teach us true compassion, not just mechanically do to us what we have done to others. And it must aim at bringing us back to God – it can never be solely retributive, harming us just because and to the degree that we have harmed others.

How can we hold these things together? We can do so only if we do not take retributive talk literally, as laying down unbreakable rules – that is the whole point of Jesus' teachings about the divine Law in the Sermon on the Mount. It is rather that those who are indifferent to others must find out what it is like to be treated with indifference. They must learn empathy, real identification with the pain of others which indifferent acts have caused. But empathy is not best learned by torturing someone. It is best learned by experiencing what it is like to be another person, so that you commit yourself to doing something, by effort and hard work, to make things better.

There are three conditions of merciful punishment. It must aim at changing character. It must require hard work to make restitution. And it must have the prospect of ending.

It is possible that character will not be changed, but will harden. Souls may sink further into hatred and greed. It will then be important that their hatred and greed bring them no advantage or satisfaction. They will become bitter, enraged individuals, forever seeking new pleasures and failing to be satisfied. They may be described as tormented and destroyed by the flames of their inordinate desires, or as locked into the darkness of their own loneliness and hatred of others. Even then, the possibility of escape remains, of discovering the unsatisfactoriness of their lives and vowing to change.

Could such a state continue for ever? Perhaps it would best be described as 'age-long' (the exact translation of *aeonios*, the New Testament word usually translated as 'eternal'). It may continue as long as the person fails to feel the suffering of such an existence enough to want to change it.

Judgment, we might say, is a state in which it becomes clear what sorts of persons we really are – proud, resentful, self-deceiving and egoistic, or genuinely devoted to the welfare of others. The Gospels use two main metaphors to describe this state. The just, the penitent, the humble, the innocent enter the kingdom, where they sit at a great feast with Abraham and the prophets. The selfish, the unforgiving, the arrogant, the cruel are locked out in darkness. Or the just are gathered into a barn, while the unjust are thrown onto Gehenna, the flaming rubbish dump outside Jerusalem.

Nobody thinks there will be a literal feast, or that we will live in a literal barn. We will not go into literal darkness or be thrown on a fire for burning rubbish. There will, however, be a division: on the one hand, happiness and security; on the other loneliness, torment and destruction. Happiness is the state of those who are open to the love of God and allow it to transform their lives into channels of love. Misery and torment is the state of those who put themselves first and whose selves are tormented and destroyed by the passions they unleash.

Jesus teaches that these things are to some extent realised during this life. But they become clear and unambiguous in the life beyond this world. That is the judgment, not that God punishes us for ever without possibility of reprieve, but that we have to live with what we have made ourselves but have often managed to disguise from ourselves and others in this world.

Yet there is no limit to divine forgiveness – according to Matthew, 'Peter came up and said to him, "Lord, how often shall my brother sin against me, and I forgive him? As many as seven times?" Jesus said to him, "I do not say to you seven times, but seventy times seven"' (Matt. 18:21–2). Would God do less? So the door of repentance is never closed.

Regrettably Christians have often taken a harsh interpretation of Jesus' teaching on judgment by taking his parables literally, and by letting the harshest-sounding texts (like Matthew 25:46: 'These will go away into eternal punishment, but the righteous into eternal life') become the key to interpreting the others.

These texts cannot really be taken literally – we are not, after all, literally either ears of wheat or weeds. Matthew's 'punishment' may be eternal, or age-long, just as the fires of Gehenna never die, but it does not follow that we can never escape from that punishment or that unquenchable fire. And what is the reason for thinking that all can be freed from it? Most importantly, it is Jesus' teaching on what love requires – unlimited forgiveness, undying concern for the welfare of even those who hate you, and the costly love shown by the parable of the Good Samaritan. Those texts should be the key for interpreting all Jesus' parables concerning judgment. They unequivocally entail that 'it is not the will of my Father who is in heaven that one of these little ones should perish' (Matt. 18:14). If only they will repent, they will not be eternally lost.

Jesus stands in the tradition of the prophets of Israel, and he undoubtedly teaches that there will be a Judgment, that the deeds of all will be exposed, and judged by the rigorous standards of divine self-giving love. By those standards, almost all will stand condemned. Such condemnation should not be taken lightly, for it means that we are unfitted for the companionship of God and locked into the flames of our own desires and the darkness of our misanthropy.

Yet precisely because it is divine love that judges us, and because divine love is limitlessly forgiving, we can be sure that repentance and renewal of mind is always possible, even beyond death. Nevertheless we must not take it for granted, and perhaps the longer we leave it, the harder repentance becomes.

The idea of a limited time of punishment is suggested by three Gospel passages. In the Sermon on the Mount, Jesus tells a parable of being put in prison if you do not make friends with your accuser, and says, 'You will never get out till you have paid the last penny' (Matt. 5:26). In another parable, the prison metaphor is used again, and the unmerciful servant is put in prison 'till he should pay all his debt' (Matt. 18:34).

Luke records a parable of a servant who has not prepared for his master's return, and says, 'That servant who knew his master's will, but did not make ready or act according to his will, shall receive a severe beating But he who did not know and did what deserved a beating, shall receive a light beating' (Luke 12:47–8).

These are only parables, but they suggest that there are different degrees of punishment, just as there are different degrees of reward. And the punishments are of limited duration. When the doctrine of Purgatory developed in the church, it built on such texts as these, speaking of punishment as a sort of probation that is meant to lead eventually to union with God. Jesus' insistent and repeated teaching on the unqualified and unlimited nature of love strongly suggests that Sheol or Hades (the world of the dead), Gehenna or the outer darkness is more like Purgatorial fire than like everlasting Hell. As Mark's Gospel says, 'Everyone will be salted with fire' (Mark 9:49). It is possible that human souls will always resist the love of God. But it is also always possible that the power of self will be broken, and that the souls in darkness will come to accept the forgiving love of God. That is what God desires, and the good news Jesus proclaimed is that the love of God draws near to inspire our acceptance.

The paintings of the terrors of Hell on the walls of medieval churches may be much more interesting than the paintings of rather static groups of singing angels in heaven. But the doctrine of eternal Hell seems to arise from a tendency to take metaphors of great spiritual depth and turn them into literal descriptions of unbearable sadism. This is a piece of Christian re-thinking that we may need to re-think again, because it seems to contradict the gospel of the limitless love of God.

THE ATONEMENT

Along with developments in the doctrine of original sin and of Hell, the medieval Latin church developed a new doctrine of atonement, God's way of liberating humans from sin and its consequences. Though this new doc-trine was never officially defined by the church, it became a widely accepted belief, the main outlines of which were later accepted by the Protestant Reformers.

The new doctrine was classically framed by the eleventh-century the-ologian Anselm of Canterbury, in his book *Cur Deus Homo?* He rejected the previously widely accepted view of Gregory of Nyssa that Jesus' death was a ransom paid to the Devil to buy freedom for human beings. Gregory's the-ory was based on Mark 10:45 – 'the son of man came not to be served but to serve, and to give his life a ransom for many'. A simple interpretation of this statement is that Jesus was paying a heavy price by sharing in the suffering of humanity, so that humans might be united to God through him. But Gregory literalised the metaphor, and asked to whom the price was paid, and how much it was. Having asked a silly question, he gave a silly answer – the price was the death of Jesus, and it was to be paid to the Devil.[7]

Anselm's objection to this was twofold – that the Devil had no rights over God, and that it would be a deception for God to give his Son as a ran-som when in fact the resurrection would deprive the Devil of his alleged payment in any case.

In its place Anselm proposed a 'satisfaction' or 'substitutionary' theory of atonement. Because of our sin, we owe God a debt of honour that we can never repay. Jesus, being sinless, is free of such a debt. Being perfectly divine, his death has infinite merit and so can be used to pay all our debts of honour to God. God became human, Anselm argues, precisely so that he could, as man, honour God truly on our behalf, and God's demand for justice would be satisfied. Jesus' perfect obedience substitutes for our imperfect obedience and is a gift of infinite worth to the Father which can be offered on our behalf.

Anselm's theory has its own peculiarities. After all, the gift that the Son offers to the Father is given by God to God, and it is rather odd for God to require that he give himself a gift to satisfy his own honour. It would be simpler for God simply to forgive our sins without any gift. Thomas Aquinas later revised a basically Anselmian theory, allowing that God did not *require* Jesus to die before God could forgive sin. Yet such a sacrificial death was, Thomas held, an appropriate way of reconciling sinful humanity to God.[8]

It may seem that such a quasi-legal transaction, of asking someone else to honour God when you cannot do it yourself, does not really help actually to liberate you from the power of sin. More ancient ideas of Christ as the great Physician, or the healer of wounded souls, may seem to meet the human need for liberation more adequately. The cross shows the participation of God in human suffering, and it is in that sense that Christ 'dies for [i.e. because of and in order to liberate us from the power of] our sins'. But it is Christ's resurrection, the divine vindication of his total obedience to his priestly vocation, which carries liberating power. That power is conveyed through the Spirit, so that forgiveness and sanctification (setting aside the power of sin and uniting us to the divine) are two sides of the same divine act.

This view of atonement is more like that of Peter Abelard, who is often misunderstood as saying that the atonement is nothing more than a subjective change in us, and that the self-giving death of Jesus is nothing more than a good example to follow. Abelard insisted, however, that the atonement is an objective act of God, that actually brings about human redemption. But he did not see it as an act of substitution. He rather saw it as the historical act of God's participation in suffering. This act needs to be effected in each human life through the objective action of the Spirit, who unites human lives to the divine life as humans respond to the self-giving act of God in Christ. This idea of atonement as participation in God's objective act of self-giving and unitive love is well attested in the New Testament, and is more characteristic of the Greek emphasis on incarnation and *theosis* than of the ideas of satisfaction and substitution that came to mark the Latin tradition after the eleventh century.[9]

Anselm's account depends upon a strict retributivist model of divine justice. Our sin has deprived God of his due. The price of honour must be paid. Christ pays it for us, and so the demand for retribution for injustice is satisfied, albeit by someone else (Platonically, if 'humanity' honours God truly in Christ, then we may be regarded as 'included' in that satisfaction).

It was from such ideas, which Anselm was the first to set out in systematic form, that the belief arose that the church possessed an infinite treasury of merits – those obtained by Christ's death. These merits could be accessed by believers who undertook specific penitential activities, imposed by the church, and could be used either for the benefit of themselves or for others, living or dead.

The Eucharistic covenant meal of the Lord's body and blood had for centuries been seen as a sacrifice, or, strictly speaking, the making-present of the one infinitely fruitful sacrifice of the cross. Christ was the priest, and Christ was the sacrificial victim. But the idea of sacrifice was developed so that Christ was also seen as offering the merits of his death for those present at Mass, or those for whom they pray. At least in popular thought, it was often believed that the more Masses you offered, or the more penances you undertook, the more merits you could accrue.

I am not speaking here of official defined dogmas, but of widespread Catholic practices in the medieval church. Nor am I primarily concerned to ask whether these practices were legitimate or not. I am mainly concerned to point out that they were new, unknown to the earlier church, and were often resolutely contested even as they arose. However new they were, for many people they now represent 'traditional Catholic faith'. But traditions rarely go back as far as we think, and in many cases historians can date their inception with some definiteness.

PURGATORY

The writing of *Cur Deus Homo* in 1098 is one such significant date. Another is the first written mention of the word 'Purgatory' in 1170, according to the French scholar Jacques LeGoff. In his book *The Birth of Purgatory* (Scolar Press, 1984), LeGoff sets out the development of the doctrine of Purgatory from the apparent mentions of a purifying fire in the Gospels, which I have mentioned, and from some other texts in Paul, to the developed doctrine of the Council of Trent in the sixteenth century. The developed doctrine is that those who die penitent and in faith may still have temporal punishments due because of their sins. These will be like painful fire, but they are finite in duration, and souls in Purgatory will be assured of final salvation. In addition, their pains may be relieved by the prayers of the living.

What is new about this is not that there may be a possibility of salvation after death, or that the prayers of the living may help the dead. What is new is belief in a specific state or place called Purgatory, different from Hell, Heaven and Limbo (a state without the vision of God, but otherwise pleas-ant, it seems). With that development goes the thought that specific periods of remission of punishment can be obtained by the church, and offered to the faithful in return for some stated act of faith and penitence.

The Greek and other Orthodox churches have never accepted this development, which they see as based largely on visionary experiences that are fantastic and untrustworthy. Modern Catholic theologians are much more sceptical about the details of late medieval teaching on Purgatory. Yet the idea of Purgatory itself seems consonant with the central Christian teaching of the love of God. A concern that there should be some possibility of growth and progress after death towards the vision of God seems natural for anyone who believes that God wishes to reconcile the whole world to the divine through Christ. And a concern that our prayers for others should not be restricted to those who are presently living seems consonant with a divine will for universal salvation.

But the medieval insistence on pain and on physical fire grates on the sensibilities of those who see Christ as primarily a figure of love, healing and renewal, not of strict retribution. Also the restriction of Purgatory to those who die in faith (even when that is widened to include a 'baptism of desire'), and the denial of the possibility of repentance after death, may now appear to restrict the forgiving grace of God too greatly.

Many may now wish to think of a state after death in which repentance and positive learning is possible, and in which the vision of God is a hope for all who have died. Like Cardinal Bellarmine, we may pray that Hell (from which there is no liberation) is empty and that Purgatory is full of largely surprised inhabitants. And, like Gregory of Nyssa, we may pray, even if we cannot guarantee, that all may eventually follow paths that lead ever further into the infinite life of God.

There is room for much re-thinking of what Christian faith implies about the destiny of individual souls after death. The medieval Latin doctrine of Purgatory seems inadequate to many largely because it is just too definite and specific about details on which we have no precise information. It developed from early sources in Christian practice and belief, but most theologians would now say that it developed too far, and in subsequent centuries it needed to be reigned in, as indeed the Council of Trent itself attempted to do.

The Second Vatican Council introduced a number of further reforms, reducing the granting of plenary indulgences (remissions of all temporal punishments still due to forgiven sins) and refraining from specifying the precise number of days and years of punishment that can be remitted by an indulgence. Thus the 'golden age' of indulgences lasted from the eleventh century, from which the first certain evidence for the granting of general indulgences can be dated, until the 1960s. The modern Roman Catholic Church still claims the authority to grant indulgences, but has virtually abolished what the Protestant Reformers chiefly objected to, the sale of pardons for the dead with an official guarantee of success.

The 1994 *Catechism of the Catholic Church* remarks that the 'temporal punishments' of Purgatory 'must not be conceived of as a kind of vengeance inflicted by God from without, but as a following from the very nature of sin' (1472). They have the nature of 'an unhealthy attachment to creatures', and an indulgence uses the holiness of Christ and the saints to 'spur them to works of devotion, penance and charity' (1478). An indulgence has become, in effect, a promise of the church that the faithful dead will be helped to freedom from attachment to self by the virtues and prayers of the saints.

In this way, the doctrines of Purgatory and indulgences have been rethought by the twentieth-century Catholic Church, as have satisfaction theories of atonement. These doctrines developed from earlier, less specific and defined beliefs, over time, and their full flowering can be dated to the medieval Latin period after the eleventh century. At that time the doctrines had a specificity and detail that had earlier been lacking, and that has since been greatly qualified.

Some people would say that the church became clear about what had previously been obscure or only implicit in Christian faith. As new questions were raised, about whether we could pray for the dead, and whether the sacrifice of the Mass could be offered on their behalf, the church defined an answer that it had not been necessary to make explicit at an earlier date. A more critical account would say that a religious system in which remission of punishment for the dead could be obtained by paying money for the offering of a private Mass is dramatically different from the fourth- and fifth-century offering of the Eucharist as a sacrifice of thanksgiving to God for the gift of eternal life, consciously received by those who are present. Either way, the medieval Latin church re-thought earlier Christian practices and beliefs in a remarkable way. And it did so by unpacking metaphors of judgment and redemption in specific ways, which can be shown by historical study to have changed in many respects over time.

On these matters the Greek and Roman churches have differed considerably. Perhaps the most basic difference is that for the Greeks the incarnation is itself the redemption of creation, the uniting of creation, or at least a foreshadowing of that final uniting, to the divine life. But for the Romans, the cross and the offering of the life of Jesus as a propitiation for sin is the supreme redemptive act. In both cases, redemption has to be appropriated by the individual believer, but whereas for Greeks this appropriation is primarily by participation in the risen life of Christ, for Romans it is by pleading the merits of Christ's sacrificial death.

These accounts do not contradict one another. But they are different ways of understanding how God redeems the world in Christ. Each has developed in a distinctive way, and this suggests that the original texts of Christian faith leave much room for, and even encourage the development of, diversity of interpretation and understanding.

THE DEVELOPMENT OF DOCTRINE

What are the implications of all this for a plausible view of Christian revelation?

I suppose it is just conceivable that Jesus could have laid down a set of specific doctrines that would have made debate over succeeding centuries unnecessary. Any problem that arose could have been resolved just by pointing to the recorded teaching of Jesus. But Christian revelation is not now, and never has been, like that. The church has continually had to make new decisions – about what should be included in the canon of Scripture, and about how Scripture should be interpreted. In the sixteenth century the

Council of Trent decreed that only the Roman church had the right to interpret Scripture. To say that Jesus or the apostles had themselves decreed this is absurd, given that the New Testament did not then even exist. It could be held, however, that Jesus had given supreme authority to Peter and his successors to resolve disputed questions in the church. There is no evidence that Jesus did so, yet it is possible, and such a claim could be accepted on faith.

Some questions will be new, never having been explicitly raised before. The Pope may, as the Roman church claims, be protected from error when he declares, on behalf of the whole church, that some doctrine or moral affirmation is a matter of faith. But even the Pope does not simply go to the words of Jesus or the Bible. He listens to arguments, considers diverse opinions and comes to a decision.

When I say that the Christian faith is essentially committed to change, I do not mean Christians must be always changing their minds. I mean that new questions will continually arise that have not previously been considered and that require, not just repetitions of previous statements, but new decisions. Even for those who grant the Pope supreme authority in doctrine and morals, we cannot just leave the consideration of such questions to him. It is important for those who are able and willing to engage in debate and discussion, so that a general opinion may be formed.

It is important to discuss how to understand the atonement, the making-one of divine and human, which is accomplished in Christ. Understandings may have to change as more general moral and social perspectives change. Anselm found Gregory's ransom metaphor unhelpful, in view of a more developed view of divine perfection. And many of us might find Anselm's satisfaction metaphor unhelpful, since we no longer live in a feudal society where matters of giving due honour to one's liege lord are of the first importance. We need continually to re-think the idea of atonement in ways that speak to our own time. My suggestion is, as the twentieth-century theologian Paul Tillich proposed, that a contemporary account of atonement might find a metaphor of participation more helpful. God in Christ participates in human suffering, which is at least in part a consequence of greed and hatred, in order that humans may participate in the divine life, through an inner process of dying and rising to new life with Christ. Yet this too is a metaphor, and should not be taken as a final and wholly adequate grasp of the mystery of the union of humanity and the divine in and through Christ. And in all such reflections we should always bear in mind one major fact of Christian revelation – the silence of Jesus on any detailed and specific questions of this sort, which suggests that we might do well to speak tentatively of what we do not fully comprehend.

Buddhists speak of 'unprofitable questions', questions we may speculate about but which are not conducive to our salvation. Perhaps no question is wholly unprofitable, as long as we do not think that we have the only correct answer to it, arrived at just by our own reasoning or by our own private interpretation of Scripture. We need to know the full range of what others have thought, and, when we have seen that, we will see how uncertain and tentative our own private answers must be. In short, we must re-think basic Christian questions again and again, without undue attachment to the answers we are disposed to give, and without frustration at our inability to resolve them all successfully. What matters is that we have new life, and a new awareness of God, through the Spirit of Christ. This should lead us to re-think our faith with reverence and caution, as we seek continually to expand our extremely limited understanding of the mysteries of faith.

It is surprising that so many Christians seem to think that doctrines such as a substitutionary theory of atonement, or Purgatory, or the granting of plenary indulgences by the Pope, are not new decisions at all, but ancient truths deriving from Christ himself.

Against such a view, it is important to show that the institution of these theories and practices can be dated quite specifically. Their gradual development over time can be and has been documented in detail. It is demonstrably not the case that they have been believed 'everywhere, always, and by all', in the supremely vacuous phrase of Vincent of Lerins. (Vacuous because virtually nothing has been believed by all Christians everywhere. There is always some theologian who will disagree. Of course he or she can be called a heretic and then ignored. But that is just winning by empty definition.)

Some novelties are older than others, but there is no particular virtue in preferring old novelties to new ones. The relevant question to ask is why the newer changes have been made, what historical circumstances might account for them, and whether they seem to be appropriate responses to new insights or new knowledge.

What is required of the church now, as was required in the very first Christian generation, is that it sponsor and encourage informed and sensitive discussion of new challenges that might make creative reformulations of older doctrines appropriate. The medieval Catholic Church to a large extent did this, and the Council of Trent, as I hope I have sufficiently shown, embodied many new creative formulations and definitions of Christian beliefs. But far greater changes were to lie ahead.

FREEDOM OF RELIGIOUS BELIEF

One of the greatest changes in the Roman Catholic Church – one that the Jesuit theologian Karl Rahner calls the greatest caesura in the church since the abandonment of Torah – was the full acceptance of individual freedom of thought and belief.

The church often used to be nervous of private speculation and claims to spiritual experience. It licensed the torture of heretics and called for spiritual crusades against infidels and unorthodox groups like the Albigenses. It was intolerant of Jews and Muslims and of any deviation from the authority of the church. Even as late as 1832, in the encyclical *Mirari Vos*, Pope Gregory XVI denied that there should be freedom of worship or of the press. Paragraph 14 of the encyclical reads,

> This shameful font of indifferentism gives rise to that absurd and erroneous proposition which claims that *liberty of conscience* must be maintained for everyone. It spreads ruin in sacred and civil affairs, though some repeat over and over again with the greatest impudence that some advantage accrues to religion from it. 'But the death of the soul is worse than freedom of error,' as Augustine was wont to say. When all restraints are removed by which men are kept on the narrow path of truth, their nature, which is already inclined to evil, propels them to ruin. Then truly 'the bottomless pit' is open from which John saw smoke ascending which obscured the sun, and out of which locusts flew forth to devastate the earth. Thence comes transformation of minds, corruption of youths, contempt of sacred things and holy laws – in other words, a pestilence more deadly to the state than any other. Experience shows, even from earliest times, that cities renowned for wealth, dominion, and glory perished as a result of this single evil, namely immoderate freedom of opinion, license of free speech, and desire for novelty.

These are strong words, but they are outdone by the syllabus of eighty errors that were condemned by Pope Pius IX in 1864. The following small selection gives the flavour of the whole. Each of these propositions was condemned as false:

15. Every man is free to embrace and profess that religion which, guided by the light of reason, he shall consider true. – Allocution "Maxima quidem," June 9, 1862; Damnatio "Multiplices inter," June 10, 1851.

16. Man may, in the observance of any religion whatever, find the way of eternal salvation, and arrive at eternal salvation. – Encyclical "Qui pluribus," Nov. 9, 1846.

17. Good hope at least is to be entertained of the eternal salvation of all those who are not at all in the true Church of Christ. – Encyclical "Quanto conficiamur," Aug. 10, 1863, etc.

77. In the present day it is no longer expedient that the Catholic religion should be held as the only religion of the State, to the exclusion of all other forms of worship. – Allocution "Nemo vestrum," July 26, 1855.

78. Hence it has been wisely decided by law, in some Catholic countries, that persons coming to reside therein shall enjoy the public exercise of their own peculiar worship. – Allocution "Acerbissimum," Sept. 27, 1852.

79. Moreover, it is false that the civil liberty of every form of worship, and the full power, given to all, of overtly and publicly manifesting any opinions whatsoever and thoughts, conduce more easily to corrupt the morals and minds of the people, and to propagate the pest of indifferentism. – Allocution "Nunquam fore," Dec. 15, 1856.

80. The Roman Pontiff can, and ought to, reconcile himself, and come to terms with progress, liberalism and modern civilization. – Allocution "Jamdudum cernimus," March 18, 1861.

In these documents the ancient alliance that is found in Plato between a claim to knowledge of absolute moral truth and the suppression of dissent is strongly re-affirmed. As in Plato's *Republic*, there is a small number of men (and for the Catholic Church it was always men, not women) who have privileged access to the truth. They are the 'guardians' of philosophical/religious and moral truth. It is their responsibility to ensure that people are taught the truth, which – in a strengthening of Plato's doctrine – is essential for eternal salvation. Moreover, any opposition to the truth can be attributed to corruption and to devilish attacks on faith, so it is, and must be treated as, evil. For that reason reading and discussion must be carefully supervised, and error, being dangerous to the soul, must not be granted any rights. Permitting the freedom to err is not worth the death of a single soul, and therefore freedom of belief and worship is dangerous, not desirable, and should not be tolerated.

At this stage I simply wish to point out that this complex of attitudes is not confined to religion. It was not associated with religion in Plato, or in other notably repressive societies like that of Russian communism or German National Socialism. What it requires is a belief that truth matters desperately, that people are naturally inclined to evil and that they need to be trained and restrained if they are to keep to 'the narrow path of truth'. So you could believe, for example, that social equality is an absolute moral imperative, that people are naturally inclined to inequality, that this is an evil impulse, and so people need to be forced to be equal by whatever social sanctions are necessary. That is what happened in Stalin's Russia. Something not wholly unlike it happened in the European Catholic Church. For Gregory XVI and Pius IX, the way to eternal salvation is narrow and known by few, and people need to be protected from their own corrupted impulses, by persuasion, restraint and – if necessary – compulsion.

I will discuss this complex of attitudes in the eighth chapter, when I begin to deal with liberal Christianity, a peculiar object of Pope Pius's animosity. But it should be noted that all these papal pronouncements have been rescinded by the Second Vatican Council. That council's Declaration on Religious Liberty states, 'The Vatican Council declares that the human person has a right to religious freedom' (*Vatican Council II*, ed. Austin Flannery, Dominican Publications, 1992, p. 800). *Gaudium et Spes* declares that 'the Holy Spirit offers to all the possibility of being made partners, in a way known to God, in the paschal mystery' (p. 924). This is explicitly said to be true 'not for Christians only but also for all men of good will in whose hearts grace is active invisibly'. *Lumen Gentium* states that 'those who, through no fault of their own, do not know the Gospel of Christ or his Church, but who nevertheless seek God with a sincere heart, and, moved by grace, try in their actions to do his will as they know it through the dictates of their conscience – those too may achieve eternal salvation' (p. 367).

The Roman Catholic faith is still said to be the one true faith, to which all must adhere if they conscientiously see it to be so. But conscientious disagreement is permitted (it is presumably not the unbelievers' fault that they honestly disagree). And it is asserted that what is most important for salvation is 'good will', or following conscience with a sincere heart. In such cases, it is affirmed, grace may be active invisibly for salvation. It is no longer necessary for all to submit to the Roman pontiff in order to be saved. This constitutes a major change in thinking from that of the fourteenth- to nineteenth-century popes, which was itself a major development from the rather modest and disputed papal claims of the first Christian centuries.

The history of the Roman Catholic Church illustrates very well the way in which basic Christian doctrines need to be re-thought in new historical contexts. For Roman Catholics, the Pope and the magisterium of the church provide guidance and encouragement for such re-thinking. And, as I have shown, they often take the lead in engaging in it – even if they sometimes deny that they are changing anything.

For some Christians, however, that lead has too often issued in repressive, harmful or unjustifiable decrees and definitions to be entirely trustworthy. In the sixteenth century, the church was to split yet again, and large numbers of believers were to reject the teaching authority of the Pope. Protestant Christianity was born.

Chapter 7

By Faith Alone

T he Word of God takes personal form in Jesus of Nazareth. Personal relationship with Christ is a form of direct personal knowledge, which transforms the life of the knower, just as any intense personal relationship transforms the participants. By the commitment of faith, human estrangement from God is overcome and the Spirit of God unites us inwardly to the love of Christ. For the Protestant Reformers, the church is the invisible communion of all in whom the Spirit works to enable us to love Christ and to share with him in the love of the Father, the source of all.

THE BIBLE AS THE STANDARD OF PROTESTANT FAITH

In 1440 Johann Gensfleisch invented printing by movable metal type. Some years later he printed a version of the Holy Bible, now known as the Gutenberg Bible. This was a discovery that was to change the face of Christianity. It was not long before a great many people, not just clergy, had access to the text of the Bible. Soon they were able to read it in their own languages, not in the Latin of the official Vulgate version. The church still claimed the sole right to interpret the text. But once the text got into the hands of the general literate public it became much harder to stop individuals interpreting it for themselves. That is the hallmark of Protestant Christianity. The Bible is available to all in a language they can understand, and they are encouraged to read it and interpret it for themselves. Christianity was re-thought as a religion of the book.

The Protestant Reformers did not wish to leave the church; they wished to reform it. Virtually everyone agrees that some reforms were needed to remedy widespread abuses, most famously the abuse of selling indulgences for money. But as Reformers looked to the Bible as the source of true doctrine, it seemed to them that a very different view of the church than that which had become common in Western Europe was to be found there.

The Roman Catholic Church had developed a doctrine of the church as one visible institution, defined by the communion of its members with the Bishop of Rome (except for the awkward case of the Eastern Orthodox churches). The Pope, as successor of Peter, had the divinely appointed role of defining correct doctrine in faith and morals. Membership of the church was by baptism; continuance in it was by confession, penance and communion.

The Reformers failed to find these doctrines in the Bible. Certainly there was a church in the New Testament, but the church seemed to be a fellowship of those who were disciples of Jesus. Paul had founded many churches, and they seemed to be more or less autonomous local fellowships, where prophecy and speaking in tongues were common, and where leaders were appointed in accordance with their particular gifts from among the congregation. There were links with the apostles, just as missionary churches today preserve links with the original missionary organisations. But, partly because of the difficulty of communication, local churches functioned more or less autonomously. They were influenced by, but did not seem to consider themselves under the authority of, the Jerusalem apostles. Indeed James, leader of the church in Jerusalem, who sent out envoys to persuade local churches to obey Torah, was repudiated as troublesome by Paul, and no doubt local churches came to their own decisions about this and other matters of concern. Over the years the churches came to be organised under five patriarchs, but the early patriarchates seem to have constituted a federal organisation rather than a top-down institution.

As the Reformers read it, the New Testament churches were local fellowships that accepted Jesus as Lord and Saviour, as redeemer from evil and giver of eternal life. There was no mention of a class of celibate priests, offering the sacrifice of the Mass for the souls of the living and the dead, and being informed of the truths of faith from a central source.

FAITH AS PERSONAL ENCOUNTER

Classical Protestants seek to base their doctrines and practices on the New Testament. To them, that suggested that the church exists, as both

Luther and Calvin held, wherever the gospel of Jesus as Saviour is preached, and the two sacraments of baptism and the Lord's Supper, both mentioned in the New Testament, are celebrated. There is no magisterium, no teaching office, of the church. There is no hierarchical priesthood. There is no class of celibate priests and no religious elite, whether monks or nuns, who have higher spiritual standing than others. There is no control by any central authority over the content of faith. There is only the preaching of the gospel, and faith in Jesus.[10] As Luther put it, justification (acceptance by God) is by faith alone, by a living trust that Jesus died and rose to redeem humanity. To make the point, Luther inserted the word 'alone' after the word 'faith' into his German translation of the letter to the Romans, chapter 3, verse 28, which actually reads, 'We hold that a person is justified by faith apart from works prescribed by the law.' It is ironic that he had to change the biblical text to make it say what he wanted!

In any case, he was adamant that salvation cannot be accomplished or helped by good works, penances, obedience to the Pope, or attendance at Mass. It is a matter of the relation of the believer to Christ the Lord, not needing any intermediaries, any visible institution or any teaching authority. The Mass remains, for Luther, a rite that makes Christ truly present, and for the person of faith it is a way of expressing and strengthening the personal union of disciple and Lord. But mere attendance at its performance does not save, and it cannot be offered in private to save those who are not present. So the pulpit, as the place where the word of God is read and preached, takes precedence over the altar.

The Reformers tried to make the Mass (or the Lord's Supper, as many call it) a focal event for the believing community, where the presence of Christ is celebrated (or where, for extreme Protestants, Jesus' sacrifice on the cross is devoutly remembered). It is a service of communion for all present, a meal that is a foretaste of the feast of the kingdom of God. So to have a Mass celebrated by priest on his own for the sake of someone who is not present is to miss the meaning of the rite. It is to replace a celebration of a truly personal relationship with what was often referred to as a 'quasi-mechanical' conveyance of merit. And to adore or carry in procession a consecrated and reserved Host is to disconnect the sacrament from the personal act of God in communion.

In this respect, Reformed practice tried to make the sacrament more constitutive of a local community and more communicative of a personal relationship than a rite efficacious simply by its private performance. Whereas the Mass had become, for some, the observation of the elevated Host far away and almost hidden by a choir screen, the Reformers wanted the community to come together and share the life of the risen Lord in fellowship. And they were concerned that people should know what was going on. Preaching assumed a new importance, and the rite was conducted in the local language with the active participation of those present (most of these reforms were to be implemented by the Catholic Church at the Second Vatican Council).

Luther said, 'Christ's kingdom is a hearing-kingdom, not a seeing-kingdom.'[11] It is by hearing the word that one comes to saving belief. Without that, all rituals and all images are empty. Luther did not ban images or rituals entirely. But in Lutheran churches images were often removed, walls whitewashed, and in Reformed (Calvinist) churches the stone altar was replaced by a wooden communion table. The central artistic image of Lutheranism is not a painting of the passion or a statue of the Virgin, but the sound of Bach's musical settings of the words of the Bible.

PROTESTANTS AND PLURALISM

For classical Protestants, it is still right to speak of a catholic – a universal – church. But that church is the company of all who trust in Christ, located in thousands of different fellowships of different sorts. Thus Protestantism is essentially pluralistic, in acknowledging many forms of Christian fellowship, without any one central authority. It is essentially diverse and is logically bound to permit many ways of understanding the gospel and the Bible, since it accepts no authoritative interpreter of the Bible.

It did not work out like that in practice. Since the New Testament is a diverse and unsystematic assembly of Gospels and letters, there are many possible ways of interpreting it, and once Protestants decided to make the Bible the only test of faith, all those ways were tried.

That is not odd or unexpected. The oddity is that each of them tended to declare itself to be the one true interpretation, to the exclusion of the others. Lutherans excluded followers of Calvin. They both excluded Zwinglians. And hundreds of denominations sprang up, most of which excluded everybody else.

For political reasons, the organising principle of Protestant faith came to be that the ruler of a state or nation would choose a form of belief, and the members of that state would then find themselves obliged to profess it. They could move over the border, where that was feasible, and profess a different form of faith. But acceptance of pluralism was not a marked feature of the classical Protestant world in Europe. That had to wait until the founding of America as a secular state, when religion would truly become a matter of free choice. Even in America, however, there was much local intolerance as various Protestant churches tried to ban others as heretical and dangerous.

It is clearly very difficult for Christians truly to accept full freedom of belief. In the contemporary United States of America, freedom of belief exists. Yet hundreds of churches do not hesitate to exclude those of their members who have the 'wrong' beliefs and to deprive them of teaching positions in their training colleges. It looks as if everyone is free to start their own church, but within it they can be as intolerant as they like.

The irony of all this, within Protestantism, is that the whole Protestant movement exists because it asserted the right of dissent (from the Catholic Church), the importance of free personal decision (a personal decision of faith in Jesus, not simply baptism into a religious group), and the rejection of an authoritative teaching authority (the magisterium of the church).

The problem is that Protestants still believed that salvation is, literally, a matter of life and death – eternal life and eternal death. The way to eternal life is much more rigorous than the traditional Catholic requirement of being a good member of the church, making confession and attending Mass. It is really believing, with the whole heart, that Christ is your personal Saviour.

In order to do that, you must know who Christ is, what salvation is, and be confronted with the necessity of making a personal decision for faith. Preaching, and preaching the truth, becomes vital for salvation – whereas, for most traditional Catholics, it did not matter much whether you never heard a sermon, or whether the Mass was in a language you did not understand. For Protestants, everything had to be made plain, and everyone had to understand it. Protestantism became a didactic faith, and preaching had to be precisely correct.

The source of this correctness, in the absence of the Pope, had to be the Bible itself. The text had to be self-interpreting and clear, and all preachers had to do was expound it correctly – to say what the Bible itself really says.

The strange thing was that when they did this they came to many different and conflicting conclusions.

Most classical Protestants did not in fact derive all their doctrines from the Bible alone. They accepted the decisions of the first ecumenical councils of the church. They accepted, for instance, that Jesus was fully God and fully man and that the Trinity was three persons in one substance. They also tended to accept some specifically Western doctrines, as formulated by Augustine – that humans are born with original guilt, that the 'saved' are predestined by God and that human free will is compatible with such pre-destination. Many of them accepted a theory of atonement that derived from Anselm, as adjusted by Calvin, that we can only be saved because Jesus died 'in our place', to pay the penalty of death that God's justice required for our sins. (Aquinas, it may be recalled, denied the necessity, but not the actu-ality, of such a payment, and the Orthodox do not make this account central to their understanding of the death of Jesus.)

So Protestants did not in fact rely on Scripture alone for their doctrines, as they sometimes claimed. They relied on a number of traditional inter-pretations of Scripture, interpretations that got more and more specific and exclusive, until in the end some of them relied on Luther, some on Calvin, some on Zwingli and some on other less famous but equally cantankerous interpreters of the allegedly 'self-interpreting' Scripture.

This is a matter that requires some explanation. How can it be that a faith that insists that even general councils of the church can err may in practice insist on the exclusive correctness of one man (like Luther) as inter-preter of the Bible? The Protestant rule must surely be that, if the church has erred, then any interpreter of Scripture can err, including you and your own church. The Protestant rule is that anyone may be mistaken. This does not mean saying, 'I think I am wrong.' But it does mean saying, 'I am not certain I am correct.' You must allow that, while you do not agree with other views, you could be the person who is mistaken. An admission of personal and institutional fallibility is built into Protestantism. But it does not always seem like that.

The rejection of any infallible teaching authority, and the establishment of the right to dissent on grounds of conscience seem to me the distinctive marks of Protestant Christianity. They seem to entail the provisional nature of most doctrinal beliefs, especially very complicated ones – meaning that we admit our interpretation could be mistaken. This in turn entails pluralism, in the sense of acceptance of a diversity of interpretations of the faith.

FAITH AND INTELLECTUAL ASSENT

The fact that many Protestants seem to be absolutely certain of their beliefs, even when they know that a majority of other Christians disagree, and that they find themselves unable to live together with people who have different interpretations of doctrine, is a mystery. It can only be accounted for by thinking they have been so influenced by the Latin tradition that they think three highly questionable things, which their own faith should undermine. They think that people can only be saved by believing correct doctrines, they think that the commitment of faith requires theoretical certainty and they think that there is some set of doctrines that needs to be defined as correct by some authority, which can then exclude and condemn contrary views as heretical. But none of these beliefs is really consistent with the basic character of Protestantism. They are precisely the beliefs of the Catholic Church that Protestants denied, and that traditional Catholics used to condemn and exclude Protestants.

In classical Protestant thought, these three beliefs are put in question by a strong emphasis on the importance of personal commitment to Christ, and on personal experience of the risen Lord or of the Spirit. This arises from Luther's emphasis on justification by faith, that is, by living trust in Christ, and from Calvin's emphasis on faith as giving assurance of final salvation. Whereas faith in Catholicism is primarily an assent of the will to the authoritative teachings of the church, for Luther and Calvin it is a perfect trust in Jesus, and especially in his death as atonement for our sins. Protestants typically speak of 'making a decision' for Christ, whereas Catholics tend to think that, if you are baptised, there is no specific, decisive decision to be made. You just naturally grow in the faith to which you belong.

Although Protestantism, I have suggested, remained largely intellectualist, it gave to personal experience an importance it had not previously had. Of course there were devotional movements in the Catholic Church, and mystics who claimed direct experiences of God. But to profess the faith was to be baptised, probably as an infant, and accept the teachings of the church. Personal experience remained a matter for you and your confessor.

For classical Protestants you must be confronted with the need of personal salvation from sin. You must consciously and explicitly commit yourself to Jesus as Saviour. You must have the experience of 're-birth' in the
Spirit, whereby Christ comes to be known to you as an inner personal and
renewing presence. This emphasis on personal choice, on commitment and
on dramatic and inner experience of the Spirit, with the concomitant down-
grading of all external rituals, religious imagery and such things as bodily
prostrations and pilgrimages, re-draws the lines of faith in a radical way.

Faith becomes a purely inner encounter with a life-transforming Spirit,
for even the act of commitment is possible only when the Spirit evokes it.
God encounters you in the preaching of the gospel. God convicts you of sin.
God impels you to bow before him in repentance. God brings Christ to birth
within you. And God gives the assurance of eternal life.

All this is a drama played out within the soul, and it is hidden from the
eyes of the world. Protestant churches, or meeting rooms, need no orna-
ments or images, for the dramas of the Spirit are played out in the secret
places of the heart. The true, holy, universal and apostolic church is not a
visible institution with a visible head. It is the invisible communion of those
whose hearts have been claimed for God, by God, whose membership is
unknown and whose head is invisible to the public gaze.

Luther and Calvin were clear that good works, the attempt of humans to
do good things, were irrelevant to this inward drama of the Spirit. They
should have been equally clear that the acceptance of correct doctrines, the
attempt (as Protestants thought) of humans to formulate correct beliefs, are
irrelevant to the drama of salvation. But they were not.

The point is that if God saves you by predestinate grace, God does not
have to wait until you believe all the right doctrines before salvation can take
effect. You are not saved because you have correct beliefs. You are saved
solely by grace, through faith. And that faith is just the inward assent to the
work of the Spirit, as it unites you to the divine life, the life of Christ.

Good works may follow from faith, as the Spirit empowers you to goodness. Correct beliefs may follow from faith, but only insofar as those beliefs
are immediate entailments of true faith. It is not, for instance, entailed by
transforming encounter with the risen Lord that the doctrine of double
predestination, of God predestining some to salvation and some to damnation, is correct. The Chalcedonian definition of Christ's person is not
entailed either, though it would be necessary that the new life that comes

through Christ truly unites you to the divine life. There may, however, be various ways of trying to spell this out more completely, if you were inclined to do so.

Faith, in the Protestant sense, does not require theoretical certainty, especially about widely disputed doctrines, and it does not require acceptance of a set of 'correct' doctrines. Moreover, since God will save whomsoever God will, there is no set of doctrines and no institution that we must defend at all costs, in order that the faith will survive. Heresy need not be suppressed as a danger to human souls. For salvation is purely in the hands of God, and if it is the divine will that the gospel should be preached effectively, then it will be, whatever humans may do. Toleration becomes a Protestant Christian virtue when it is recognised that, for the vast majority of Christians, Protestants are the heretics, and intolerance would wipe them out. More importantly, since salvation is by grace not human works, we do not need to guard the truth by policing the souls of men and women. God will ensure that God's purpose is carried out. And, if Jesus is any model, it is not by violence and repression that it will be carried out. Salvation is by the grace of God, which is neither hampered nor hindered by the plans of men and women. And it is appropriated not by assent to a complex set of doctrines, but by faith, by living trust in Jesus as personal Saviour.

INSPIRATION AND SCRIPTURE

Of course to trust in Jesus you must believe that Jesus existed and had a specific personality or character, that he did and taught specific things. So there must exist a trustworthy record of Jesus' life. That argument is strong, though even then, if what is important is personal relationship to a living Lord, the information about the historical character of that Lord does not need to be very detailed. It might be a positive advantage to have different accounts and assessments of Jesus, showing the ways in which he affected very different people.

However, classical Protestants usually went on to say that the Bible can be trustworthy only if it is given by God, and, since God cannot lie, the text must be true in every detail. It is true that God cannot lie, but why should it be thought that the text is actually given by God? Divine dictation has never been part of a Christian view of most of the Bible. What is required is something both vaguer and more subtle. If God wishes us to know and love the divine in and through the person of Jesus, then God must ensure that we know that person in sufficient detail to be able to identify him. So God must ensure that there exists a reliable tradition or traditions about the historical Jesus. But how God ensures this, and in what form, is not entailed by these requirements.

All Christians agree that the New Testament contains records of the life of Jesus from very near apostolic times. All agree that they provide the best evidence we have for the life of Jesus. All Christians agree that the evidence must be reliable or trustworthy. It is reasonable to think that God ensures that such a reliable record exists. The question is: how?

God could dictate it; but that does not seem compatible with the varying styles and authorship of the texts, and the fact that some texts are occasional letters written to churches. It is also in tension with the fact that Jesus did not write or dictate anything himself – which suggests that dictation is not the means of Christian revelation.

God could preserve it from all error, but that is incompatible with the varying accounts of incidents in Jesus' life (see chapter 1). It is also in tension with the results of archaeological and historical study, which throw doubt on many historical accounts in the Old Testament.

An alternative possibility is that God could ensure the general reliability of the New Testament, exercising a guiding influence on the selection of Gospels and letters that go to make up the canon of the New Testament, so that the rather subjective emphases of one account are balanced by complementary emphases of other accounts, and the whole is sufficient to give a clear account of how Jesus can be a channel of the divine life.

This is vague, because it does not say exactly when or how God exerts such influence. It is subtle, because it suggests that 'reliability' is necessary only insofar as it preserves what is necessary for a saving relation to God through Christ – and that, too, is left undefined. Presumably we need to know that Jesus was a man filled with the divine Spirit, and therefore was wise, spiritually powerful, and loving. He was empowered to forgive sin and to inspire his disciples. His vocation to be God's Anointed was genuine. He died voluntarily, for the sake of the redemption of the world, and was raised from death. These are the things we need to know if we are to relate to God through him as mediator. It would be reasonable to think that God would ensure these things were recorded reliably.

But reliability does not entail that an account is without any error. It entails that the accounts are accurate and full enough to give a correct impression of Jesus' character, and of his death and resurrection. But this suggests that God's influence works through the process of gathering together the documents that were to make up the New Testament, as well as through the writing of them. And that influence must continue to work through subsequent history, to ensure that a saving relation to God remains a living possibility, not just a recorded historical fact.

In other words, it seems reasonable to think that whatever form of inspiration or guidance God exercised in the composition of the Bible will continue in the history of the church. God may not preserve the church from all errors, but God might well guide the church so that it remains a vehicle of saving knowledge of God, a community in which the Spirit acts.

A REFORMED AND LIBERAL CHURCH?

There is an evident tension in the frequent Protestant claim that the Bible is inerrant and the sole source of authority whereas the whole Catholic Church seems to have become irredeemably corrupt. The tension is that if God worked through groups of humans over many centuries to write and compile the biblical documents, it is strange to think that God ceased to guide the church at all over the next thousand years.

We can ease that tension by denying the total inerrancy and sole sufficiency of the Bible, and also by denying that the church is irredeemably corrupt. In practice this is what Protestants have largely done. In accepting the theological interpretations of the councils and of Augustine, they accept some tradition of interpretation in addition to bare text. And the Protestant movement is meant to be one of reform, not of denial. When Luther pinned his ninety-five theses to the door of the castle church in Wittenberg in 1517 – an event that many see as the crucial beginning of the Protestant Reformation – he did not intend to found a new church. He hoped for reform within the Catholic Church. He hoped that the church, as the set of many communities that accept the apostolic faith and celebrate new life in the Spirit of Christ, would remain the divinely mandated way of salvation. But the Reformers believed that many errors had crept into the Western church, and some of these were re-affirmed at the Council of

Trent. They included the doctrine of papal supremacy over councils of the church, doctrines of merit and indulgences, the invocation of saints, especially of Mary, and the veneration of relics and images.

When the Reformers rejected these doctrines, they did not reject the church. They claimed to be returning to the original apostolic faith, and often tried to model their churches on New Testament accounts. That faith had never been lost. It had just been overlaid by practices and beliefs that were no part of the apostolic faith.

The apostolic faith was never quite as the Reformers pictured it. For a start, it had no New Testament, and so could hardly be called a 'biblical church'. It also undoubtedly contained many Jewish Christians, who upheld the strict observance of Torah. It was much more closely related to Judaism than were the Protestant churches, which regrettably tended to be anti-Jewish. And it almost certainly had never formulated views like substitutionary atonement, Chalcedonian Christology, predestination, sacramental theology and all the complicated versions of the 'second coming' that many Reformers seemed to be fixated with.

Still, the idea of a return to apostolic faith is a powerful one. It is a traditional Catholic view that the deposit of revelation ended with the death of the last apostle. It might be useful advice to say that no doctrine should be regarded as absolutely necessary to Christian faith unless it was part of the apostolic faith. Our only written evidence for that is the New Testament. So, while the Reformers may have thought that too many of their doctrines were apostolic when they were not, and though some of them may have had an exaggerated view of the inerrancy of Scripture, one may feel a great deal of sympathy with the recommendation that the New Testament is the only source of doctrines that are strictly necessary to Christian belief.

This would not commit us to accepting that everything in the New Testament has to be believed today – I have argued that such a position is insupportable. But it might commit us to saying that no belief is absolutely necessary to being a Christian if it cannot be supported by the New Testament. That, we have seen, leaves a lot of room for disagreement and development, and it would leave even the incarnation and the Trinity open to many diverse interpretations.

If that is so, Protestants should allow much diversity of interpretation of the texts, and should be very careful not to claim certainty in matters that are highly disputed among intelligent readers of the texts. Perhaps the besetting heresy to which Protestants are prone is to claim certainty in matters that do not allow of certainty, and to fail to see the diversity of Scripture, and the necessity of following some interpretation of it which will not be found in Scripture itself and is bound to be less than universally appealing.

Surprising as it may seem to some, Protestantism is thus essentially liberal, in the classical sense of allowing, and even encouraging, diversity of interpretation, the right of dissent, and personal freedom of belief. It calls for liberty of conscience, as a condition of its own existence – even though it sometimes practises intolerance of disagreement within its own fellowships. It calls for the equality of all before God. In rejecting a central teaching authority and in insisting upon an open Bible, which all can interpret for themselves, it undermines any spiritual hierarchy – even though it has reinforced many social hierarchies in its church organisation. It calls for fraternity and brotherly love and fellowship, in rejecting any distinction of clergy and laity, any special class of 'religious', and in stressing the participation of all in the communion service and in the running of the churches – even though some of its tracts are still filled with vitriol against Christians of different persuasions.

Liberty, equality and fraternity were the ideals of the Protestant Reformation, even though they were rarely put consistently into practice. Today those words do not suggest Protestantism, but something more revolutionary, something that was to destroy the feudal order and to challenge a Christian faith that had become perhaps too closely associated with it. Europe was about to be changed by a force even more powerful than the Reformation, though the Protestant Reformation prepared the way for it. Before it, Christian faith, in all its forms, was to tremble. The Enlightenment was at hand.

Chapter 8

Critical Faith

Christ is the Way, the Truth and the Life. So Christian faith is absolutely concerned with truth. Liberal faith holds that truth is not best discovered by simple acceptance of authority. It requires appeal to evidence, free debate, acceptance of fallibility, and attention to new insights. A commitment to seek truth is important; a claim to possess it may rather be arrogant. A full grasp of truth lies in the future; in that sense Christians are always seeking to understand more of what Christ truly is, and will not assume that they already grasp it completely.

'TO CRITICISM EVERYTHING MUST SUBMIT'

In 1784 Immanuel Kant wrote a little essay called 'What Is Enlightenment?' in which he said that 'enlightenment is man's release from his ... inability to make use of his understanding ... without direction from another. *Sapere aude!*: "have courage to use your own reason" [it actually means "Dare to know"] – that is the motto of enlightenment.'[12]

This was not a new thought. In 1277 the Bishop of Paris had condemned 210 propositions that some academics in the University of Paris had supposedly propounded (some alleged views of Thomas Aquinas were included). They included the assertion that 'man should not be content with authority alone as a means of acquiring certainty', and that 'we should believe nothing that is not known in itself or cannot be explained by known principles'.

But thirteenth-century Europe was not yet ready for the reception of such ideas. It was not until the eighteenth-century American and French revolutions that the idea of democracy, of all people thinking for themselves in politics as well as in morality and religion, came to seem a real possibility. In 1740 King Frederick II ('the Great') had introduced at least a degree of liberty of the press and freedom of worship to Prussia. For that reason Kant rather sycophantically called the age of enlightenment 'the century of Frederick' – though Kant stressed that it was really an age in which the obstacles to enlightenment were gradually being reduced.[13]

What did Kant mean by using your own reason in matters of religion, politics and morality? Kant epitomises his view in the *Critique of Pure Reason* (preface to first edition), in the pithy phrase, 'To criticism everything must submit.'[14] His essay on enlightenment is not a licence for everyone to think anything they please. It is actually a very restricted plea for the freedom of scholars to publish their 'carefully tested and well-meaning thoughts'. In religion, he holds that no group or church is justified in seeking to bind their successors to views that are laid down as unchangeable and exempt from public criticism. No state is justified in 'supporting the ecclesiastical despotism of some tyrants' over others. And each person must be free to make use of reason in matters of conscience.

The challenge to the traditional views of the Catholic Church, and also of many Protestant groups, is clear. These four principles define the Enlightenment attitude to Christian (and any other) faith. Every belief must be open to public criticism. No system of belief should be laid down as unrevisable in principle. No one system of belief should be made mandatory by any state. And there should be complete liberty of conscience in religion (compatibly with the prevention of harm to others and the maintenance of social order).

It is these principles, and not any specific Christian beliefs, that define liberal Christian faith. Holding them is compatible with holding a raft of ancient and rather conservative beliefs – for instance, about the divinity of Christ, the Trinity and salvation by the grace of God – as long as those beliefs are open to criticism, revisable in principle, and not imposed on others. But it is not compatible with belief in an infallible and unrevisable source of unchangeable doctrines, whether Pope, councils or Bible. It is precisely what Pope Pius IX's 'Syllabus of Errors' condemned.

Like most thinkers of the Enlightenment, Kant was an intellectual elitist. He thought that most people were prone to superstition, laziness in thought and supine conformity. What enlightenment required was a cultivation of human intellectual powers in the right way and to the fullest extent. It was hard work, and the criticism he espoused was not a negative or cynical rejection of all authority, but a disciplined and informed critical enquiry into the proper methods and limits of human knowledge.

THE IMPACT OF NATURAL SCIENCE

A large part of the impetus for this sort of informed criticism came from the extraordinary growth of knowledge in the natural sciences. The Aristotelian science that had dominated late medieval thought had been decisively over-thrown. Close observation and careful experiment had triumphed over the massive intellectual authority of Aristotle, which had been defended by the church. The Galileo affair of 1633, when the Inquisition forced Galileo to say that he would no longer publish his Copernican view of the solar system, had become an icon of the struggle between new observational science and old authoritarian cosmology.

Newton's formulation of the laws of motion and mechanics completed the rout of Aristotle. A system of science that saw the universe in terms of entities striving to reach their proper goals (their formal and final causes) was decisively replaced by an acceptance that the universe is best under-stood in terms of the non-purposive action of bodies in accordance with general and impersonal laws of nature.

At a more popular level, belief that God, angels or demons might act in specific and unpredictable ways at any time was replaced by belief that things happen because of impersonal laws, not because some spiritual agent suddenly decided to make them happen. Importantly, the new science pro-duced results – it enabled new inventions to be made, since what was pre-dictable could in principle be controlled and shaped to meet human needs. Humans discovered that they could, at least to some extent, control their material environment, and improve it. No longer was nature a sacred realm that should not be interfered with. It was a mine of usable materials that could be exploited for human welfare.

So the new science was a major source of a tendency to reject ancient authority (which had proved to be wrong) and rely on observation and experiment. It also inspired the idea of progress, that human life could be improved by technological invention, and material standards of living could be raised to new heights. And it bred a reliance on the free exchange of ideas and the critical examination of evidence as the best method of discovering truth about the physical world.

Later, in 1859, when Darwin's *Origin of Species* was published, an even more decisive change in the human view of nature occurred. The evolutionary view that things had become more complex by mutation and selection over many generations, and that human intelligence and knowledge had developed from much cruder and simpler beginnings, completely reversed the traditional Christian view that humanity had 'fallen' from an original perfection in Eden.

In the light of this quite new knowledge of the universe, Christian views of God's creation had to change radically, a process that has not even yet been consolidated. Where the traditional beliefs of ancient religious authorities could be seen by most informed and scientifically minded observers to be outmoded, appeals to tradition began to lose their force. It began to seem that new knowledge was more reliable than ancient tradition. Criticism of old and established views began to seem necessary if there was to be any chance of arriving at truth.

For some, Christianity itself was called in question by this new critical approach to knowledge. Some writers claimed that nature can be adequately explained by appeal to non-purposive laws of nature, without any appeal to a creator. Some claimed that evolution, which works by random mutation and selection by environment, rules out any ideas of moral purpose in nature. Thus the Enlightenment can make the idea of God seem superfluous, and undermine the idea of a morally oriented or goal-directed creation. It can make miracles seem to contradict the belief that everything proceeds in accordance with universal laws of nature. And it can make the idea of any intervention by God in the universe seem to be in conflict with a new belief in the apparently closed causal system of the natural universe. In that sense, the new science was a challenge to traditional Christian beliefs, and to any religious beliefs at all.

I have considered this challenge in detail in *Pascal's Fire* (Oneworld, 2006). There I suggested that the new science does not in fact undermine religious faith, that the existence of laws of nature may be taken to point to a wise and rational creator, and that evolution is perfectly compatible with belief in a cosmic purpose of great value. But even if science is compatible with Christian faith, the traditional forms of that faith must change quite markedly.

What this means for Christian faith is something that has to be spelled out by placing Christian beliefs about incarnation, resurrection and salvation in a completely different context, in a universe physically different in almost every detail from that imagined by the biblical writers. It is no longer sufficient to repeat traditional beliefs. Hypothesis tested by observation and experiment provides us with reliable knowledge about the universe. Any acceptable Christian faith must cohere with that knowledge. So it is not just some passing cultural fashion that leads to a demand for a re-thinking of Christian faith in a scientific context. It is the demand for truth that requires us to be critical of any religious views that predate or conflict with the best knowledge of the universe and of human nature that is available to us. And, since scientific knowledge itself changes and grows rapidly, that process of critical re-thinking must be expected to continue for the foreseeable future.

THE IMPACT OF CRITICAL HISTORY

The critical approach required by new knowledge in the sciences quickly passed over to the study of history. In the classical world, histories had been written largely as the presentation of heroic or morally worthy examples, or to bolster the prestige of particular people or places. The more amazing or fantastic were these tales of the past, the better they were liked. Accounts of the past tended to grow in detail and in wonder as time went on. But as the critical examination of evidence had been important in establishing progress in the natural sciences, so such methods began to be applied to available records of the human past. By 1776, historians like Edward Gibbon, who wrote *The Decline and Fall of the Roman Empire*, were insisting on a close examination of the evidence for any historical assertions. They were exercising suspicion of any sources that were prejudiced in favour of supporting a particular cause ('history is written by the victors'). And they were insisting that we should not claim more certainty about what happened in the past than the evidence allowed.

Critical study of sources would clearly have a great impact on religion if the new historical methods were to be applied to the Bible and the pronouncements of the church. For this reason Canon Pusey of Christ Church, Oxford opposed a proposal to introduce an Honours School of Theology in the University of Oxford in 1870, because, he said, it might mean that the Bible would be studied 'like any other book'. By that time in universities study of a text meant subjecting it to ruthless criticism and letting the argument go where it would. For, as John Stuart Mill suggested, in disputed and contentious matters the best way of attaining truth is to promote informed argument and critical discussion.[15] It is only by meeting the strongest criticisms and producing rationally defensible reasons that any opinion can confidently be asserted as true. Even then, the degree of confidence should be proportioned to the sort and degree of evidence and argument that can be produced.

For many years, particularly in England, critical study of the Bible was viewed with great suspicion as 'German methodology'. Many insisted that the Bible, being the word of God, should be exempted from historical or literary criticism. But how do we know the Bible is the word of God? Or how do we even know that there is a God?

The thirteenth-century Catholic Church had an answer. Reason could demonstrate the existence of God, and, by the proofs of his miracles and resurrection, the divinity of Jesus. Reason could go on to show that Jesus had founded the church and endowed Peter and his successors with authority to teach the truth. So Christian faith is entirely rational. Having established the authority of the church by reason, it is reasonable to accept thereafter what the church says.

The trouble is that the first step in this argument, that reason could demonstrate the existence of God, was based on arguments from Aristotle, who had just been shown to be an unreliable guide. Immanuel Kant was widely believed when he undertook to refute all possible rational arguments for God. And as for the 'proofs' of the miracles recorded in the New Testament, they will not be proofs any longer if the New Testament cannot be shown to be based on reliable historical evidence. Critical historians will look with some suspicion at accounts written from only one biased viewpoint, will be sensitive to the presence of conflicting accounts of the same events in the text, will be aware of how religious accounts of the past in general tend to exaggerate and embroider the facts, and will be very suspicious of accounts of amazing things happening in the past that have no parallel in contemporary experience. So critical historians are liable to discount accounts of miracles in the Bible, or at best to say that the evidence for them is not strong enough to build any secure foundation of religious beliefs on them. We might believe in faith that they happened. But then we can hardly appeal to them to support our initial faith!

So, for critical thinkers, reason cannot prove the existence of God, it is very uncertain whether miracles happened, and there is no written evidence that Jesus endowed the successors of Peter with authority. In fact, as I pointed out in the first chapter, there is some evidence that Jesus did not expect Peter to have any successors at all.

It follows that you must logically allow that the teachings of the Bible and the church can be reasonably disbelieved. And that epitomises the critical argument – no historical statement upon which Christian faith is said to be founded can be established beyond reasonable doubt. Not only is there a logical possibility of reasonable doubt, but we know there are millions of reasonable people who do doubt the Christian account. They used to be called infidels and heretics. But in a critical age we simply have to admit that they weigh the probabilities differently.

Any Christian faith that is critical must live with reasonable doubt and with acceptance of reasonable diversity. That position is a logical consequence of Protestant doubt of various Catholic doctrines, and of Protestant inability, despite the most desperate efforts, to get agreement on what the Bible really teaches. But the consequence did not become clear until the eighteenth century, when it led to conclusions the Reformers did not foresee.

This leads to acceptance that the Bible must indeed, as Pusey saw, be studied like any other book. For Christians, it will be a book that contains the only written records of the life and teaching of Jesus, and so it will have a peculiar importance. It is not unreasonable for Christians to think that God may have inspired the writing and editing of the Bible in a special way or to a special degree. But, if we are seriously concerned to discover the truth about Christian faith, we need to ask by whom and for whom particular biblical texts were written, how they were put together and what in them is essential for faith and what may rather be an expression of limited cultural perspectives of the time. We need to pursue critical biblical scholarship seriously. To refuse to do so is to be afraid of finding the truth.

The critical method is not an attack on a truth that is known with certainty, that is essential for salvation and that has to be defended by force if necessary. Criticism exposes the fact that the truths of faith are not known with absolute theoretical certainty, that acceptance of all the assertions of the Bible is not necessary for salvation (some biblical assertions may actually be false) and that truth is better defended by informed critical enquiry than by brute force.

Such enquiry is not at all a form of easy scepticism. It requires that I seek to know all the available facts that are relevant to religious claims. I must consider them sensitively and without distortion, as far as I can. I must be aware of, and evaluate, differing assessments of probability. I must have learned, through practice and discussion, what it is to make an informed judgment of probability, and what hidden background beliefs may be influencing my judgment. Only then am I in a position to make an informed judgment. This is a difficult and demanding process, and it is wise never to consider that I have finally completed it.

The liberal view is that such criticism is the most appropriate path to truth and that censorship and repression are symptoms of ignorance and fear, masquerading as paternal concern for those who are unable to think for themselves.

CRITICISM, REVELATION AND AUTHORITY

The chief traditional argument against such a critical Christian faith is that it is radically unrealistic to expect most people to think for themselves. Traditional faith is hierarchical, giving doctrinal authority to a small elite. Yet the Enlightenment is also elitist in its own way. The elite are those who have the time for, and are capable of, critical argument. What about the millions who have not the time, interest or ability for critical religious thought (and that is, as Kant and Hume saw, almost everybody)? Would they not be well advised to rely on authority?

Kant seems to overstate his case considerably when he says that enlightenment consists in using your own understanding 'without direction from another'. It would be absurd to work out quantum mechanics for yourself without taking a great deal of direction from competent physicists. It would be equally absurd to tackle some historical question without learning a great deal about historical methods from a competent teacher.

It is reasonable to expect that there should be something to learn in matters of religion, so that some direction from others will have a proper place in Christian faith, some reliance on testimony, and some acceptance on trust of matters to which most individuals do not have direct personal access. It seems to be a central part of most religious faiths that some individuals have privileged access to knowledge of truths about God and the divine purpose in creation.

It is reasonable to think that, if there is a God, such knowledge would be revealed in some form by God, and the revelation would have to be given to a specific person or group of persons. In that sense revelation and some form of authoritative statement of revelation is a central part of religious belief. One reason some Christians do not like the term 'liberal' and feel opposed to the Enlightenment is that it is taken to exclude the possibility of revelation. This leaves a very reduced view of Christian faith and is probably why past papal pronouncements were opposed to what they called 'liberalism'.

Such exclusion of revelation is not, however, an essential part of the call for freedom of thought that is made by critical enquiry. Indeed, we need to be critical about the exclusion of revelation from enquiry, as well as about any particular account of the nature of revelation. What is needed is an account of authority that can take due account of revelation but is compatible with informed critical enquiry.

If we look back at the arguments of the Papal Bull *Mirari Vos*, we find that what worried the Pope was the spectre of 'indifferentism', the view that truth does not matter, that all views are just matters of personal opinion, and no one belief is to be preferred to any others. But on this matter liberal thought can be in complete agreement with the Pope. Truth is of absolute importance. That is precisely why it is of the greatest importance to find and pursue the most appropriate way of discovering truth.

In the sciences, it is an established fact that this way is that of testable hypothesis, close observation and repeatable experiment. In history, it is a matter of making probabilistic judgments, proportioned at least to some extent to available evidence and testimony. In religion, the final appeal is to personal experience and knowledge of God, and the attainment of human fulfilment, in its intellectual, moral and psychological aspects.

But traditional religion involves many historical judgments, and in religious documents like the Bible statements have been made about scientifically ascertainable facts. On such matters, the criteria of knowledge used in history and in natural science must be accepted. In addition, there are innumerable disputes among more or less equally intelligent and informed religious believers. In such a situation, the best hope of arriving at truth is to promote a process of public critical debate. The result of that might be to discover that the main items of religious belief are no more than theoretically probable and are always subject to rational dispute.

This is not unusual in human affairs. In politics and morality the same result applies. All moral assertions are rationally disputable, and none can be established beyond the possibility of reasonable doubt. Yet we often need to be totally committed to one political or moral view in practice. As Bishop Butler said, 'Probability is the very guide of life,' and we must often be prepared to stake our lives on a probability, knowing that others may take a different position.[16]

This means that it is reasonable to accept some beliefs on authority: in science, on the authority of leading scientists; in politics, on the authority of experienced people of practical wisdom; in morality, on the authority of informed and sensitive moral agents; and, in religion, on the authority of those we believe to be people of prayer, wisdom, charity, learning and experience of the divine.

So far, one may agree with Pope Gregory XVI. But we may also wish to reserve the right to disagree in conscience even with an authority we accept in general, if a question arises on which we have formed a firm, informed and reasoned opinion.

That is a position that the Protestant Reformers were bound to support, if they were going to disagree with the authority of the Catholic Church. What they often did not see or accept was that the Bible is in just the same position, logically, as the Pope. There are many different views in the Bible, and we may in conscience, and for what we think to be good reason, disagree with some of them. Once you allow criticism of authority, you cannot forbid criticism when it touches the authority you accept. In this sense, all Protestants are in principle committed to accepting the conscientious right to disagree, even while allowing that it is reasonable to accept some interpretations and doctrines on authority. And in this sense, all Protestants will be liberals, though they do not always seem to realise the fact.

THE VALUE OF DISAGREEMENTS IN RELIGION

It follows that those who take different views on religion from us cannot be regarded as just evil and corrupt teachers who imperil the soul and corrupt the mind. We will therefore be inclined to believe that conscientious disagreement does not lead to the death of the soul, and that 'the narrow path of truth' is not quite so certainly and indisputably grasped by our favoured authority as we may have thought.

I may believe, and commit my whole life to, the belief that Jesus is the Son of God. But if I accept that others conscientiously disagree with me, and that my belief is not theoretically indisputable, I will be less inclined to think that disagreement is dangerous and evil and that people will be condemned by God (and should therefore be condemned or persecuted by me) if they do not agree with me.

It could be termed an axiom of critical faith that honest error does not lead to the death of the soul. A correlative axiom is that religious truth – which is after all about God, the ultimate mystery – is not likely to be obtained with absolute theoretical certainty by any human mind, since human intellects are so puny and limited. So the best way to seek truth, and avoid harm, in this area is to allow the expression of many differing views, some of which will help to purify my own of error, and some of which may help me to be clearer about what is centrally important in my own faith.

Freedom of thought does not spring from or lead to 'indifferentism'. It arises from a serious concern to avoid errors to which I may be blind, and to discover truths that I, and my tradition, may have overlooked. Disagreement and diversity could then be encouraged, insofar as they co-exist with charity and sensitivity and concern to find a truth that is vitally important but difficult to discern. I can remain firmly committed to my own Christian tradition, while being in a position to respect the conscientious disagreements of others and to learn from them wherever possible.

This will mean being prepared to re-think my own tradition, but it will not mean that I must be constantly thinking of giving up my strongest beliefs. It will mean, however, that tolerance, charity and intellectual humility will be recognised as important intellectual virtues, firmly founded on faith that Christ is the way, the truth and the life. Since Christ preaches love and not hate, reconciliation and not violence, such a truth does not need defending by force, and it would be inappropriate to defend it in that way.

Since I have criticised one or two past popes, I will end by emphasising that such a position was firmly and unequivocally declared by the Second Vatican Council of the Roman Catholic Church, and this means that the largest Christian church in the world is now committed to at least the major propositions of a liberal and critical faith – even though not all its leaders may like to use those words.

Chapter 9

Eternal Life in the Midst of Time

Close to the heart of Christian faith is a specific sort of moral commitment. That commitment is to the love that is disclosed in the life of Jesus, a love that can become an operative power in the lives of disciples, and that will ultimately triumph over evil and death. This is the active character of the divine life, and it places eternity in the midst of time, as it is mediated through humans who turn to the God revealed in Jesus Christ.

GOD AND FACTS OF SCIENCE AND HISTORY

The word 'liberal' has many strands of meaning. I have expounded two strands, and held that they are positive contributions of post-Reformation thought to the Christian heritage. First is the acceptance of the freedom to dissent, to follow one's own conscience and to practice one's own faith. This was a fundamental strand of Protestant thinking, and it is also biblically based on Jesus' unflinching criticisms of some Pharisaic religious belief and practice in his own day.

Second is the propriety of close empirical observation and experiment in establishing truths about the physical cosmos, and the propriety of informed critical enquiry and argument based on consideration of available evidence in weighing claims about historical facts. The fact that there are four different Gospels, and many diverse perspectives on Christian belief in the New Testament, suggests the necessity of critical comparison for a mature biblical faith. The fact that Christian claims about Jesus are rooted in history suggests that a sympathetic but critical study of history is genuinely important to Christian belief, and that Christianity has nothing to fear from such a study, as long as it is carried out without strong prejudice.

Non-liberal Christians reject either or both of these positions. They may deny that there should be freedom of religious practice or expressions of belief. They may deny the theory of evolution on the ground that it is not in the sacred text, or deny that historical methods of investigation can be applied to the Bible. Liberal Christians may have a wide range of views on the content of their faith, but they will be affected by critical science and history to some extent. The problem of liberal Christianity is the problem of how extensive such effects will be.

At the radical end of the spectrum are those who think science and history have sole sovereignty over all factual questions. Then religious faith would not speak of facts at all. No questions about the origin, causal structure and end of the universe will be relevant to Christian faith. Even the historical life of Jesus will be irrelevant to faith. Insofar as the existence of God, or at least of a God who makes any difference to the universe, is taken to be a fact, Christian faith will be in no position to say that God exists. Doctrines and stories about God and divine acts in history will have no factual content. They may be taken as expressing deep attitudes and emotions, or as advocating in picture form ways of life and moral commitments.

This is the view taken, though not quite consistently, by the German theologian Rudolf Bultmann, and more consistently in the twentieth century by the English theologian Don Cupitt.[17] For Bultmann, Christianity contrasts inauthentic with authentic life, calls the believer to choose authentic life and conveys the power to live authentically. Bultmann held the view that the resurrection of Jesus is not a historical event. It is the proclamation of new life, and liberation from despair. The preaching of the resurrection *is* the resurrection. Past history is irrelevant. Nevertheless, he also held that God confronts us in a unique way through an encounter with the risen Christ, in the proclamation of the gospel of the cross and resurrection.

The Swiss theologian Fritz Buri held that this retention of a historical element of Christian uniqueness is not tenable, and that humans can be presented with the possibility of authentic life without the preaching of the cross. The Christian form of that presentation is only one of many possible symbolic forms for speaking of authentic and inauthentic existence. There are many religious forms, and, since none of them has factual content, they can be viewed as different life-pictures with a more or less equivalent role in placing existential possibilities before men and women.

Consolidating such a view, Don Cupitt holds that Christian beliefs do not tell us about facts. They evoke and sustain loving attitudes and ways of life. They are 'myths' whose function is to articulate and elicit deep moral and emotional commitments.

Such a ruthless way with facts does not appeal to many Christians. It may well be true that religion is primarily a matter of practical commitment rather than a purely intellectual exercise. That is important to remember, when believers tend to get passionately involved in arguments about abstract intellectual doctrines like that of the Trinity. Yet it is usually felt that practical commitment should be appropriate to the facts in some way. So most believers suppose that there exist facts that are not facts of empirical science or history.

The most obvious fact of this sort is the fact that God exists. God is spiritual, not material, so empirical science cannot directly deal with God. God has no body, so no agent of allegedly divine acts can be observed, and divine motives are inaccessible to the historian. God may have some effects on the universe and on history, but, since no divine agent can be seen, measured or tested, any testimony to such acts will be ambiguous and disputable. Anyone who thinks that all facts are material or historical facts will deny that such agency exists and seek to explain such alleged acts in other ways – as just anomalous physical events, perhaps, or as illusions.

Belief in God may have many roots, but in the end it will probably depend on a claim that someone has apprehended a spiritual reality clearly enough to be a reliable witness to the divine presence and nature. Christians think that the prophets apprehended God in visions and through experiences of 'possession' or inspired speech. They think that Jesus had a particularly clear and intense apprehension of God as Father. And they think that followers of Jesus through the ages have apprehended God, whether as an imageless reality in contemplative states, as mediated through the personal presence of the risen Christ, or as known in the inward activity of the Spirit.

God can be experienced as a transcendent reality, mediated in and through many finite states, in nature, in history and in the creativity and mystery of inner personal experience. God is known, not only in discrete and startling experiences of the holy, but also in a general interpretation of experience as encounter with a transcendent reality of commanding value and awe-inspiring power.

God is not, however, knowable through scientific observation and experiment. A scientist will always quite properly look for a purely natural explanation for any event. Yet the existence of God has some implications for science. God is not demonstrable through a critical study of history, and a critical mind will always find reason to doubt whether any historical event is an act of God. Yet if God was in Christ, reconciling the world to the divine being, then God does act in history, and that will have implications for the historian.

Faith in God is not *based on* science or on history. But it calls for a certain sort of interpretation of facts about the cosmos and about history. It calls for an interpretation of empirical reality as a realm in which spiritual presence is manifested and spiritual purposes are realised.

CHRISTIAN FAITH IN THE CONTEXT OF MODERN COSMOLOGY

Christians need to speak not just of informed critical enquiry, but of informed critical commitment. Committed to the existence of a supreme transcendent reality and value, and to the possibility of its apprehension in nature, in history and in personal experience, Christians will see nature, history and inner experience as carrying intimations and signs of such a reality.

With regard to science, most Christians will not be able to accept any account of evolution that excludes the providence and purposes of God, or any account of the laws of nature that excludes the possibility of divine influence.

Most Christians will, for example, exclude any account that makes physical laws universal, exceptionless and exhaustively explanatory in a sense that leaves no room for purposive explanations. They will exclude any account of evolution that sees it as entirely random, non-purposive, accidental or unrelievedly horrendous and cruel.

On the other hand, Christian beliefs about the nature and purpose of God will be modified by what appears to be the fact of many billions of years of cosmic evolution of the cosmos from unconscious simplicity to integrated complexity and consciousness, probably to be followed by more billions of years of descent into freezing lassitude. And beliefs about divine providence will be modified by acknowledgment of the suffering and extinction of millions of animal species, brought about by the laws governing the evolution of life. Science will not destroy belief in God. But it may affect human ideas of divine providence and purpose by giving greater knowledge of the sort of universe God has created.

Within the New Testament, in the first chapter of the letters to the Ephesians and Colossians especially, the writer puts Jesus into a cosmic context. Jesus is seen, not just as a young Jew, but as the human manifestation of the archetype of all creation, by whom and in whom the whole cosmos was created. 'Christ' is interpreted, not just as a human being chosen to implement God's purpose, but as a cosmic power 'in whom all things hold together' (Col. 1:15–20) and in whom the whole cosmos ('all things, whether on earth or in heaven') will be reconciled to God. The eighth chapter of the letter to the Romans speaks of 'the creation' waiting with eager longing to be set free from its bondage to decay (Rom. 8:18–21).

All this fits well with the prologue to John's Gospel, speaking of Jesus as the cosmic *Logos* of God 'made flesh', and with the visionary chapters of the book of Revelation which look for the creation of 'a new heaven and a new earth'. The Christian story is not just the story of a young man unjustly put to death. It is the story of a cosmos formed in the image of divine wisdom, of that wisdom taking finite form in the person of a human being, and participating in the life of the creation in order that the whole cosmos should be renewed, freed from decay and brought to participate in the divine nature.

From New Testament times, therefore, the Christian faith has been concerned with the whole cosmos and its relation to the divine. Now we know that the cosmos is an immensely greater arena for divine redemption than the New Testament writers could ever have guessed. The cosmic vision of Christianity needs to be reformulated in the light of what we now believe about evolution and cosmology. This will not undermine the gospel, but it may set it within a context that brings out the depth and width of its vision.

We now know that if we talk about an incarnation of God in Jesus, we are not talking about a culminating event at the end of time. We are talking about an event fairly early in the history of the universe, on one tiny planet, among a lineage of primates who have existed as hominids for between five to ten million years and have evolved from single-celled organisms that existed on earth about four billion years ago.

This means we must re-think much of our imagery of creation, of heaven and of the coming of Christ in glory at the end of time. The creation is a multi-billion-year development from the primal simplicity of the Big Bang through the formation of atoms and complex molecules, to replicating organisms, the development of central nervous systems and brains, and the onset of intelligent consciousnesses, perhaps in many different forms throughout the universe. There could be millions of years of evolution still to come, and perhaps God's plans for intelligent life have hardly begun.

Heaven, life in the knowledge and love of God, is a possibility for all intelligent conscious beings. If 'everything on heaven and earth' is to be united in Christ, that Christ must be infinitely greater than the human Jesus. Christ must be, as John's Gospel saw, the eternal *Logos* of God, the divine Wisdom whose form is infinite and who is before all time. But that infinite form can be truly embodied and manifest in the human person of Jesus, for us and for our salvation. How could we restrict the divine power and say that this is the only finite form the *Logos* could take? The finite forms of the *Logos* may be many and diverse. We can say the divine Wisdom is truly embodied in the human Jesus, that Jesus is God for us. But the eternal Word may take forms we cannot imagine, and humans may play a relatively small part among the richness of created lives that will share in the life of God in heaven.

Belief that Christ will appear in judgment becomes a symbol of hope that the whole cosmos will culminate, after aeons of time, not in a whimper of cold emptiness, but in the ultimate destruction of evil, and the incorporation of all the good that has ever been into the unending life of the God who was truly seen on earth in Jesus. This will almost certainly take place beyond the boundaries of this physical cosmos, which will eventually cease to be. The 'new creation' will be in other forms of time and space that we can hardly begin to imagine. It is not surprising that Paul felt himself unable to say what the 'resurrection body' would be like (1 Cor. 15:35–6). It will not be some slightly modified version of our present human body. It will be, as Paul says, glorious, incorruptible and as unlike us as wheat is from the seeds from which it grows.

This calls for an expansion of Christian vision. It is most unlikely that a human Mary and Jesus will be at the apex of heavenly existence, as they are in most traditional pictures of heaven. They are more likely to be human representatives of a wide diversity of intelligent life-forms.

Our iconography of heaven must change. The cosmic purpose of God is unlikely to be centred on human beings. It may well be concerned with the flourishing of many forms of sentient life, and humans may be just a passing stage even in the evolution of life on earth. The human Jesus will not be the consummation of creation, though he can be regarded as the ideal exemplar of a truly human life in relation to God.

The important Christian fundamentals can still stand firm. God is a creator of unlimited love and compassion. The destiny of humans, as of all intelligent creatures, is to be liberated from self and to share in the divine nature. Jesus is the one who reveals in human history God's purpose of unitive love, a love that unites finite lives to the infinity of God. Jesus' life founds a new society, the church, within which God's Spirit lives and acts. Jesus is the human incarnation of the divine Word and Wisdom, and the one who unites human nature to the divine. But we have no idea of what we shall see when we see him as he is. We only know that, through divine power and love, we shall then be conformed to his image of glory (cf. 1 John 3:2: 'What we will be has not yet been revealed. What we do know is this: when he is revealed, we will be like him, for we will see him as he is').

This gospel cries out for an evolutionary cosmic vision, the vision of a universe that is drawn towards intelligence and love by the perfect Good from whom it derives and on whom it depends for its existence. This Christian vision is that the Supreme Good, the ultimate mind that actualises in itself and enjoys supreme goodness, draws the material universe towards itself and enters into the universe, perhaps in many forms but specifically on this planet in the form of a human person, so that there shall be on this planet a foreshadowing of the final cosmic goal and the growth of a new community of the Spirit that will keep the vision of that goal alive. Modern science can bring the Christian gospel alive in a new way, teaching us more about the grandeur and glory of the creation as it moves on its multi-billion-year journey into God.

CHRISTIAN FAITH AND CRITICAL HISTORY

Though modern science can be seen as a challenge to Christian belief, in this way it can give a new and vibrant life to Christian faith, seen as the disclosure of God's purpose in a vast and awesome creation. In a similar way, critical history can challenge many over-confident claims about the historicity of the Bible. But it also can help to encourage a better appreciation of the ways in which the eternal God enters into the processes of time to lead it towards unity with the divine life.

Most Christians will not be able to accept any account of history that discounts the possibility of divine action and influence. They will reject accounts of history that are purely naturalistic – that account for everything that happens solely in terms of physical laws and human motives and purposes. They will be open to the possibility of miraculous events that transcend the normal physical regularities of nature. And they will be open to the possibility of encounters with God, especially among great religious teachers and saints, which can influence the course of history.

On the other hand, beliefs about exactly how and where God acts in history will be modified by more careful and critical analysis of available historical data. Detailed and comparative historical study will reveal the huge amount of fraud in religion, the extent to which the deeds of saints are often magnified by legendary accretion, and the degree to which we must remain decently agnostic about exactly what happened in the recorded past. Christians may well be convinced that God was disclosed in the person of Jesus and that the Gospels give a reliable enough account of Jesus' teachings and character to give new insights into the nature and purpose of God. Yet they should realise that the Gospel accounts do not give certainty about exactly what Jesus said and did, that they provide accounts from significantly different perspectives and that there can be very different assessments of such things as the status and importance of miracles, or of the extent to which Jesus' recorded teachings have been amended by later re-telling of them.

Historical assessments will range from the very sceptical view that we know almost nothing about Jesus to the very trusting view that all, or almost all, of what the Gospels tell us is accurate. This raises the important question of how much believers need to know about Jesus before they can call themselves Christians.

My own view is that we need to have enough data to believe that Jesus was a person in whom God could be authentically disclosed in a new and distinctive way. This means we need to be reasonably sure, for instance, that he taught about humility, non-violence and unlimited love, that he died for the sake of the kingdom and that he appeared to the disciples after his death. But we do not need to know that he was born of a virgin mother, that he performed all the miracles and exorcisms attributed to him in the Gospels, that he was actually tempted by the Devil and fed by angels in the wilderness or that his body rose physically from the dead and ascended into heaven in a cloud.

My view on this is affected by the fact that I think historical study can give us good (though not theoretically overwhelming) reason to believe the first set of things, but may leave us feeling that we are dealing with later additions, exaggerations and legends when we come to the second set. I accept, of course, that others may feel that much more in the Gospels is factual. But it is not necessary to accept that 'more' in order to commit yourself in faith to the God who is disclosed in the person of Jesus and in the church that seeks to make that disclosure present to each succeeding generation.

The main point is, however, that any informed critical Christian should be aware of the sort of arguments that have been widely deployed in this area. We should see that there is a range of possible viewpoints, and recognise that there is legitimate room for diversity, once we have admitted the relevance of historical enquiry.

The worst sins against historical truth are committed by those who proclaim their own understanding of the Gospels without any hint that there are other understandings in existence. They compound the felony by pretending that their account is historically established and faithful to God, whereas alternative accounts are unsound and due to lack of faith. Any responsible teaching that is based on the New Testament must be honest and open about the range of interpretations that exists of these documents. No one should claim to be certain that their own interpretation is correct, though of course one interpretation may and should be expounded and defended, as long as alternative accounts are acknowledged.

The objection to this procedure is that it seems to leave Christian faith at the mercy of the latest learned articles of biblical scholars. Will the acids of criticism not dissolve away all faith in the historical Jesus? Or at least leave one so uncertain about what happened that firm commitment becomes impossible?

The word 'liberalism' is often used within theology in a narrower sense than the one in which I have used it, to signify the work of a group of German scholars in the late eighteenth and the nineteenth century who approached the problems of historical criticism in a particular way.

In 1770 Gotthold Lessing published some of the writings of Hermann Reimarus, who had died shortly before. In these *Wolfenbuettel Fragments*

Reimarus held that the real historical Jesus had been primarily an ethical teacher, who had believed that the end of the world was imminent. After his death the disciples hid his body, and, realising that the world was not ending, the church began to construct a mythical Christ that bears little relation to the historical original.

Two major themes of nineteenth-century German liberal thought are presaged here. One is that Jesus was important primarily as an ethical teacher. The other is that the dogmas of the church are later Hellenistic constructions that belong to mythology, constructed by human imagination in response to deep human needs, but which a more scientific view of the universe renders obsolete. Though these themes were often referred to by their proponents as constituting 'liberal theology', it should be clear that this is a much more restricted definition of 'liberalism' than the one I have provided. This third strand of liberalism was indeed affirmed by those who were liberal in the first two senses (accepting freedom of belief and informed critical enquiry, especially in science and history). But the third strand by no means follows from the first two and is best regarded as just one possible form of liberal theology – and a form that has largely been superseded, precisely by later critical investigations.

Underlying nineteenth-century German liberal theology is the belief, made explicit by David Friedrich Strauss, that nature and history both consist of a closed causal nexus of purely natural causes and effects.[18] Miracles do not occur, and any beliefs Jesus had about the end of the world were deluded. So the importance of Jesus had to lie in his moral teaching. Nevertheless, the myths about Jesus that developed later may express in narrative form archetypal ideas about the processes of history and human moral goals which are of great psychological value. In this form of liberalism, historical and metaphysical claims, about exactly what happened in the past or about the ultimate nature of reality, are kept to a minimum. The important core of Christian faith lies in its moral teaching. But in this area, too, the critical methods of the Enlightenment raised great problems for Christian belief.

CHRISTIAN FAITH AND THE AUTONOMY OF ETHICS

One of the most important German liberal theologians was Adolf von Harnack (1851–1930). In his presentation of Christian faith, he abandoned almost all claims that Jesus was the incarnate *Logos*, that God was Trinitarian and that Jesus died for the sins of the world. He held that in the ideas of 'God the Father, Providence, the position of men as God's children, the infinite value of the human soul – the whole Gospel is expressed'. This is not a total reduction of Jesus' teaching to morality, of the sort of which the philosopher Immanuel Kant might be accused. An objectively existing God and some sort of providential divine action in history give special force to Jesus' teaching that the kingdom of God, 'the rule of the holy God in the hearts of individuals', is the goal of history. Harnack spoke of Jesus' message as being a message of 'eternal life in the midst of time', so that morality is love of and trust in God, not just keeping a set of ethical principles.

Immanuel Kant, who is in many ways the supreme German philosopher of the Enlightenment, had held that ethics is wholly autonomous, and the idea of moral autonomy provides an important strand of Enlightenment thought, a strand that can very easily come into conflict with religious faith. In fact the idea of moral autonomy sometimes provides a fourth sense of 'liberal'. In addition to freedom of dissent and expression, acceptance of scientific and historical methodology, and reference to a specific German school of theology as 'liberal', 'liberalism' is often taken to stand for the rejection of external authority in morals. I shall try to show that there is a qualified sense in which such moral liberalism is acceptable to Christians. But it needs to be carefully distinguished from the more extreme view that you can decide to act in any way you choose, as well as from the view that there is no place for moral authority at all in Christianity.

For Kant, autonomy is that property of the human will by which it legislates its own moral law. Ethical principles can be known without any reference to religious beliefs and they do not depend for their validity on any external or revealed authority. Moreover, God does not enter into the moral life in any experiential way. All alleged experiences of God are fanatical illusions, and appeals to divine grace are craven admissions of human weakness. Harnack did not follow those opinions. For him, Jesus discloses in his life and teachings a 'higher righteousness', the demand of a transformation of the heart to receive and mediate self-giving divine love. Jesus mediates that love in a real and powerful way, enabling his disciples to become the beloved children of a personal and passionate God. So there is a place for moral disclosure in Christian faith, and a place for experience of God that is ethically relevant.

Nevertheless a certain sense of moral autonomy is important for Harnack. In making particular moral decisions, it is not enough to accept some rule on authority, whether it is in the Bible or promulgated by a church. We may be guided by the judgments of others, who may be wiser or more experienced than we are. But in the end we are responsible for forming our own moral beliefs. So the ethical authority of Jesus is not a matter of laying down particular rules that have to be obeyed. Jesus already had the 613 rules of Torah, and did not need to add any more. Jesus' authority lay in the vision he provided of a new life in the kingdom of God, the community of the divine Spirit. That new life could be summed up in two simple rules – love of God with the whole heart, and love of neighbour as oneself (Matt. 22:34–40). These rules provide a more rigorous and testing way of applying all the particular rules of Torah. They also provide a way of moving beyond all such particular rules, as the church did when it abandoned observance of Torah and tried to live just by 'the law of Christ', which is the law of total love.

Such love cannot be laid down in a set of rules – which have to change to adapt to new situations. It is laid down in the example of a life of healing, forgiveness, non-attachment and passionate care for others, especially the poor and outcastes of society. The moral authority of Jesus is the life he lived and the death he died, surrendered in self-abandoning hope for the coming of God's rule in the hearts of men and women.

Jesus not only reveals the character of that love as the character of God. He made and makes it possible for individuals to practise such love, insofar as they receive from him the Spirit of God, and God's love takes form in their inner lives. This is 'eternal life in the midst of time', the life of God incarnated in the society of those whose hearts are ruled by divine love.

For Harnack the Christian myths that turn Jesus into a divine being, a God-man, have the function of giving imaginative and emotional form to what might otherwise be rather abstract doctrines of the Fatherhood of God, the moral goal of history, the role of Jesus in disclosing and mediating the higher righteousness, and the infinite dignity of humanity. The intricacies of conciliar definitions are inadequate philosophical attempts to convey simple practical truths about a loving God who wishes to implant the divine love in the hearts of all those who turn to God in trust.

Harnack and his teacher Albrecht Ritschl both saw Christianity (especially in its German Protestant form) as the perfect religion, a form of inner ethical monotheism, a morality of the heart and spirit. The place of Jesus is in being the supreme exemplar of this morality, and the founder of the community whose vocation was to incarnate the higher morality of love and fellowship in the world.

These writers tended to be unsympathetic to grand metaphysical schemes, or to any metaphysics at all. So they saw the Trinitarian and Christological dogmas as empty speculation, unimportant to faith. They were also unsympathetic to mysticism, or to claims by special individuals to have direct knowledge of God. They preferred to think that the basic religious experience was moral experience, interpreted within the Christian community.

Like Immanuel Kant, by whom they were deeply influenced, they saw religion as primarily practical, a system for promoting a loving way of life. Unlike Kant, they did not see God as just a postulate for assuring agents that virtue would be rewarded in the end. They saw the experience of God as Father as an important one, one that is implicit in moral experience itself, seen in threefold form as apprehension of absolute duty, experience of an inner divine power making for righteousness, and a hope for the victory of love in a broken world. This is a distinctively Christian view of what morality is, and it depends essentially upon a living faith in God, the God whose character is uniquely revealed and whose presence is uniquely mediated by the historical Jesus.

The religion of a morality of love, revealed and mediated by the person of Jesus, is very different from the sort of fully autonomous morality that Kant recommended. Kant left no place for revelation or for experiences of divine grace, and he thought that moral rules could be worked out by reason applying the principle of possible universal agreement (the Categorical Imperative). Ritschl and Harnack gave God a more constitutive place in moral life. The personal God gave real imperative force to the morality of love. The person of Jesus revealed what love really requires. The resurrection of Jesus (whether physical or not) revealed what God's love promises. And the Spirit of God helped to make love possible.

This is a distinctively Christian view of morality. But it is not a morality that derives its moral rules directly from the Bible or from the church. Both Ritschl and Harnack adopted a fully critical attitude to religious authority and to the Bible.

THE BIBLE AND ETHICS

A critical approach to the Bible puts in question any appeal to the moral teachings recorded in the Bible as coming directly from God, and therefore as unquestionable and authoritative. The Bible can be seen as primarily a record of the testimony of those who have been touched by a sense of God, or who feel themselves to have been possessed by the Spirit of God, rather than as the very words of God. We are free to see their testimony as expressing all the limitations of knowledge and understanding of their own culture, historical situation and psychology. They may indeed have been possessed by the Spirit of God, but that did not simply over-ride their own rational and moral views.

So when we read of the command to exterminate all Canaanites who do not simply surrender to the Israelites, together with their children and cattle (Deut. 20:10–18), we are free to see that as an extremely primitive understanding of what God, the Supreme Good, requires. When we read that adulterers and disobedient children are to be stoned to death (Deut. 21:18–21; 22:22) we are free to say that these are the moral codes of early tribal societies, not the commands of God.

Moral insight develops, at least sometimes. The Bible itself records some decisive advances in moral understanding. Ezekiel records that people should be punished only for their own sins, not for the sins of their fathers (Ezek. 18:4) – a crucial moral advance. The 'Lex Talionis' limits retribution to an eye for an eye, not just unlimited vengeance on a whole family. And, most decisively for Christians, the Sermon on the Mount (Matt. 5–7) goes further and recommends turning the other cheek, love of enemies, and non-resistance to those who do evil. It has proved extremely difficult for Christians to interpret Jesus' teachings in a practical way, but there is no doubt that such teachings render any literal application of Old Testament rules obsolete.

Once a whole set of biblical rules has been seen to be subject to criticism and rejection, it is hard to prevent criticism of the New Testament as well as the Old. Released from the binding authority of both church and Bible, eighteenth- and nineteenth-century thinkers set out to see if they could find some sort of rational basis for morality. Various strategies were attempted. Solutions ranged from seeing morality as an attempt by the weak to restrain the ravages of the strong (Nietzsche), to seeing it as a cultivation of social

sentiments (Hume), as enlightened self-interest (Butler) or as a set of principles that could be universally agreed and adopted (Kant).

Most of these proposals agreed with Kant's assertion that morality
should be autonomous, in the sense of not being dependent on prior
religious beliefs. Kant's stronger sense of autonomy, that the human will is
a law unto itself yet naturally acts on universally justifiable principles, was
not widely shared. Some thought that an appeal to universal moral principles was merely a confidence trick used to obtain social cohesion in societies
of aggressively competing individuals.

It became clear that morality does not collapse without religion.
But there are various accounts of what morality is, and general views of
human nature and its place in the cosmos are relevant to which account you
are likely to accept. Morality is not after all autonomous, in the sense of
being totally independent of whatever views of human nature you hold. If
you think humans are accidental by-products of a process of random
genetic mutation, it would not be rational to hold that there are absolute
obligations to act on strictly impartial principles, at any personal cost. If, on
the other hand, you think humans are created by God to know and love God
for ever, it would not be rational to hold that you should invent whatever
moral principles you think fit (or that you should have no moral principles
at all).

It is in that sense that Christian belief makes a difference to moral belief.
If you believe God has created you for a purpose, the most reasonable way
to act will be to aim to achieve that purpose. Indeed, that will become a matter of strict obligation. For Christians, Jesus' own life discloses what that
purpose is – it is to love God, and to heal, forgive, reconcile and help others,
especially those in greatest need. A life of Christ-like love is the basic
Christian obligation, based on the disclosure of the moral demand of God
in the person of Jesus.

It is important to add that this will not be just a matter of obeying a strict
command as if from some arbitrary dictator – that is Kant's rather perverse
interpretation of 'heteronomy', a term under which he includes acting in
obedience to the commands of God. For orthodox believers, however,
God's commands are not just arbitrary dictates. In the Christian and in the
Jewish view, they are for the good of creatures ('Keep the commandments of
the Lord your God and his decrees that I am commanding you today, for
your own well-being': Deuteronomy 10:13). They delineate what acts make

for the welfare and flourishing of persons, who are creatively to actualise many of the positive potentialities God has given them. It is in such creative activity that humans are to 'be like' the creator God. They are to be co-creators with God of the good things of the created world.

The human response to God is not one of craven submission. It is, ideally, one of reverence, gratitude and love – reverence for the beauty and perfection of God, gratitude for the gifts of creation, and love for the One who gives the divine life in love that personal beings should flourish and be happy.

Where Kant is right is in pointing out that Christian morality is not slavish obedience to arbitrary rules set down in the Bible. Where he is wrong is in thinking that Christian morality can be worked out by reason alone, without reference to Jesus Christ. What is required is the key that Paul provides for understanding Christian morality. That key is simple: 'The letter kills, but the spirit gives life' (2 Cor. 3:6). God wills the welfare of creatures. In Jesus he gives a decisive clue to what this involves. But specific moral rules, whether they are found in the Bible or propounded by the church, may carry with them limitations of perspective and insight that need to be modified by new knowledge or experience.

NATURAL LAW

In fact the main Christian tradition has never been content to take its ethical principles just from the pages of the Bible. The Catholic tradition of 'Natural Law' has focused rather on the doctrine of God as creator.[19] Assuming that the purposes of nature are the purposes that God has placed in nature, the church has based much ethical teaching on the principle that the purposes of nature should not be frustrated, but should be held inviolate. By looking at natural human inclinations, implanted by God, the main moral guidelines that govern human life can be discovered by reason.

With the acceptance of evolutionary science, however, such appeals to nature may also need to be re-thought. In a biological process that is based on random mutation and natural selection, many of the ways in which 'nature' works will not be in accord with the purposes of God in creation. God can certainly be seen as setting up such a process in order that personal, responsible and intelligent communities should come into existence. But the way nature works can no longer be taken as a definitive guide to how humans should act responsibly. For nature is partly random and many of its specific processes are indifferent to moral concerns.

So an informed scientific view of nature needs to identify those processes that are 'natural', in that they occur in accordance with scientific laws, but that should nonetheless be eradicated or modified by any morally concerned person. The growth of cancer cells, for example, is natural, but should certainly be frustrated. Why should such growth be frustrated? Because it frustrates the deeper purpose of God in creation that personal life should flourish.

The moral criterion, in other words, cannot be simply that a process is physically present or even normal. Each physical process must be assessed in terms of its contribution to the existence and flourishing of personal life, of moral awareness and the capacity for social relationship. There is still a place for Natural Law thinking in a scientifically understood universe. But we need to be clear that what is taken to be 'natural' is not just what happens in nature – and even less what might seem to be a 'purpose' of nature itself, which has no purposes – but what God intends to generate through the general processes of nature. The moral criterion will, in short, be personal flourishing in a just society and not simply the maintenance of a given physical structure. It is by reflection on the purposes of God that nature is meant to subserve that we can come to a reasonable view of how we should deal with the natural world. That will mean more 'interference with', and modification of, physical structures, than would have been envisaged in medieval times. But that is hardly surprising, since we have had the technology for such change only within the last century.

The new ethical dilemmas and possibilities that scientific technology has opened up are not envisaged by either the Bible or by traditional Natural Law thinking. So our moral principles need to be continually re-thought. Nevertheless, the Bible and tradition lay down the general Christian orientation of such thinking. That orientation does not lie in any specific moral rules, which may well be rendered obsolete by new understandings of nature. It lies in the consideration that God creates the cosmos in order that personal life should flourish, that Christ gives special emphasis to care for the poor and the oppressed and that the Spirit acts to unite all creation ('everything in heaven and earth') to the divine life 'in Christ'.

Armed with these principles, the Christian moral vocation is to think creatively and responsibly about how these goals would be best attained, insofar as human action can help to attain them. For Christian morality, there is an objective goal of human flourishing in relation to Supreme Goodness, and the human task is to be co-workers with God in working towards that goal. Christians may have given up a specific 'law of God' (a Torah), but there is a powerful and distinctive Christian morality, and to embrace it is to embrace at least one form of Christian faith.

A CRITIQUE OF EXTREME HISTORICAL CRITICISM

It is important, for this view, that the historical Jesus should be to some extent accessible, and that his character, teaching and proclamation of the kingdom should be historically ascertainable. The conditions under which a critical historian could achieve that were set out by Ernst Troeltsch, as three basic principles of critical historical method.[20] First, the principle of criticism is that, since belief must be proportioned to evidence, and historical evidence is nearly always disputable and can be interpreted in more than one way, no historical fact can be established with more than probability. Second, the principle of analogy is that things in the past have probably proceeded in much the same way as things in the present, so you must assess the probability of past occurrences in the same way that you would assess the probability of their occurring now. Third, the principle of correlation is that historical events cannot be considered in isolation, but must be seen in their social and cultural context, if their significance is to be properly understood.

These principles, it must be said, are not self-evident. It is true that if we are trying to obtain a purely neutral account of the past we may be happy to say no more than that 'such and such might have happened, but not everyone agrees, and of course it might not have happened'. But scepticism is incompatible with trust and loyalty. Sometimes we are challenged to trust in what someone says, even when it cannot be evidentially established, as a token of our loyalty and commitment to that person. If Christians believe that Jesus is the one who shows that God is unlimited love, that his presence is authentically known in the churches and that he is the proper object of devotion, it is very odd to say that we will only accept as true those things which a non-Christian, who might even believe that there is no God and that all prophets are deluded, could agree with. Commitment to God, and specifically to the God revealed in Jesus, entails a certain degree of trust in the reliability and truthfulness of the early Christians who compiled the New Testament. While the principle of criticism might lead us to be cautious about the details of some biblical accounts, it would not be reasonable to say that Christians should only accept what a neutral (i.e. non-Christian) historian would accept as established beyond reasonable doubt. The principle of criticism must be balanced by a principle of reasonable trust in the veracity and sincerity of the New Testament writers.

Similarly, the principle of analogy has very definite limits if the Christian claim is precisely that Jesus is uniquely the revelation of God in history. It would be odd if that was true and yet there was nothing in Jesus' life or teachings that could not be paralleled in the contemporary world. The uniqueness of Jesus suggests that there might well be some things about his life that have no analogy to the everyday events we are now familiar with.

The principle of correlation, too, cannot be accepted by an orthodox Christian in such a way as to rule out all divine or spiritual influence on the physical world. While it is helpful to place historical events in their social and cultural context, it is not acceptable to rule out all spiritual influences, or all actions of a personal God, in principle. So while it may be right to be critical, to seek analogies with present experience and to seek to see things in their total context, it is not defensible to rule out initial trust in the veracity of those who recorded the originative events of the Christian faith, to rule out the uniqueness of the events surrounding Jesus or to rule out any possibility of extraordinary divine acts in history. To rule out such things is prejudice, not principle. What the critical Christian historian must seek to do is to balance critical method against trust in God's action in Jesus, and find a path between uncritical acceptance of every historical claim made in religion, and rejection of all religious claims as false and deluded. This is not easy, and the German liberal theologians would now be generally judged to have overlooked several factors in their own assessments of the life of Jesus.

For a start the biblical records of miracles were largely discounted, or at least regarded as liable to be greatly exaggerated and often legendary. For such records are always no more than probable, they portray events radically unlike the events with which we are familiar today, and they come from a culture that tended to accept accounts of marvels and wonders much more readily than anyone would today. It followed that the records of Jesus' life, of exorcisms, healings and miracles, were judged unlikely to be accurate. Ritschl,

Troeltsch and Harnack all agreed that the element of the miraculous in the Gospel accounts is not crucially important – though the resurrection appearances pose a problem here, since they do seem rather crucial to the subsequent development of Christianity. Those appearances, however, were judged to be more in the nature of visions, of a communal, vivid and enduring sort, than the raising of a physical body from the tomb. If, however, we are rather sceptical of methodological scepticism, we may wish to say that God could manifest his healing power through the person of Jesus, and that the resurrection can be intelligibly seen as a disclosure of the ultimate spiritual destiny of all humans, and of the primacy of spiritual over physical reality. Miracles are not ruled out for a critical historian, though they may be approached with various degrees of caution or scepticism, depending largely on the nature of your other background religious beliefs.

For the German liberals, John's Gospel, in which Jesus constantly refers to his own person as the object of faith, could be discounted as an accurate record or even as an authentic amplification, of Jesus' actual teaching. In the synoptic Gospels Jesus does talk, rather, about God, the coming of God's kingdom, and the way of life those who look for the kingdom should adopt. In those Gospels, Jesus' parables, his rather extreme aphorisms about conduct, and his cryptic teachings about the imminence of the kingdom are very probably accurate, if only because they are so difficult and unexpected. In these respects, however, the liberal account perhaps overlooked the fact that some of Paul's letters, which are earlier than the Gospels, display the same sort of interest in Christ's cosmic role as the divine Wisdom that is found in John's Gospel. In addition, the themes of *Logos*, of divine Wisdom and even of personal embodiments of Torah in human lives are parts of Jewish tradition, and are not alien imparts from Greek philosophy. The historical evidence that Jesus was primarily a moral teacher is not strong, and the German liberals claimed, ironically, to know much more about the historical Jesus than their methods should have allowed. But what they claimed to know is not in fact supported by the New Testament documents, which stress the unique authority and cosmic role of Jesus above all else.

Finally, the principle of correlation suggests, correctly I think, that Jesus will be most helpfully understood as a Messianic Jew. Yet the German theologians almost wholly failed to see the distinctive Jewishness of Jesus. So they tended to see Christianity as something entirely distinct from, and an important advance upon, Judaism. As Albert Schweitzer was to say, they tended to see Jesus as an enlarged version of their own Protestant selves and ideals.

For them, Jesus was more of a universal moral teacher than a Messianic claimant. However, it should be said in their favour that the morality they had in mind was an inner, God-directed and God-dependent morality. There is a spiritual sublimity in the idea that true religion lies in the practice of loving-kindness and mercy, commanded, evoked, enabled and eventually to be fully realised in the human heart by God. Faith is not the assent of the intellect to complicated doctrines, but moment-by-moment trust in the power of a morally demanding and merciful God. Jesus is the point in history at which the nature of the demand and the promise of its eventual fulfilment are disclosed. He is the founder of a community in which the future rule of God becomes partially present, in a new and distinctive way, the way of the Spirit working within the heart.

In Ritschl, Troeltsch and Harnack, Reimarus' accusation of fraud on the part of the apostles and his complete rejection of divine action and revelation have disappeared. Divine providence does exist, though it rarely, if ever, breaks the laws of nature to produce amazing miracles like turning water into wine. Revelation of the divine nature does exist, though it is not infallible and free from all possible doubt. The apostles were genuine and faithful disciples of Jesus, as an overwhelming disclosure of God's character and mediator of the Holy Spirit, though they probably did not regard him as personally divine.

THE GERMAN LIBERAL RE-THINKING OF CHRISTIANITY

To what extent are these theologians successful in rescuing history from total scepticism, and in providing a firm foundation for Christian faith? I think what they show is that Christian faith cannot be *based on* history, as though we could just take the biblical accounts as wholly accurate and base our faith on that. Faith, for them, is a practical commitment to morality seen in a distinctive way, as response to an absolute moral demand, an enabling moral power and a providential directing of history towards the moral goal of a society of fellowship, compassion and free co-operation. This commitment provides an interpretative framework for history. The available evidence must be consistent with it and must support the interpretation in an intelligible, but rather unspecific, way. That is all the person of Christian faith has a right to require of critical history, and a fully critical attitude to history can support such a view of faith.

These German 'liberal' theologians show that critical historical method does not necessarily lead to total scepticism, or to constantly wavering opinions. A prior conception of faith in a morally demanding and merciful God can be brought to history as an interpretative framework, and, though it can be tested in various general ways, history is unlikely to provide a final decision on whether that prior conception is acceptable or not.

The German liberal re-thinking of Christian faith is that Christian faith is primarily practical commitment to a way of seeing morality, and to a way of seeing history as the progressive realisation of such a morality. It is not a matter of speculative doctrines about the inner nature of God, or of claims to special experiences of God. It may turn out, however, that we need to say rather more about God and the nature of God's action in the universe, and rather more about possible ways of apprehending such action, than these German theologians allowed. In brief, metaphysics (talk about the ultimate nature of reality) and mysticism (talk about ways of apprehending God) may be more important than they thought.

Harnack's treatment of Eastern Orthodox and Roman Catholic forms of faith was less than fully appreciative. He saw the religion of the Catholic Church as a 'total perversion' of the simple trust, humility and fellowship, the 'dependence on God and freedom in him', that he thought the gospel proclaimed. He saw the Orthodox doctrine of 'deification' (*theosis*) as sub-Christian and as belonging to 'the lowest class of religion'.[21]

Such harsh judgments flow from his conviction that 'the Gospel, as Jesus proclaimed it, has to do with the Father only and not with the Son' (lecture 8). So Christological dogmas have, he thinks, lost all connection with the historical Jesus. They replace direct faith in Jesus with theoretical dogmas. And they replace the simple moral teachings of Jesus with what he calls 'pharmacological' notions of ontological union with divine substance. Harnack wants simple personal relationship and moral commitment, not metaphysical and impersonal speculations about human and divine substances.

However, things are not so simple. Harnack says that Jesus 'was himself what he taught', that he had a unique knowledge of God and a unique vocation to do God's work. He is the 'personal realisation' of the gospel, and in him 'the divine appeared in as pure a form as it can appear on earth' (lecture 8). How is it that Jesus was uniquely able to embody the kingdom in his own person, that he had a unique knowledge of God and a unique calling from God and that the divine appeared in him in a uniquely pure way? How is it that he alone among humans shows 'eternal life in the midst of time' and was raised from death to life and glory, as Harnack affirms?

However much Harnack disliked metaphysics, some metaphysically persuasive account of Jesus' uniqueness is required if such statements are not to be mere poetic exaggerations of what were in fact rather ordinary events in the life of a rather ordinary religious reformer. And some account of the possibility of unique knowledge and experience of God is required if Jesus is to be accepted as a reliable and authoritative guide to a truly moral way of human existence.

Two other nineteenth-century German thinkers, Hegel and Schleiermacher, argue for notions of faith that stress the primacy of metaphysics and experience, respectively. But before I turn to consider them I will suggest that the positive contribution of Ritschl, Troeltsch and Harnack to re-thinking Christianity is to have located moral commitment (not intellectual assent to correct dogma, not ritual practice and not unusual and ecstatic personal experiences) as the central concern of Christian faith, and to have given a new interpretation of what Christian morality is.[22] In short, such a morality is not a set of specific moral rules, but a view of morality as encounter with a transcendent personal moral will, who demands a concern for the welfare of all human beings without exception (we might now say, of all sentient beings without exception) and a realisation of the personal potentialities in which human flourishing consists. These demands are absolute. But God is compassionate, and the divine mercy is infinite. On such a view, the history of religion, or at least of authentic religion, is the record of such moral encounters, and of a gradually broadening and deepening understanding of them.

While historians must be content with probabilities, must be sceptical about the literal veracity of many ancient records and must subject Scripture to the same critical criteria as any other text, they can find enough evidence to support the belief that there is such a supreme moral will, which has been at least partially apprehended at various times in history. And they can find enough evidence to support the belief that Jesus has the unique historical role of decisively revealing that view of God and of morality, and of inaugurating the community or set of communities in which the divine love can be mediated in a new and deeply inward way.

Insofar as Jesus is the place wherein the divine is disclosed, made known and accessible, Jesus can be regarded as the mediator of God to humanity and the medium of God's historical actions for the welfare of God's creatures on earth. This is one major form of what has been called liberal Protestant Christianity. It is a re-thinking of Christianity that is true to the roots of Christian belief in the Hebrew Scriptures (however much it misunderstood Judaism). It is needed whenever Christians find themselves arguing angrily over intricate and complex points of dogma. Its motto could well be the statement of the prophet Amos: 'I hate, I despise your festivals, and I take no delight in your solemn assemblies ... but let justice roll down like waters, and righteousness like an ever-flowing stream' (Amos 5:21, 24). The kingdom of God is a moral kingdom in which all can find fulfilment and happiness, and in which all will do so by conscious relation to God as the Supreme Good and the well-spring of compassionate and joyful love.

Chapter 10

Apprehending the Infinite

The starting point of contemporary Christian faith is an experienced liberation from hatred, greed and ignorance, brought about by a vision of transcendent goodness in and through the risen Christ. Such a liberating apprehension needs to be worked out tentatively yet creatively in relation to the modern scientific and historical worldview. That is the view of a long cosmic evolutionary process within which the divine life can be expressed and become the matrix of a transformation of the cosmos itself to participate in the life of the eternal God. That expression, that matrix, and that goal to which all creation strives, is Christ. To be a Christian is to place all your faith in that vision and that goal.

THE NEED FOR METAPHYSICS

The German liberal theologians were right when they pointed out that history shows there are few unchanging elements of revelation, that the gospel calls us often to discard old traditions and drink the new wine of freedom in God, and that Christian revealed morality is a life of self-giving love, not an adherence to ancient and limited moral rules.

They did not see so clearly, however, that this morality of a growing moral insight into the will of God for the universal flourishing of creatures needs to be based on a firm doctrinal or metaphysical foundation. There needs to be an objectively existing God of supreme perfection, who reveals the divine nature and purpose in the person of Jesus, and who continues to work in the church to complete the flourishing of humans by uniting them to the divine life. There needs to be a metaphysics of God, of revelation, of incarnation, of the Spirit and of the ultimate goal of the cosmos. Perhaps their witness in a Germany that was just about to descend into the abyss of two world wars and the obscenity of National Socialism was muted by their failure to provide a firm doctrinal basis for Christian moral commitment. Their critical voice was heard, putting in question many traditional tenets of Christian faith. But their call for a liberal morality of love was partly compromised by their own belief in German (Aryan) cultural and intellectual supremacy, and partly weakened by their inability to found their morality on any metaphysical base that could countermand the myths and lies of the Nazi propaganda machine.

This was because they agreed with Kant in holding that faith should not be made to depend on metaphysical assumptions, for Kant was thought to have destroyed any metaphysics that transcends the bounds of experience. And they agreed that specific moral rules should not be accepted on scriptural authority, for historical criticism reveals the fallibility and culturally bounded nature of many moral beliefs of the biblical writers. Faith lies in the adoption of a distinctive view of a theistic and inner morality, defining a set of attitudes that serve as an interpretative framework for human experience. In this, they agree also with Kant's definition of religion as 'seeing duties as divine commands'. But unlike Kant they give a personal and active God a constitutive role in this view of morality, and stress forgiveness and loving personal relationship more than mere command.

Their use of critical–historical method, however, raised some questions that troubled Ernst Troeltsch. He entirely agreed that it was important for Christians to accept such a method when dealing with biblical texts. But it increasingly came to seem to him that historical method, if consistently applied, could not lead to a discovery of one 'essence' or 'kernel' of Christian truth, as Harnack had argued. It could not lead to any claim that Christian faith was wholly unique, so that Christianity is the 'only perfect spiritual religion', as Ritschl had argued. Nor could it support the view that the consciousness and knowledge of God possessed by Jesus was different in kind and degree from that of any other human beings, before or since – yet this was the 'historical' fact that, for them, replaced a dogmatic definition of Jesus' divinity.

Troeltsch came to think that there is no one essence of Christianity, since each age and culture tends to see the essence, or vital core, of Christian faith differently. He also argued, with much reason, that Christian historians had not studied other religious views in enough detail to make any serious comparative judgments about uniqueness – their dismissive view of Judaism and Islam was certainly wholly inadequate. And the inner psychological states of human minds – such as Jesus' allegedly unique consciousness of God – are beyond reliable discovery by any historians. No historian can ever be in a position to say that, as a result of historical study, we are entitled to say that Jesus is in principle superior to every other human being in some aspect of his inner knowledge of or relation to God. I am not saying that claims about Jesus' unique consciousness of God cannot be made. But they cannot be based on critical and impartial historical study alone.

In the end Troeltsch came to think that Christianity was, not the one absolute and perfect religion, but the best religion for Europeans (and especially for nineteenth-century German Protestants). Other cultures, he supposed, perhaps saw things differently, and history cannot adjudicate between such basic differences.

Something more than appeal to critical history was required for Christian faith, since such an appeal could not justify the belief of many German liberal theologians in one unchanging essence of faith that is unique and absolute and that is founded on the inner consciousness of a man who lived long ago in a very different culture.

HEGEL AND THE DIALECTIC OF HISTORY

The German philosopher who tried to provide a metaphysical basis for Christian faith was Georg Wilhelm Friedrich Hegel, who did not hesitate to do what Kant said could no longer be done, and set out a description of the nature of ultimate reality-in-itself, a system of transcendent metaphysics.[23] For Hegel, there is one Absolute reality, which he called *Geist* or Spirit, but it lies beyond history, and its reality cannot be established by pure historical research. Its nature is to be known, not by a purely 'historical' appeal to the life of a long-dead person, but by Reason (*Vernunft*) reflecting upon the whole of human history and penetrating to the hidden basis of history in Absolute Spirit.

Spirit cannot be definitively or exhaustively expressed in any one moment of history, since the whole of history is its self-expression. Yet each historical epoch discloses something of its infinite nature, in a way that is accessible to human knowledge. Whereas Kant held that we can never know reality-in-itself, Hegel replied that we can know it, but only in partial, limited and developing ways. We really do apprehend the Absolute, but in ways suitable to our faculties of cognition. As history develops, we develop, supplement and revise our apprehensions, on the whole moving towards fuller knowledge, but with occasional reversals of insight.

There is no one essence of faith, then, but many culturally limited perspectives. These are not just contradictory views. They are all parts of a continuing dialectical process, in which each age has the possibility of assimilating the insights of the past and moving on to a new synthesis of understanding. We understand religious views much better when we see them in their historical context, when we see how they have developed, partly by reaction against their immediate past, and partly by integrating past knowledge into a new creative and imaginative leap into the future.

We will never have absolute and final knowledge within history. But that does not mean that everything is relative, that each view is as good as every other. We can discern a progress, a moral and intellectual development from the arbitrary taboos and myths of origin held by pre-literate tribes to the rational morality and scientifically tested theories of modern science.

The direction of progress is discerned by Reason, but Reason does not provide some sort of rigid and unchanging conceptual scheme into which all human knowledge and experience must be fitted. On the contrary, Reason is fluid, imaginative and creative. It thrives on dialectical opposition – on paradox – and in seeking to resolve such oppositions it never ends at a final or unrevisable position.

Unfriendly critics sometimes say that Hegel believed that the progress of Reason had come to its fulfilment in Hegel's own philosophy. But that is unfair. Hegel did think that he had discerned the fact that history was the self-manifestation of one underlying cosmic Reason, and that this was a new stage in the self-understanding of the universe. But he did not think that ended the process. The inner logic of his position is that the dialectic must continue, probably without end. For we can grow for ever in our understanding of Spirit, but we will never wholly comprehend it.

This may seem like a very ambitious exercise in speculative philosophy, and indeed it was. But what was important for Christian faith was that Hegel saw it as a Christian philosophy, and indeed as a philosophy suggested and inspired by the Christian faith, and in particular by the doctrine of the Trinity. The Trinitarian basis is this: Spirit 'in-itself' is the one and only source of all things ('the Father'). Spirit 'for-itself' is that which is generated from the source as a sort of externalisation or objectification of its reality. By projecting itself as object, Spirit comes to know itself objectively ('the Son'). Here, however, Hegel is not just thinking of the eternal Word or *Logos*; he is thinking of the created cosmos itself. In this cosmos, Spirit manifests and realises what is only potential in its own inner being. And in that manifestation there is a necessary estrangement or alienation from the divine source, so that the 'creation' is also, and necessarily, a 'fall' into otherness and separation. Finally, Spirit 'in-and-for-itself' is the return or reconciliation of the cosmos to its divine source, the apotheosis of creation. Estrangement is overcome and, by the uniting of the cosmos to Spirit, Spirit itself gains a new and richer sort of reality. From being a solitary and largely potential source of reality, it now embraces in its own being a community, or many communities, of finite spirits, harmonised and fulfilled in the divine life, which has now become fully self-actualised and realised in relationship. The whole cosmic process can be seen as the actualisation of love as a shared relational reality, which is, of course, the inner nature of the divine, of Absolute Spirit.

The Christian roots of this ambitious philosophy are clear. It gives to history an importance it had never before had, as the self-expression of the life of God. It gives a new but powerful exposition of what it means to say that 'God is love', interpreting love in relational terms, relating God to beings that are truly 'other' than God and are thus free to accept or reject relationship. It provides a total context within which the various diverse expressions of Christian faith can be understood as historically situated responses to new knowledge and cultural configurations. It locates Christian faith intelligibly within a general picture of world religious and cultural history. And it dispenses with the need to know the 'inner life' of Jesus, since the specific and public Messianic context of Jesus' ministry becomes more important to understanding the rise of Christian faith than any inner psychological events that may have been going on.

HEGEL AND CHRISTIAN FAITH

This all sounds very positive. Yet Christian theologians have been very ambivalent about Hegelian philosophy. This is partly because it seems to many not so much to be an interpretation of Christianity as a replacement for it. Why, in this grand cosmic vision of self-expression and cosmic reconciliation, should the person of Jesus be of any particular significance? It is true that the cross and resurrection are potent symbols of the entrance of God into the suffering of the world, and of the final regeneration of the cosmos in the life of God. But are they merely symbols, replaceable by a deeper purely philosophical understanding? That is the accusation that has often been made against Hegel, and it is not without justification.

Even the idea of the Trinity becomes a picture of the genesis and apotheosis of the whole cosmos, not a truth about the inner nature of a God who transcends this and every cosmos. So the particularity of God's involvement in the life of Jesus can become lost in a general speculative grand narrative of cosmic history. Some would say that where God, the Father of Jesus Christ, is replaced by an undifferentiated Absolute Spirit, Christianity has been left behind.

There has also been a widespread feeling that Hegel's cosmic vision is just too optimistic to match historical reality. Where he would see an inevitable progress leading to the full historical flourishing of self-conscious Reason, many historians can see only a chaos of conflicting imperialistic powers, probably doomed to self-destruction in the near future. The contemporary fashion is to decry any attempt at holistic vision and grand narrative, to deny the existence of Absolute Spirit and to present a much more piecemeal, fragmented and adventitious view of nature and history. The name of Hegel has almost been forgotten in contemporary philosophy and theology, lost in the fog of obsolete European colonial ambitions, belief in the superiority of German culture, and pre-1914 optimism that the world was inevitably moving towards peace and harmony.

Hegel has had an enormous impact on Protestant theology, albeit in unattributed or disguised forms. His philosophical system of Absolute Idealism dominated philosophy in Germany and Britain at the beginning of the twentieth century and was influential in Sweden and in America. But it faded away in face of the German descent into barbarism under Hitler, the growth of a rejection of all grand metaphysical speculation, and the rise of more sophisticated versions of materialism or scepticism about the objective existence of any distinctive spiritual reality.

GOD'S INVOLVEMENT IN HISTORICAL TIME

Despite these weighty reservations, there are elements of Hegelian philosophy that may form a permanent contribution to Christian thought. As Aristotle was baptised into thirteenth-century Christian faith, so a generally Hegelian approach, qualified by a greater humility about the powers of human reason and by the greater knowledge of the universe given by modern science, may be a way of re-thinking Christianity in an age that is for the first time truly aware of global history and of our planet's place in the immensity of the cosmos.

The most radical move Hegel made was to make Spirit the basis of the historical process as a whole. For most of Christian history since Patristic times, it was assumed that God was changeless and perfect, complete in being without the universe, and indeed fundamentally unchanged by anything that happened in the universe. The perfect divine nature certainly did not share in the suffering of finite creatures, and it was neither enriched nor diminished by anything that happened to them.

This was always rather a strange view to hold for a religion based on the assertion that 'the Word was made flesh', that God suffered and died on a cross and that the Spirit works within human lives to 'fill them with the fullness of God' (Eph. 3:19) and bring them to share in the divine nature. It looks as though God does enter into creation, even becomes one with at least part of it, suffers by the divine unity with creation, and changes by bringing finite beings to share the divine nature in loving relationship.

The central gospel is that human and divine natures are united in an especially intimate way. This unity is fully realised in Jesus. To say that Jesus is the Christ does not just mean that Jesus is a man who is designated as anointed King of Israel. It means that Jesus is the human manifestation of the eternal Wisdom of God, and as such he is designated Lord of the church, head of the body of God in the world, the community in which divine–human unity is ever more fully to be realised. This unity is shared by all those who become parts of 'the body of Christ', and the whole of creation is destined to be united 'in Christ'. In this unity, the divine shares in the sufferings and the joys of finite creatures, and the human shares in and contributes to the relational love within God that is made possible by the creation of genuine 'other' persons between whom love can flourish.

In Hegel it is never quite clear whether Absolute Spirit is separable from the universe, or is just the pattern and inner purpose of history itself. It is possible that Hegel's God can disappear into the immanence of the historical process, and in Karl Marx it did so, also being, as Marx said, 'turned on its head' at the same time.[24] So a Christian version would insist more strongly that God is infinitely more than the universe and has an inner life that transcends the universe completely. Nevertheless, in agreement with Eastern Orthodox theologians, we may wish to say that the inner life of God is wholly beyond human understanding, and all we can know is how God is in relation to this universe. We can believe that this really is how God is in relation to us; it is not just an illusion. But we can never say that this is the whole of God and that the whole is fully understood by us. The inner being of God remains a mystery beyond intellectual comprehension.

For Hegel, history both expresses and changes God, as it realises aspects of the divine that would otherwise have remained potential in the divine being, and as God truly relates to these aspects in new and creative ways. It is compatible with this view to say that God also has a proper divine actuality even without creation, and certainly without this specific universe. So we may not wish to say that this universe is necessary if God is to be conscious of the divine nature. However, there is a great deal of force in the thought that, if God is to realise the divine nature as love – in the sense of relation to truly free personal agents – then the creation of some universe in which true freedom is possible will be needed.

The sort of love that obtains between God and created persons – a *kenotic* love that enters into humility and suffering, that seeks those who are lost and reconciles those who are estranged – is not possible solely within the being of God itself. Because of that, the creation of a universe is the necessary condition of the actualisation of kenotic love in God. A stronger stress on the value of personal relationship leads to involving God more in time and change than classical theologians like Aquinas thought. We may not want to follow Hegel in the detail of his philosophy, but this is a move that he was the first major philosopher to make.

HAS HISTORY A GOAL?

For Hegel, the creation of the universe entails its estrangement from God. We may wish to declare agnosticism on this topic, for how could we know, with our very limited faculties, what is truly necessary for God or for a universe that God creates? It does seem, though, that the *possibility* of estrangement is implied in the existence of truly free and self-determining agents.

The existence of such freedom is another highly contentious part of Hegelian philosophy. Many commentators hold that he sees history as a predetermined and necessary progress towards an inevitable goal – the goal of the full self-consciousness of Spirit. The fact is that Hegel is unclear about this, and exhibits the same sort of ambivalence about freedom and predestination as does the Christian tradition in general. But it is possible to accept Hegel's view that the ultimate source of all reality is Spirit, and that Spirit expresses something of its potential nature in and is changed by that expression, while also accepting the radical freedom and responsibility of finite persons.

If we do so, we must accept a modification of any view of history as the self-expression of God. If persons in history are free, then history cannot be predetermined, and it cannot simply express what God is and wills. There may be a pattern and purpose in history, but finite agents will be able to obstruct that purpose. Hatred, greed and wilful ignorance will obstruct God's purposes of love, self-control and growing wisdom. How far this will be so we cannot tell.

In the New Testament, it seems clear that many writers thought that 'the world' was opposed to God and was destined for destruction. Far from a continual progress towards peace and harmony, the world would end in a cataclysm of destruction. God would not ultimately be defeated, even though the original divine purpose for earth was frustrated. For God would create a new heaven and earth, in which evil would be excluded and righteousness would rule.

Yet there are also indications of another view – that the Spirit would work among men and women so as to gradually increase their understanding, and that the world would grow in Christ until it was fully reconciled to God. This seems to be the implication of the first chapter of the letters to the Ephesians and to the Colossians.

The fact is that if humans are truly free we cannot say which of these views will prevail. We know what God wants – progress to a society of peace and the flourishing of all the creative potencies of the earth. We know that people can either progress towards or impede this goal. We know, from the tragic record of history, that God permits them to impede the goal. We know, in faith, that God's purpose will ultimately be achieved, though perhaps only in a 'new creation' after this one has ended.

It seems, then, that with a full belief in freedom we cannot accept Hegel's thesis of an inevitable progress towards a goal achievable in history. The point is made with particular savagery by the rapid descent of the cultured and urbane Prussian state, which Hegel eulogised, into the catastrophe of the National Socialist Third Reich.

God can place before us the goal of a society of free and loving persons, and make the pursuit of the kingdom binding upon us. But God will not guarantee its actualisation in the normal processes of history. Those facts have important implications for the particularity of Christian revelation in Jesus. Within the terms of Hegel's own philosophical system, we would expect understanding of God, of morality and of spiritual truth to grow continually. It would not really make sense to speak of a 'final' revelation, especially one at what now seems to be a fairly early point in human history (remember that for the first Christians Jesus was believed to have appeared at the end of history). We would always be looking for fuller revelations and leaving the past behind for a better future. That is one reason why Christian theologians have often regarded Hegel with suspicion, and suspected him of replacing Christian revelation by a philosophical system.

The Christian view of history is not that it is a purely adventitious chaos, without a central narrative. There is a central narrative. God ensures that free responsible agents will evolve from the material universe, plans that on this planet they shall freely develop a world community of friendship in the love of beauty, and promises that such a community will exist as a consequence of their actions. But the narrative has been obscured by the fact that the agents that did develop have largely used their freedom to frustrate the intended goal. So what we see is a confused picture of moral progress and destructive hatred. The kingdom has been deferred, perhaps until the whole history of this planet has finally come to an end. History is not a continual progress towards perpetual peace, but a confused battle of ignorant armies fighting in self-created darkness, of goodness continually crucified and of love struggling in a world of pain.

In such a world the goal of history must appear, if it appears at all, a dimly perceived ideal among the distortions of hatred, greed and pride that have derailed the progress of history. God may disclose that ideal in the ambiguities of history, but the ideal will be a foreshadowing of a goal that is now beyond history and at its end.

The idea of a particular and decisive revelation becomes intelligible when the total process of history is seen to have deviated from the divine intention in such a marked way that history in itself can no longer directly disclose what God is and wills. The incarnation of the divine Wisdom is a particular event that breaks through the general alienation of the world from God. It is not a historical objectification in which God comes to know the divine nature for the first time. It is a life in which God expresses what the divine objectification in time truly is, for the first time. It therefore becomes the standard of human life united to and interpenetrated by the divine life, and the model for a process the Spirit will sustain for the rest of human history. Jesus will never become irrelevant, for the model of his life provides the definition of the character of the divine Spirit. And the Spirit is the power that salvages human lives from the wrecks of corrupted time and enables them to be, at least to some extent, channels of the divine life and foreshadowings of lives fully redeemed and taken into God.

THE CREATIVITY OF REASON

How do we know all this is true? In Hegel, it seems as though history is known as the progressive self-manifestation of Absolute Spirit through Reason. But the Christian provenance of the Hegelian system should not be underestimated, and even Hegel's conception of Reason is not untouched by his Lutheran training and commitment. The point can be made by trans-lating 'Reason' (*Vernunft* – for which there is no exact English equivalent, in the sense in which Hegel uses the term) with the biblical word 'Wisdom'. Then we can say that the Wisdom of God, which is the pattern of all cre-ation, is recognised by the wisdom of the human heart, made aware of that pattern by God. Hegelian Reason is not an empirical principle of sticking to the evidence, or a rationalist claim that certain truths are self-evident and clear and distinct to reason alone. Hegelian Reason is the imaginative intu-ition that can hold together differing poles of a dialectical, continually changing, diverse and growing set of understandings of reality, and move on to an original synthesis that can hold such diverse understandings together in one total perspective, which will in turn have to change dynamically as history progresses.

When Hegel uttered the infamous statement that 'the Real is the rational, and the rational is the Real', he could be interpreted to mean that finite reality is patterned on eternal Wisdom. The creative synthesising activity of the human mind, created in the image of divine Wisdom, can discern the inner spiritual structure of reality – though always only partially and from limited and continually changing perspectives.

This seems to me a very fair statement of a fully Christian position on the role of the human mind in understanding a reality that is patterned on, and contained in, eternal Wisdom, the Christ.

Yet it is true that Hegel often spoke as though the particular events of the life of Jesus were more like symbols of general philosophical truths than indispensable data for revealing what divine Wisdom is really like. And he often spoke as though he had unravelled the ultimate nature of God and the universe in a way that was superior to a rather outdated Christian traditional philosophy, with all its myths and quasi-Hellenistic perspectives.

It is not altogether surprising that some later German theologians eschewed speculative metaphysics and tried to see Christian faith in more down-to-earth historical terms and with a basic practical, not theoretical, commitment as its essence. What is needed, however, is not less metaphysics but a metaphysics that is more aware of its indebtedness to revelation and that is rather more tentative about having reached an assured grasp of the ultimate nature of reality.

SCHLEIERMACHER AND EXPERIENCE OF GOD AS THE BASIS OF FAITH

Despite the complexity and richness of Hegel's metaphysical system – or perhaps because of it – many Christians felt that Christianity was not primarily a grand explanatory philosophical scheme, outlining the nature of ultimate reality. Nor was it a special sort of moral commitment, which happened to owe much to the example and inspiration of Jesus. Both these views missed out, or at best underemphasised, the distinctively religious element in Christian faith. That primary element was experience of God, an experience that has the power to change and re-orient the lives of those who have it.

The main theological spokesman for such Christians is Friedrich Schleiermacher (1768–1834), a contemporary of Hegel in Berlin. He is often termed 'the father of liberal Protestantism', even though his views contrast, sometimes strongly, with those of Hegel, Ritschl, Harnack and Troeltsch. Since these writers, and other German theologians of the same century, also disagree with each other quite strongly, the term 'liberal Protestant' is perhaps not very helpful. What unites them is acceptance of historical–critical methods as applied to the Bible and Christian doctrines, together with a preparedness to re-think the ancient creeds and formulations of dogmatic theology. What divides them is almost everything else, including especially their ideas about what is of primary importance for the Christian faith. In fact in Scheiermacher a fifth sense of the term 'liberal' is found, quite different from the four strands I have noted thus far – namely, the project of basing all religious beliefs on personal experience. That is certainly one strand of liberal traditions in theology, but we must be careful not to assume that all liberals will agree with it, and we should note that it is just one possible liberal strand, that can be clearly distinguished from the other strands I have mentioned.

Schleiermacher is certainly responsible for a stress on experience as the vital element of Christian and of any properly religious faith. In *Religion: Speeches* (1799), he tried to define the essence of religion in general, and proposed that religion is 'a sense and taste for the infinite'. It is an intuition of 'the whole', mediated through some particular experience. It is not primarily conceptual knowledge (knowledge that something is the case), and it is not primarily moral commitment. It involves both of these things, but its distinctive and essential core is the 'intuition and feeling' (*Anschauung und Gefuhl*) of the infinite. Echoing William Blake's 'Auguries of Innocence' of 1789, Schleiermacher wrote, 'To be one with the infinite in the midst of the finite and to be eternal in a moment, that is the immortality of religion' (Second Speech, final sentence).

Schleiermacher has been accused of pantheism and subjectivism – pantheism because 'the whole' or 'the universe' seems to be taken as the object of worship and devotion, rather than a God who is other than the universe, and subjectivism because feeling is a state of mind, rather than contact with an external reality. But Schleiermacher cannot be both a pantheist and a subjectivist, since pantheists make assertions about the universe whereas subjectivists are simply immersed in inner feelings.

Of course he is neither. He reacted to accusations of pantheism by modifying his definition of religion in his major work, *The Christian Faith* (1821). There, he wrote that the 'essence of piety is this: the consciousness of being absolutely dependent, or, which is the same thing, of being in relation with God' (para. 4). The 'sense of the infinite' has now become 'the consciousness of absolute dependence'. Faith has an object, and it is something that is absolutely independent. The object of faith is not the universe, which consists of a collection of mutually dependent parts. As in Hegel, the infinite includes, rather than excludes, the finite, but it is other and more than the finite.

As for 'feeling', Schleiermacher does not have in mind a purely subjective state with no intensionality, no reference to an external object at all. Many, if not all, feelings have objects (the external referent of the feeling, as opposed to what it feels like). It might catch Schleiermacher's meaning better if we spoke of 'apprehension' or 'perception' rather than of 'intuition' (*Anschauung* normally means 'apprehension'). He is trying to describe a sort of apprehension whose object is not a particular finite object, but the infinite and unbounded, beyond all finite change and limitation. Such an object cannot be conceptually described, but it can be apprehended, and its apprehension is a form of union with it, a union with eternity in a moment, and with infinity in the palm of a hand. It is a union that, as Plato said, makes us immortal, so far as that is possible for any human life.

The link with Plato is not accidental, for Schleiermacher's romantic vision of a discernment of eternal truth in the midst of time is also the Platonic vision of the Good amid the shadows of the cave. Such a vision can be spoken of only in metaphors and images. Concepts that seek to pin down, analyse and precisely define reality fall into paradox when they seek to describe such an object. It cannot be grasped by concepts, but only by union. And that union, utterable only in metaphor and simile, is for Schleiermacher the heart of religious discernment.

Plato, living in a world of many gods, and seeing religion largely as a set of myths and rituals for the ignorant and superstitious, did not associate his quest for the vision of the Good with religion. Schleiermacher made it the heart of religion, for the Christian God had long been said to be one and veiled in mystery, yet accessible through a transformation of the human heart by the condescension of divine love. In his Pietistic tradition of Protestantism, Schleiermacher had learned that the Spirit of God can change and mould the human heart, evoking in it a love and devotion to God that is warm and deep, but not primarily concerned with correct doctrine. The sense of absolute dependence of which he speaks is a changing of the heart to feel the infinity of the divine being as intimately present, embracing the finite self in its unconditioned love. Plato's unchanging Good has become a living and acting presence. The rule of the Good (the kingdom of God) enters and transforms the heart (Jesus said, 'The kingdom of God is within [*entos*] you': Luke 17:21). The unity of divine and human is sensed, beyond words, and the infinite is mediated in the finite forms of time, insofar as they are taken up to participate in its reality and power.

Whatever this is, it is not subjectivism, and it does not reduce faith to being a matter of purely internal experience and sentiment. It tries to locate the essence of religion in a personally transforming apprehension of a unique reality that is infinite and beyond all limitation.

EXPERIENCE OF GOD AND REDEMPTION

But if this is the essence of religion, what is distinctive about Christian faith? It is that, in Christianity, 'everything is related to the redemption accomplished by Jesus' (*The Christian Faith*, para. 11). Redemption is a passage from an evil condition to a better one, and Jesus is redeemer because he alone was never in need of redemption but the Spirit that he communicated to others brings about their redemption. One way of interpreting Schleiermacher's thoughts on this topic is to say that Jesus incorporates, from the beginning of his life, that perfect union of divine and human that is the result of, or is the very nature of, a clear and full apprehension of the infinite. Redemption is the move from a state in which we are not conscious of the infinite, but are lost in a world of desires and obsessions, to a state in which all things are seen in the infinite, and even our own personality is one with the infinite because of our entire and immediate dependence upon it. Jesus was not in need of redemption, because his 'God-consciousness', which, as Schleiermacher says, 'was a veritable existence of God in him' (para. 94), was complete and perfect from the first.

In us, however, such a God-consciousness needs to be implanted and developed gradually, in face of our selfish desires and pride. This happens through the activity of the Spirit in the church, wherein the Spirit inwardly communicates to us the power that was in Jesus to apprehend and love God fully.

Schleiermacher's style can be difficult to follow, and it is unclear how far he is simply putting fairly traditional Christian doctrines in new ways, and how far he is proposing a quite new approach. But it is clear that he does not feel committed to the conciliar definitions of the incarnation and the Trinity, treating them with a certain amount of scorn. And he does want to make the essential core of Christian faith a certain sort of experience, the experience of 'redemption' by an apprehension of God that is non-conceptual and that transforms the knower by a re-orientation of 'feelings' and inner attitudes.

If the salvation of the soul is freedom from self-regard, hatred and greed, and conscious union with a God of unlimited love, then it does not have to depend on the intellectual acceptance of a complicated set of correct beliefs. It could depend rather on an encounter with the love of God which liberates from sin and makes you a more loving person. Such an encounter may not provide you with intellectual certainty. Indeed it may make you less certain that your intellectual understanding of God is anything like fully adequate or complete.

It is perhaps the early Lutheran idea of salvation by faith that first suggested that Christian belief may be based upon an encounter with the love of God which convicts of sin and engenders a new spiritual birth. Faith is a committed personal response to revelation. And revelation is a personal disclosure of the power and goodness and beauty of God. It is a disclosure of supreme goodness and beauty that evokes in the believer a love of the good and beautiful and redeems believers out of the world of hatred and greed in which they have been trapped.

For Christians, such a disclosure occurred to the disciples around the person of Jesus, as he was encountered and remembered by them. That disclosure, or a whole series of disclosures, was expressed in the Gospels, presented in the light of the resurrection and further experiences of the risen Lord in the church. Such disclosures indirectly presuppose the experience of Jesus himself as an experience of God as Father and of the divine Spirit as the energising and creative power of his own life.

Christian tradition has been built up over centuries as the primary experience of redemptive encounter with God in Jesus has been placed within the ever-changing contexts of more general understandings of the universe and of human history.

Personal experience witnesses to the fact of present encounter with God through the person of the risen Christ in the community of the church. Such experience is always limited by the psychological and social situation of the disciple. That is why it needs to be controlled by some awareness of wider communal traditions that include many different personal perspectives, traditions that can distinguish between the ephemeral and the enduring in matters of worship and devotional understanding. It needs to be controlled also by the normative canon of Scripture, which provides the personal paradigm and the general parameters of Christian understanding.

On this understanding, the primary data of Christian faith thus lie in forms of experience – the normative experience of the apostles (and, underlying that, the presupposed experience of Jesus himself), the historical experiences of the church, and the personal experience of the individual disciple.

Apprehensions of God are necessarily interpreted in terms of the concepts available to us. We could not have a feeling of absolute dependence, for instance, if we lacked the concept of 'dependence' and if we could not distinguish conceptually between the relative and the absolute. But those concepts do not control the apprehensions. Concepts give form and shape to our apprehensions, but without the apprehension concepts would be purely abstract. And we will probably have to amend or qualify our initial concepts in the light of new apprehensions that occur to us.

Christian doctrines may be founded on experience, but such experience is not a matter of purely personal subjective and wholly non-rational feeling. It is controlled by the normative experiences of Jesus and the apostles, it is tested by the long and changing experience and reflection of the church, and it is given intellectual content by the concepts and values that we bring with us to all new experience and that are usually inherited by us from a long tradition of reflective and creative thought.

EXPERIENCE AND INTELLECTUAL BELIEF

On this view, revelation is not a set of truths, given in some pristine text, preserved without error for all time. Nor is it a set of truths propounded by meetings of leaders of the some church. The church and the Bible witness to a normative divine disclosure in the person of Jesus, and they elaborate ways of developing our understanding of it, in the light of new knowledge and experiences in different historical contexts. But such elaborations are not themselves parts of revelation.

This form of Christian faith proposes that the basis of a reasonable religious belief is experience. The special character of religious experiences is that they are transforming experiences of transcendent reality and value. There may be many such forms, and they do not all exist within systems that would normally be called 'religious'. People can have a sense of transcendent significance in works of art, in the contemplation of nature, in a sense of moral obligation and in the claim of other persons upon them. The religious sense is distinguished by its attempt at integration and discipline. The transcendent value it seeks to apprehend covers every aspect of experience, not just the moral or aesthetic. It aims to integrate all these aspects under one all-inclusive idea. Moreover, it becomes an object of disciplined attention in its own right. Religions set out disciplines of mind and heart that are intended to increase awareness of the Supreme Good in itself, beyond all the ways in which it impacts on particular sorts of human experience.

Different religions do this in different ways. For Schleiermacher, the monotheistic religions are superior to polytheistic religions, because they are more developed intellectually and morally. Among monotheisms, Christianity is the purest and most perfect form, since it is not limited to one race (Judaism) and not tainted by a 'strongly sensuous content' (Islam) (all this in para. 8). These judgments seem inadequate and unacceptable today, but they show an attempt to distinguish between forms of religion in terms of a development towards universality and spirituality.

The living heart of faith may be a liberating encounter with Transcendence. But what is meant by liberation has to be worked out by ethical reflection, and how you interpret Transcendence depends upon how you see the relation of the Transcendent to the cosmos as it is understood by the natural sciences, and upon ideas of what a Supreme Value should be. So religious experience is inseparable from ethical and intellectual belief and reflection.

It is not the case, as Schleiermacher sometimes seems to imply, that all Christian beliefs can be spun out of a feeling of absolute dependence. There are sources of belief in history, in empirical observation and in moral reflection. For the believer, all these things must be brought into relation with what seem to the believer to be apprehensions of a spiritual reality of transcendent value. That relation will be one of mutual modification, as diverse patterns of belief, evaluation and personal experience are integrated more or less well into general models of understanding that are themselves in a state of flux and development.

Faith is not theoretical certainty. It is not unreserved assent to the truth of a set of propositions. It is practical commitment to a set of values, to the best that I know, in awareness that certainty is not available. What kind of faith is that? It is faith in goodness, personal commitment to a search for goodness and beauty, a search that is inspired by a specific disclosure of such goodness and beauty that has occurred in my experience.

Is such a disclosure and such a search inadequate? Yes, always. It is highly unlikely that I should have perceived what absolute goodness really is. It is much more likely that I should have a partial and limited vision of goodness. In saying my vision is inadequate, I am not saying it is totally mistaken. It is, as far as I can see, correct. But I know that I cannot see very far. So my beliefs are always open to revision by further disclosures or insights, or by new knowledge. In fact it is very important that I remain open to the possibility of such revision. If I think that absolute truth is probably beyond me, and that my understanding is very limited, then I am obliged to keep trying to understand more widely and deeply, and never to give up the search.

There is a danger of a cynicism that undermines every perception of goodness and leaves us unable to make any moral commitments at all. This can be best avoided by a belief that there is goodness to be found, and that we are able to perceive it in part, if not fully. The whisper of destructive cynicism, telling us that there is no such thing as goodness, is different in kind from the counsel of humility, telling us that our present perception of goodness is limited and partial. The former says that there is no goodness to be found. The latter says that, precisely because supreme goodness exists in reality, it may be hard for us to discover, and very hard for us to grasp in any adequate way. So the condition of practical faith is a belief that goodness exists and is supremely worth striving for, together with awareness that we are yet a long way from comprehending it. The temper of faith is self-deprecating and joyful, not cynical and destructive.

In the person of Jesus and in the experience of the Holy Spirit, Christians discern the highest and most challenging goodness that they know. But they understand it very inadequately, and almost always fail to see many of its implications. There is yet much more to learn and understand.

This is where Christian faith should start – not with doctrines, but with a living encounter with the Spirit of Christ, leading to a deeper self-awareness, a love of the Good and Beautiful, a personal creative participation in goodness and beauty, and a hope for a closer union with the Good that can sublimate the transience of time. But interwoven with this quest is and must be an intellectual attempt to see the true nature of human existence in a cosmos that is generated by Supreme Goodness. Hegelian Idealism represents one such attempt, made in the light of the new critical and scientific thinking of the Enlightenment. It may have proved too grandiose and arrogant, but there remains the necessity of constructing a similarly cosmic vision, albeit more tentative and open, that can provide the metaphysical framework for modern Christian faith. In a combination of themes drawn from Hegel and Schleiermacher we might find the outlines of a positive re-thinking of Christianity for the world after the Enlightenment.

Chapter 11

Christianity in a Global Context

Through the prophets of Israel, God becomes known as a morally demanding will, concerned to establish conscious relationship with creatures through their free co-operation with the divine will and their love of beauty, truth and friendship (the kingdom of God). Jesus is, for Christians, the 'fulfilment' of the prophetic tradition. In his person the kingdom is actualised in history, as his human mind and will is interpenetrated with the divine Spirit. It is in this sense that Jesus is Son of God and Christ, the one in whom God's will for liberation and union is enacted. In and through him, God is disclosed as limitless love, sharing in the suffering of creatures and willing for them eternal unity with the divine. In and through Jesus, God acts to liberate from hatred, greed and ignorance and to unite human lives to the divine.

Jesus proclaims that the kingdom has drawn near. The kingdom is the presence of the Spirit of Christ, the new covenant of the heart, the society of the Spirit. It grows secretly in human hearts and spreads throughout the earth. The churches proclaim it, but cannot be identified with it, for the Spirit blows wherever it will.

THE MORAL CRISIS OF LIBERALISM

The decisive factor in the history of the twentieth century, which is still gathering strength at the beginning of the twenty-first century, is the fact of globalisation. By this I mean primarily the way in which every part of the planet is now entangled with every other part. At the beginning of the twentieth century, travel to distant parts of the globe was difficult, often impossible. Now anthropologists studying forest tribes in New Guinea arrive after a flight of a few hours to find helicopter bases already set up in the jungle. In 1900 the intellectual resources of faraway cultures were largely locked away in untranslated and inaccessible manuscripts. Now we have access in our own homes to the knowledge of the world, in translation and with commentaries, via satellite and computer networks. The toys of British children are made in China, and British telephone calls are routed through Bangalore. Multinational firms can move factories to any part of the globe, and waves of immigration transfer populations from one part of the world to another.

In such a globalised context, Christianity has to be reconceived as one stream of religious life in a wider global pattern. When this is done, the rather sobering fact is that the success of Christianity, as the largest religion in the world, seems to be largely due to its connection with past forms of imperialism. Its first major expansion came through its adoption as the official religion of the Roman Empire. Later Spanish acquisitions in South America spread Catholicism more widely, and European, especially British, imperialism led to the cultural dominance of Christianity in many parts of the world. Countries that resisted imperialism also resisted the Christian faith that went with it. Most notably, East Asia, India and the Islamic world – a competing world of imperial expansion – remained resistant to Christian hegemony.

This alliance with empire has been a mixed blessing, since it associated Christian faith in the eyes of many with thoughts of military conquest and world domination. Yet within the Gospels there is a very clear condemnation of violence and the lust for power. Jesus condemned not only killing, but even anger, and told his hearers not to resist evil (Matt. 5:22, 39). He taught his followers that if they wished to be great, they must be the servants of all (Matt. 20:26). There is an inbuilt moderating influence on power in the Gospels, and, though Christian faith may have partly spread through imperial expansion, it also carries an unmistakable message that such power must be humanised and redirected for good. In the twentieth century Christianity, as a world religion, was still struggling to maintain a balance between assertions of cultural superiority and a rediscovery of its core values of loving service and liberation for the poor. But it is arguable that it was a century in which the faith was slowly disentangled from many old imperial associations, and its centre of gravity began to move from the West to the Southern and Eastern hemispheres.

In Europe and North America, rich scientifically advanced cultures developed within which the Enlightenment values of freedom of belief and critical enquiry flourished. I have argued that such values were rooted in the religious upheavals of the Protestant Reformation, but they also unleashed almost uncontrollable destructive forces. Reason and belief in objective goodness, two pillars of traditional Christian faith in a wise and good creator of the universe, came under critical scrutiny. For some critical thinkers, goodness was seen as simply the realisation of individual desires, whatever they are. Reason was seen, by David Hume among others, as the slave of desire.[25]

The desire for power, to be realised through superior strength, was legitimated, and the way was prepared for the two most destructive wars in world history. By a terrifying perversion of the Hegelian vision of a dialectical historical progress leading to the implementation of a truly just society, Marxist-Leninism advocated the violent overthrow of liberal societies to make way for the dictatorship of the proletariat. In reaction, fascism advocated a nationalistic and authoritarian rule of the strong, the dictatorship of the Führer. In the clash between these dictatorships, a generation of Europeans and their allies throughout the world came to the brink of extinction.

The twentieth century showed that liberalism is not enough. What is also needed is some positive conception of the Good that can inspire devotion and positive commitment. Both communists and fascists could appeal to a great cause, worthy of the self-sacrifice of its devotees. But in both cases the conception of the Good was fatally flawed, because in the end it relied on the appeal to naked power and contingent desire. An adequate conception of the Good should be one that discerns what is intrinsically and supremely worthwhile, and that sees that the goal of realising such a good cannot be attained by means that are themselves violent and destructive. In a liberal society such a conception can only be embraced on a voluntary basis, but Christians might well think that it is of the greatest importance that there is a strong and effective witness for good in a society that permits the widest possible freedom.

Towards the end of the twentieth century it was still doubtful whether, in the Western world, there was such a widely shared conception of the good. The growth of philosophies of materialism continued to throw doubt on the very idea of goodness itself. Humans were often seen as accidental by-products of a blind evolutionary process whose desires – basically of lust and aggression, with an admixture of limited altruism – had been genetically determined millions of years in the past, and had now become largely counter-productive. The very idea of a shared or objective good disappeared.

The growth of liberal or critical Christianity failed to reach the general public, who consequently tended to see Christianity as an outmoded set of pre-critical beliefs. This was not helped by the rapid growth of fundamentalist Christian groups, especially in the United States, who, in turning against the negative aspects of liberalism, turned against liberalism itself, in all its forms. So faith became acceptance of whatever was written in a sacred text, beyond the reach of reason and flying in the face of science and a reasoned concern for the welfare of all sentient beings.

When 'Western values' are spoken of in a global context, people often have in mind a set of societies in which there is a widespread scepticism about any objective values, and in which the stress on individual choice threatens to undermine all bonds of social unity. Christianity is seen as a failed and largely obsolete minority interest, existing in tension with the dominant scientific and moral trends of Western cultures. Yet the West talks of 'human rights', 'democracy' and 'freedom' as though they are moral absolutes that the West has a destiny to safeguard – even though secular Western culture has undermined any basis for speaking of moral absolutes at all. So these absolutes are widely seen as subterfuges for protecting the sort of freedom from interference and freedom to accumulate wealth that maintain the social and economic superiority of the West at the expense of the rest of the world.

Such cultural confusion may be the price that a liberal society has to pay for the freedom it prizes. But there is a place for an assertion of the value of persons as beings whose distinctive capacity is to realise positive potentialities for good in co-operation with others. In fact at the heart of liberalism, particularly as it is found in Immanuel Kant and John Stuart Mill, is the belief that the freedom of the individual is important precisely because it makes possible the realisation of personal and cultural excellences, of moral and intellectual virtues, for all.[26] The question of whether such a belief in the unique value of the personal can be sustained in face of the more extreme liberal belief in the relativism of desire is one of the crucial moral and religious questions of the modern world. It is the moral crisis of liberalism.

TRANSCENDENTAL PERSONALISM

When Kant propounded his theory of moral autonomy, he did not have in mind a belief that individuals are free to decide for themselves what desires to follow. His moral theory was as far as it could possibly be from the view that individuals are free to invent morality in accordance with their dominant desires.

He argued, however improbably, that Reason itself could legislate universal moral principles that all ought to agree with and that are absolutely binding, whatever individuals happened to desire. Reason did not merely try to work out what desires were preferable for a happy life, or what compromises might have to be made between the competing desires of various individuals in order to get a secure and stable society. The voice of Reason was absolute, and Kant asserted what he called the 'principle of autonomy' in the belief that Reason spoke in every individual and should not be subject to the whims and taboos of tyrants or traditions.

Kant was in fact asserting the Protestant principle that every person has the right to follow conscience rather than defer to external authority. He argued that the voice of conscience is clear and absolute. It is not some genetically programmed or socially reinforced compulsion. It is the voice of Reason, the same Reason that sustains the life of the cosmos itself. When Kant saw duties as divine commands, that for him had an intensity and seriousness that is hardly possible for a fully secular moralist.

While the voice of Reason is not subject to the power of desire, it is not unrelated to desire. Kant knew well enough that humans have desires, goals and distinctive capacities. In the *Metaphysic of Morals* (not the more widely read *Groundwork to the Metaphysic of Morals*) he states that the necessary ends at which Reason aims are the happiness of others and the perfecting of one's own physical and mental powers. The notion of 'self-perfecting' is central to Kant's moral philosophy. He accepts the Aristotelian principle that it is mental capacities that are most distinctively human, and that the best life for humans is one in which such capacities can be freely expressed. The orientation of the mind to knowledge and understanding, to the creation and appreciation of beauty, to empathy with others in shared experience, and to co-operation with others in common pursuits – these are the perfections that a liberal society will encourage, but never compel, humans to pursue.

For Kant, the Categorical Imperative sorts out which of these perfections can be universally willed, for all people at all times. Most of us might think that this stress on the universal is rather Procrustean, since different perfections might be appropriate for different people, and in different degrees. But the main point is that for Kant freedom from external authority is important, not just for its own sake, but for the sake of the pursuit of personal perfection that it enables. Freedom to dissent is necessary in the face of authoritarian systems that restrict knowledge and repress creative thinking. Informed critical enquiry is necessary to help place knowledge on firmer foundations and to motivate a continual search for deeper truth. Moral autonomy is necessary to counteract reliance on rationally unjustifiable and repressive traditions and rules. In all these aspects, critical freedom exists in the service of the flourishing of the human person and the perfecting of the life of the mind. The justification of a liberal society lies in its commitment to moral personalism, to the widest possible realisation of personal excellences in a society committed to the pursuit of the common good.

What does this have to do with Christianity? More than many people might think. It is not, in my view, an accident that Kant lived in a Christian environment. His commitment to the moral importance of the human person, to the realisation of distinctive human excellences, to the ideal of making such realisation possible for all, and to the obligation to orient such commitment to the pursuit of the common good – all these elements form part of what might appropriately be called a transcendental personalism. This is a humanism (though I prefer the term 'personalism' to make the point that persons are not logically limited to the human species) that makes persons and their flourishing of fundamental moral value. But it is transcendental in that it holds that human persons have unique value because they exist in the image of, and in potentially conscious relation to, the supreme personal reality of the divine.

Without such an ontological primacy of the personal, humanism might be seen as an arbitrary, even self-interested, preference for the human species. Talk of 'distinctively human excellences' might be seen as an elitist form of cultural snobbery – after all, for the great Utilitarian Jeremy Bentham, pushpin – billiards – was as good as poetry. The desire that everyone should pursue such excellences might be seen as a form of repressive liberalism, paradoxically insisting in the name of freedom that everyone should do the same sorts of things, and have the same basic sorts of desires, as oneself. And talk of a 'common good' might be seen as a concealment of the conflicts of interest and desire that in fact characterise all societies.

Humanism, in the sense of valuing human persons for their distinctively human – or better, personal – qualities, needs a stronger foundation than an arbitrary preference for the human species and for what Mill called the 'higher pleasures'. Christian personalism provides such a foundation, in its core belief that the whole universe is the creative expression of a supreme personal reality, and that its purpose is the emergence of communities of persons who can ultimately share in the understanding, creativity, compassion and bliss of the creator. For such a view, human lives have a purpose, which is part of the purpose for which the whole cosmos exists. That purpose is primarily to come to greater knowledge of truth, beauty and goodness, to love the good and beautiful, as it is found in the created order, in the lives of other persons and supremely in the being of the creator itself. The duty of obedience to law is transformed by the attraction of love for the personal ground of all being. Human persons are loved, not because they are supremely good, but because the God who is supremely good wills that they should grow and flourish and that we should help them to do so. On this view, humanism is rooted in the purpose of the cosmos itself that personal values should flourish; it is motivated by love for the beauty of the supremely personal reality that underlies all things; and it is sustained by the hope that persons will finally achieve their proper perfection in unity with God.

Christianity, from this point of view, is fundamentally the belief that in the personal reality of Jesus humans have seen a foreshadowing of the purpose of the cosmos. They have seen expressed in Jesus' life and death a self-giving love that puts the flourishing of persons first. They have seen in Jesus' remembered person the normative finite image of a personal reality that appropriately invites total devotion. And they have seen in Jesus' resurrection a prefiguring of their own final destiny to find true personal fulfilment in God.

In all the cultural confusion of the liberal West, there is a way to be found between a reductive liberalism that finds the springs of human

behaviour in desire and the lust for power, and an anti-scientific funda-
mentalism that reacts by clinging to a non-liberal, literalistic interpretation
of ancient religious texts. Such a way would seek to re-establish a transcendental personalism, founded on a vision of God as a supreme, self-giving,
unlimitedly loving being, whose nature and purpose have been disclosed to
humans in and through the personal reality of Jesus Christ.

PERSONAL AND RELATIONAL IDEAS OF GOD

The struggle to re-think Western Christianity in the twentieth century has
been a struggle to find a mediating way in face of the strongly competing
ideologies that have made Western society a battleground of deep intellectual and moral divisions.[27] Christian thought has always been influenced by
the prevailing philosophies of various cultural epochs, and the post-
Enlightenment West is no exception. But in the modern world there is no
one accepted philosophical authority, as that of Plato was in the early
church, and as Aristotle became in the medieval church. Modern philosophy has split into a number of different schools, and each of them has influenced Christian thought in some way.

One stream is that of those who seek a metaphysical base for Christian
theism. By 'metaphysics' I mean a systematic attempt to state the ultimate
nature of reality, and the kinds of things that are real. Materialism would
count as metaphysics, as would any common-sense view that the things we
see and encounter around us are the ultimate realities, not dependent on
anything beyond other things of the same sort. Theistic metaphysics holds
that the ultimate reality is personal or spiritual – conscious, intelligent and
of supreme value. Most Christians believe that the whole physical cosmos
depends entirely for its existence on such an ultimate reality. Yet Christians
have conceived the ultimate reality in various ways.

The classical Christian view of God has been derived from Plato and
Aristotle, and was formulated in detail by Thomas Aquinas in the thirteenth
century. There is an important strand of neo-Thomist thought in the contemporary world, especially among Roman Catholic theologians, that seeks
to retain the major insights of the classical view in a new scientifically
informed context.[28] For it, God is 'Being-itself', or Pure Being, infinite,
immutable, timeless and containing all possible perfections in a higher

manner. The advantage of such a view is that it avoids all anthropomorphic pictures of God and is committed to interpreting passages about God in the Bible in a non-literalistic way. But it suffers two major disadvantages. One is that the Aristotelian terminology used by Thomists is precisely the terminology that was found unhelpful or even misleading by modern science, and so it is difficult to make it fully coherent with scientific views. The other is that it does not allow God to engage in, or be affected by, the sufferings or joys of the created cosmos, and so is seen by many as having a rather 'passive' and impersonal view of God. Thomists have ways of responding to these points. But it seems to me that the post-sixteenth-century emphasis on the reality and importance of time and history, together with the biblical emphasis on the importance of the incarnation and passion of Christ, suggests the need for a more dynamic concept of God which will see God as more fully personal and involve God fully in the events of history and of finite consciousness.

Most Protestant theologians have felt the force of this suggestion and have sought to propound an idea of God who is more involved in time and history than the Thomist God seems to be. Theologians like Rudolf Bultmann, Paul Tillich and John Macquarrie have reformulated Christian doctrines in terms of concepts that derive from Hegel.[29] As I noted in the preceding chapter, Hegelian Idealism is now generally thought to have been too ambitious, giving a view of history that was too neatly systematic and rationalistic, and a view of reality that owed too much to armchair speculation and needless obscurantism. Hegel was, however, a major influence on twentieth-century Protestant theology. His Trinitarian view of Absolute Spirit (*Geist*) as the ultimate source of all being, objectifying itself in the physical cosmos, and reconciling the cosmos to itself in fully conscious awareness, is reflected in John Macquarrie's account of the Trinity as primordial, expressive and unitive Being. His view of the divine infinity as including the cosmos as part of its self-expression is reflected in Karl Barth's conception of God as including temporality in the divine being, and of redemption as the reconciliation of the whole creation to God. His view of history as the developing disclosure of Spirit is reflected in Wolfhart Pannenberg's stress on total history as the objective revelation of God, which is only fully understood at its culminating point.

Most theologians would, not surprisingly, reject Hegel's apparent claim that his philosophy finally disclosed the truth about reality, of which the

Christian religion spoke in mythical or story form. But many would accept that Hegel had taken the Christian doctrines of Trinity and incarnation, fall and redemption and constructed a philosophical framework within which time and history play a constitutive part in the divine nature. Within such a framework, God has a history, and is involved with the cosmos in a way that classical accounts, founded on Greek ideas of divine immutability, timelessness and impassibility, could not permit.

Hegel overestimated the attraction of his philosophical system and underestimated the extent to which his views depended upon Christian revelation of the nature of God in the person of Jesus. But he did open the way for twentieth-century theologians to see God as dynamic, truly creative, and in responsive relation to the cosmos (my own views on this are most fully presented in *Religion and Creation*, Clarendon Press, 1996, esp. parts 3 and 4).

This general approach was taken in a slightly different direction by Process philosophy, formulated by A.N. Whitehead.[30] This philosophy used some Hegelian ideas, combined with ideas from Leibniz and a knowledge of mathematical physics, to expound an ambitious metaphysical scheme in terms of which reality is to be understood. Charles Hartshorne and John Cobb are representative of a group of theologians, mostly in the United States, who have used Process thought to reformulate Christian doctrines.

God is not seen, as in Hegel, as the only ultimate cause of the world. Rather, the world consists of a large, possibly infinite, series of momentary events. These events arise by 'prehending', or by having their inner states causally influenced by, the set of events that preceded them, recombining them in a new and creative way, and almost immediately passing out of existence as the newly originated events are incorporated into a new set of events that follow them. So reality consists of a process of events or 'actual occasions', not of substances that endure through the change of some of their properties. In this system, God is the primordial reality that sets out the array of possibilities from which the events of the world will select what is to become actual. God is also the consequential reality that 'feels' or experiences the totality of new events as they arise and perish. And God's consequential nature will influence the course events take, insofar as they are affected by and do not oppose such influence.

Christian interpretations of Process philosophy tend to focus on the cross as the symbol of God's love. They show how God persuades reality towards good outcomes, without actually determining them, and how

God shares in, by actually experiencing, all events. 'God', wrote Whitehead, 'is the fellow-sufferer who understands.'

As with Hegel, Process philosophy has been chiefly influential, not so much as a system to be accepted as a whole, but as a source of new insights and ideas that Christians can use. Whereas the classical tradition had denied that the divine nature could suffer, much Protestant theology now holds that it is important to Christian faith that God fully enters into the sufferings of the world. This is a central part, for instance, of the theologies of Jurgen Moltmann and Karl Barth.

As Christian faith seeks to relate to modern scientific discoveries, Process thought has also contributed significantly to the work of scientist-theologians like Ian Barbour and Arthur Peacocke.[31] For such theologies the life, death and resurrection of Jesus, while being historical events, are primarily symbols of the general nature of God's relation to the cosmos as a persuasive influence that leads to the emergence of new complex forms of conscious being, possessing their own real creativity and freedom, but being directed to a general goal of responsible, personal and conscious existence.

Process-influenced views of God are often called 'panentheistic', meaning that the cosmos is part of the being of God, though God transcends the physical cosmos. All the events that together make up the universe enter into, or are part of, the being of God, who can both influence and transfigure them within a wider divine experience. Panentheism drastically modifies the form of classical theism that denies all change in God, and all real relationship of God to the cosmos. For many theologians it still seems right to preserve a certain 'distance' between a sinful and estranged world and the supreme goodness of God. They would not be happy with saying that this universe of sin and alienation is actually part of God, or with supposing that all real causal influences come from the atomistic 'events' of which the universe is composed, and not from God. Nevertheless, there are prominent New Testament themes of the final unity of all creation 'in Christ', which imply that all will be 'in God' in some sense. Paul Tillich seems to have caught the spirit of this when he spoke of 'eschatological panentheism', belief that in the end, if not now, all things will exist in God.

Perhaps it should be recognised that the models of God being 'outside' the universe, or of the universe being 'inside' God, are only models, not literal descriptions, of the divine reality. Persons in the universe have their own experience and autonomy, and God relates to them as a personal reality that is supreme and perfect in itself. Yet perhaps a supreme personal reality can only be realised in relation to other persons, and in such relationship God has an inward presence to finite persons that is not merely external. So we may speak of God and finite persons as forming a relational unity of being that is more than a relation of distinct parts, yet does not destroy the real individuality of persons in relation.

The revision of the idea of God in a more personal and relational direction is an important strand of twentieth-century Christian thought. Among the diverse strands of global religion, this form of Christian theism stresses the value of persons, the existence of a supreme personal creator and the existence of a moral goal for the universe. Among the Abrahamic faiths, it stresses the relational union of divine and human, the participation of the divine in time and history, and the participation of the finite in the divine life. And it affirms the character of the divine, in whose image humans are created, primarily as self-emptying and unitive love, a love that gives itself to the uttermost in order that conscious beings might share companionship with the divine.

EXISTENTIALIST THEOLOGY

This stress on concepts of God may seem a little speculative and abstract, and it is important to emphasise that faith in the Christian God must be founded firmly in personal experience. In post-1945 Europe, especially, there was a reaction against highly speculative philosophies, and this reaction found expression in a group of theories that were broadly called 'existentialist'. Existentialism renounces the attempt to speculate about reality as a whole. It begins from reflections on what it means, or on what it is like, to exist as a human person.

Inauthentic human life is life lived in alienation from the material world, from others and from your own freedom. It leads to despair, a sense of meaninglessness, and anguish in face of death. Existentialist philosophers looked for a way of finding liberation from inauthentic existence, and for a way of living authentically, in creative freedom and self-affirmation.

There were as many ways of understanding authentic human existence as there were existentialist philosophers. Nietzsche called for acceptance that God was dead and that meaning had to be freely created by a leap of personal commitment in the face of Nothingness. Paul Tillich, at the other extreme, called for participation in the New Being, liberated from guilt, despair and fear, which had been realised in Jesus and could now give the 'courage to be' to all.

An existentialist approach in theology turns away from the objective metaphysics of dogma, from an intellectual belief in whatever facts are related in the Bible and from the attempt to found faith on historically establishable facts. It focuses on subjective experience of the human condition as one in which we are enslaved by greed, hatred and ignorance, and prey to anxiety and despair. This is the condition of 'sin', of spiritual decay and death. It is that condition to which the Christian gospel speaks, proclaiming the possibility of a new life, in which compassion, empathy and wisdom can become real, and *hilaritas*, inner joy, is found by conscious relation to an objectively existing supreme value and goal.

For such views, the gospel is not primarily about speculative theories, beliefs about past history, or submission to some external authority. It is about the present possibility of new life, of liberation from fear and anxiety, and personal participation in the Spirit of love that comes from beyond the self yet is present in the centre of the self.

This does not have to be (though it may be) an ecstatic experience of sudden renewal or of the personal presence of God. It can be a gentle, almost imperceptible, yet real re-orientation of attitudes as the world comes to be seen in a different way, as transparent to goodness rather than as shadowed by an ultimate pointlessness.

Existentialism is no longer a potent force in philosophy. It is usually seen as too subjective, too inward-looking, too unconcerned with real social relationships and with the objective material and historical conditions of human existence. As far as the Christian use of existentialism goes, it is almost certainly a mistake to reduce the gospel just to a present experience of a personal sense of alienation and liberation. Sartre turned from existentialism to Marxism, as he came to think that the social, economic and historical conditions of human existence are at least as important as concentration on inner feelings and emotions. And of course the Christian gospel is embedded in a historical reality, the crucifixion and resurrection of Jesus. It is embedded in the social reality of the church in its many historical forms, and it is committed to claims about the objective reality of a creating and redeeming God.

Existentialist themes were used by twentieth-century theologians to make the point that Christian faith is basically a choice between spiritual life and death. It is about salvation from sin and the possibility of eternal life. In a culture in which these terms had become virtually meaningless, they needed to be put in a different way. Nevertheless, we can be saved from sin only if there is a God who can save us – and that is a metaphysical or dogmatic assertion. We have the possibility of new life in the Spirit because Jesus inaugurated in history a new community in which the Spirit was made known and active in a new, inward yet also relational, way.

Christians cannot avoid either metaphysics or history. Nevertheless, in a world of competing ontologies and interpretations of history, where little is certain and much is unknown, it is important to state that Christian faith is at heart about salvation from sin (liberation from alienation), and new life in God (or life in creative freedom). It is primarily upon such liberating experiences that belief in the personal, relational and loving God disclosed in Jesus is founded.

CHRISTIANITY AMONG THE WORLD RELIGIONS

Both Tillich and Bultmann saw that, if this message was to be proclaimed in the twentieth-century Western world, it would have to be disengaged from the worldview of the New Testament, and that of the sixteenth-century Reformation too. As Bultmann put it, the 'mythology' of a Hell below ground and a Heaven above the clouds, of Satan and demons, of angels and miracles, would have to be rejected in any literal sense and interpreted in terms of spiritual symbolism. There would still be ontological and historical claims, but they would have to be more flexible and tentative, more symbolic or metaphorical and susceptible of variant interpretations, than on any literalist view.[32]

Bultmann was on the whole content to stay within the Protestant Christian tradition, wedded to a Lutheran view that the proclamation of the Word of freedom in Christ was central to a Christian faith that was religiously supreme and more or less self-contained. But Tillich was aware that once you take many of the ontological and historical claims of Christianity to be symbolic or metaphorical, and once you make the centre of faith a journey from spiritual death to life centred on the Ultimately Real, many of the old reasons for separation between religious traditions disappear. If you agree that you are not as certain of specific dogmatic formulations as people once seemed to be, and allow a number of variant interpretations, many old disputes between churches fade away. So in the twentieth century Catholics and Lutherans were able to agree on the doctrine of justification by faith, which had been a matter of violent dispute in the past. Anglican and Catholic theologians, if not their church officials, were able to agree on the doctrine of the Mass. The foundation of the World Council of Churches in 1948 was a sign of a growing awareness that traditional lines of division were becoming irrelevant insofar as more liberal attitudes to Christian faith became widespread.

Tillich also saw that this new ecumenical consciousness extended beyond the boundaries of Christianity and was part of the emerging global awareness. For religion is a global phenomenon. It has a common origin, millions of years in the proto-human past. It is concerned with human attempts to know and relate to a realm or state of transcendent reality and value. In a global history of religions, we can see the emergence of four main streams of belief over the last three thousand years, each stressing a different basic matrix for understanding the transcendent in its relation to the material world. In the Semitic tradition, to which Judaism, Christianity and Islam belong, prophets developed the idea of one morally demanding creator. Within this tradition, Christianity jettisoned the idea of a divinely revealed Law and replaced it with the model of revelation in and through the person of Jesus. Christianity also made the idea of a union of divinity and humanity central to its spiritual path, a union to be effected by love. Christianity can still learn much, however, from the Jewish insight that relation to God (the covenant) is a matter not of exclusive salvation but of a special vocation or calling to witness to God in a world of diverse beliefs and practices. And Christianity can learn much from Islam's relatively greater stress on the transcendence of God, on the basic simplicity of faith and on the priority of practice over abstract speculation.

The renouncing traditions, originating in India, of which Theravada Buddhism is the most widespread, understand the transcendent in a more impersonal way, as Nirvana, a state of wisdom, compassion and bliss. Christianity is committed to the existence of one supreme personal creator. But many contemporary Christians are learning from Buddhism the value of meditation and the disciplines of mindfulness, and the importance of learning to achieve liberation from hatred, greed and ignorance and train the mind to overcome self-centredness.

Orthodox Hindu tradition sees the transcendent in terms of an all-including cosmic self (*Brahman*), manifesting in the play (*lila*) of the universe. Many Christians would wish to stress the importance of individual personhood and of a moral goal for the cosmos more than is typical of Hindu belief in millions of re-births and an ultimate desire to be wholly liberated from the wheel of suffering. But there is much to learn from the Hindu insight that all things share in and can be expressions of the divine life, and that God, as Supreme Self, is not simply a distinct person but the all-inclusive personal ground of all being.

In East Asia a more monistic view of the transcendent as being the 'reverse side', the inner law of being of our ordinary social world, found expression in differently nuanced ways in movements such as Confucianism, Taoism and Mahayana Buddhism. Again, most Christians would stress the need for a fully personal reality underlying the cosmic moral law. But Christianity often stands in need of the East Asian emphasis on the sacredness of all life, the importance of the social virtues, and the cultivation of compassion for all sentient beings.

These four great streams of religious thought, within each of which there are hundreds of subsidiary groups and institutions, trace out four main ways in which humans have tried to relate themselves to a reality of transcendent value. They are not monolithic and self-contained realities. For in each of them important strands can be found that reflect elements more characteristic of the other traditions. Indeed, there have been many historical interactions and influences that have changed the character of beliefs and practices in each tradition.

I have traced this global development in *The Case for Religion* (Oneworld, 2004). It is possible now for the first time in history, thanks to computer technology, for anyone to have access to the classic texts of these traditions, in good translations and with reliable commentaries. Christianity can now be more fully understood in the global context of this development. For it is not a unique and isolated revelation from God, occurring in no context and with no developmental history. It cannot be understood without a good knowledge of the Jewish context in which it arose. That in turn is only rightly seen as one strand of human religious thought, with distinctive emphases but also with relative lack of stress on aspects to which other traditions pay more attention. As Christian faith changes through greater knowledge of and response to the world in which it exists, one major feature at the present time is the possibility of interacting positively with the wider religious traditions of the world.

Friedrich Schleiermacher was committed to such an approach as long ago as 1799, when he wrote the *Speeches on Religion*. But at that time there was insufficient knowledge of other traditions; he even wrongly thought, for instance, that Judaism was a spent force. In the twentieth century Hans Küng and John Hick are pre-eminent among theologians who have tried to see Christianity in global context as one set of traditions of human relationship to transcendent reality and value.[33]

If, as Pannenberg holds, Christianity is committed to a view of total history as the expression of God's interaction with the world, then we need to see history as a totality. It is not enough to tell the Christian story, for that is only one part of the history of the development of human beliefs about God. If Christian faith also requires a total worldview, and so must find a coherent relationship with new scientific knowledge, it must also find such a relationship with the claimed knowledge of the Transcendent that is found in the world's religious traditions.

Twentieth-century theologians have taken various views of how this is to be done. John Hick's 'pluralistic hypothesis' is that many major religious traditions offer paths to liberating relationship with the Real. Karl Rahner, from a Roman Catholic perspective, accepts that this is so, but maintains that the Catholic way must logically be regarded, by Catholics at least, as the most adequate path. My own views have been developed at some length in my *Comparative Theology* (Clarendon Press, 1994–2000). In general, liberal theologians (and I include some major theologians of the Second Vatican Council under this description) reject the opinion that only Christianity offers a way to salvation. Seeing how much Christian faith has been re-thought over the centuries, and how internally diverse the Christian world is, they tend to reject the model of 'Christianity' as one monolithic body of doctrines opposed to other equally monolithic entities like 'Islam' or 'Hinduism'. The religious worlds of humanity are fluid, and Christians can most reasonably believe that at every point God is present as a gracious God willing the salvation and flourishing of all created beings. Jesus can be understood by Christians as the point in human history at which a crucial disclosure of the Transcendent is given as a threefold God who has supreme creative power, who is self-emptying limitless love that shares the joys and sufferings of creation, and who wills to unite all creation to the divine life.

Precisely because that is what Jesus reveals, in his life, teaching, death and resurrection, Christian faith can never be an exclusive sect that lays down the necessity of explicitly believing in Jesus for salvation. For the very heart of the revelation of God in Jesus Christ is that the divine love has no limits.

Each person must follow their own conscience and God will honour such endeavour to follow the Good as honestly as possible. Yet for most Christians it remains true that it is specifically and normatively in Jesus that this disclosure of God's universal love is made. The other streams of religious tradition may enable Chistians to see their own tradition in a new and broader light and as an important part of the general human quest to understand human life in relation to a transcendent good. So Christian evangelism consists mainly in continuing to love, heal, serve and reconcile, as Jesus did. But it also consists in proclaiming in appropriate ways God's will that all should know and love God, and that God has shown the character of divine love specifically in the life and death of Jesus, has shown the power of the divine love in the resurrection of Jesus and has shown the path to sharing the divine love in the inward action of the Holy Spirit in (though not only in) the church. That is a Christian faith that is both liberal (affirming freedom of belief and acceptance of informed critical enquiry) and orthodox (assenting to the main declarations of the seven orthodox councils of the church).

Chapter 12

From Liberalism to Liberation

When liberalism stands alone, it can succumb to relativism and indifference. But when it is allied with transcendental personalism, it is an important part of a concern for human flourishing, and for a commitment to God as a personal ground of being that underlies and encourages the flourishing of human moral values. Liberal Christian faith is concerned above all with a search for truth and for the widest possible fulfilment of God-created personal potentialities. This sponsors a vision of the churches as positively concerned to promote societies in which such fulfilment is possible for all. The vocation of the churches is not merely to nourish the relation of individual souls to God. It is also to mediate God's will for the liberation and flourishing of all life, and, so far as is possible, to enable all things to become transparent to the glory of God.

THE GROWTH OF POST-MODERNISM

In the modern world there is an important place for a liberal and personalist Christian faith that is prepared to re-think ideas of God in a scientific age, that stresses the vital importance of spiritual and liberating experience and that is open to learn from the wider religious life of humanity. But in the twentieth century there have also been Christian reactions against liberalism. I think there are two main reasons for that.

First, there is a suspicion that the Enlightenment inevitably leads to secularism and to a loss of the sense of the importance of religious faith. Religion becomes an optional extra for those who like that sort of thing. Second, is the suspicion that liberalism is bound up with a sense of Western superiority and cultural elitism. I do not think these suspicions are well founded, just as I do not think that Christian faith is necessarily connected with the imperialism of the old Roman Empire. Yet there are historical connections here that, however contingent, need to be explained and counteracted.

It is true that there is a form of anti-religious secularism that mocks the wide diversity of religious beliefs as evidence that all religious opinions are equally absurd and unjustifiable. The freedom of expression and critical enquiry that mark Enlightenment thought have given rise to free expressions of anti-religious sentiments and destructive criticisms of religious beliefs. After the Enlightenment, membership of a religious institution does tend to become a voluntary option, and the possibility exists that most people will not opt for such membership. In that sense, the Enlightenment has led, certainly in Europe but increasingly in the United States, to secularism and to a widespread indifference to religious faith.

In that situation, some Christian writers have reacted by seeking to defend forms of thought that are critical of the Enlightenment, and that some call 'post-liberal' or 'post-modern'. I agree that liberalism, in the sense simply of freedom of belief, enquiry and criticism, is not enough. Taken on their own, such freedoms leave you without any positive moral values or goals, except that of making your own mind up in any way you like.

Of course most Enlightenment thinkers did not want such freedoms to be taken as the only, or even as the most important, values. What they perceived was that critical enquiry and argument promote and do not undermine a genuine search for truth. Liberal values, in other words, are largely instrumental to the creative pursuit of values that are truly intrinsic or worthwhile for their own sakes, values such as truth, beauty and friendship.

But where do such values come from? In the splintered world of the twentieth century, it may seem that human values are irreducibly diverse and that there can be no universal agreement on just one set of 'rational' or 'self-evident' values. 'Modernity' is sometimes said to be the view that human reason can somehow work out just one set of universal values or principles, and that all that is needed to obtain universal agreement is to distinguish reason clearly from prejudice and tradition and apply rational methods more efficiently to social and moral issues. Alisdair MacIntyre has given the name 'the Enlightenment Project' to 'the project of discovering new rational secular foundations for morality' (*After Virtue*, Duckworth, 1985, p. 117). He argues that this project has collapsed. In the face of such collapse, we need to return to our differing cultural traditions of morality, located as they are in particular worldviews and social practices, and stop looking for some universal basis for morality.

His own preference is for a basically Aristotelian approach to the virtues, as excellences that tend to fulfil the human *telos*, and he recognises that in the modern world this may mean a re-instatement of a fundamentally Christian view of reality, which can underpin the belief that there is such a *telos*, or end for humans as such. It will also mean the acceptance that there will be differing moral and religious outlooks, with no common or universal basis, and that both our morality and our basic standards of rationality will be tradition constituted. But they will be none the worse for that, since everyone else's ultimate standards will be tradition constituted also. It would seem to follow that we can and should look in the post-modern world for a conversation of differing traditions, that can lead us to expand our own tradition as much as possible by encounter with others, and that will not allow us to think that our tradition has the one ascertainable and obvious truth.

Having said all that, we may seem to have undermined the secularist claim that science has superseded religion and that universal standards of evidence and inference in effect rule out religious beliefs as obsolete. Then we can simply speak from a committed Christian position and say, 'We cannot justify our position. But neither can you justify yours. These are just different starting points, and ours is as good as yours.'

It is possible then just to take the Bible as given and to argue that any attempt to justify it is already a capitulation to secularism. biblical revelation does not need independent rational foundations. But no knowledge has universally accepted foundations, so it is no worse to start from the Bible than from anywhere else. Moreover, if Christian faith is response to divine revelation, and is directly evoked by God, we might expect that there would be no independently rational and non-theistic foundation for it anyway.

Secularism is thus challenged at its core with a view that refuses to accept its foundational principles and that insists on the epistemic right of

Christians to live and think by their own distinctively Christian (either ecclesiastical or biblical) principles. In this way a Christian form of post-modernism has become one major response to what have been perceived as the secularising tendencies of Enlightenment 'modernism'.

THE NATURE OF CHRISTIAN DOCTRINE

Post-modernism may give Christians greater confidence to speak from a committed Christian position. The problem is that it may also cut them off from conversation with their wider culture. While seeing themselves as bringing all culture under the banner of Christian faith, Christian post-modernists may in fact make Christians an even more separate minority culture and marginalise that culture in a more severe way than liberals ever did.

George Lindbeck, in his influential book *The Nature of Doctrine*, suggests that a 'post-liberal' approach to Christian doctrine is needed.[34] He proposes that we should see Christian doctrines as grammatical rules for speaking within the church community, which is a distinctive cultural/linguistic community. Professor Lindbeck divides views of Christian doctrine into the categories of 'propositional', 'experiential/expressivist' and 'cultural/linguistic'. He argues that propositional views belong to a pre-modern time, when it was thought that doctrinal propositions simply mirror external reality. The medieval church, for example, could define doctrines as universal truths that were in principle accessible to all rational persons and were establishable by reasoned proofs of God and of the reliability of Christian revelation. Such dogmatic confidence was, however, undermined by Enlightenment sceptical arguments.

Experiential/expressivist views, he says, are characteristic of liberal modernism and claim that doctrines simply express inner feelings or experiences. This certainly avoids the charge of ontological over-confidence. But it seems to reduce religious beliefs to a matter of subjective feeling and to confirm a widely held Enlightenment view that religious and moral beliefs are basically matters of private opinion.

Cultural/linguistic views he associates with post-liberalism or post-modernism, when language is seen to be constitutive of communities and views of reality. Traditions are constituted by distinctive concepts and a

whole web of conceptual relationships, which have no external foundations, but each form of life has its own characteristic internal rationality and
rules of discourse. At its extreme, such a view holds that different conceptual frameworks are incommensurable, and so it is useless to try to compare
them and even worse to try to move concepts, taken out of context, from
one framework to another. But in less extreme form this view holds that the
set of concepts we have learned in our community governs the ways we will
identify and describe both the external world and our inner feelings.
Language comes first, and basic metaphysical views and experiences will be
determined by the sort of conceptual scheme we have, in the community of
which we are part.

I am sympathetic to the proposal that there are basically different
worldviews that have no agreed common basis, so in that sense there is no
external or universal foundation for such views. Indeed, commitment to
liberalism does not entail acceptance of the Enlightenment project of finding some universal secular basis for morals and metaphysics. On the contrary, it entails freedom to choose many different projects of our own, and
so it is inherently pluralistic. Liberal Christians must accept that people are
free to have different beliefs. A Christian worldview must be quite different
in many respects from an atheistic one, and there seems little prospect of
obtaining agreement between them.

But I do not like the proposal that propositional views, which claim
objective truth, are somehow pre-modern and perhaps obsolete. Christian
faith makes assertions about objective reality, and is in that sense propositional, even if many of its formulations are metaphorical or very inadequate. No doubt dogmatic beliefs should not be imposed by force, and it can
no longer be thought that they are the only possible beliefs for intelligent
and morally sensitive individuals. Nevertheless, most Christians do wish to
affirm that God really does exist, became incarnate, is Trinitarian in being
and reconciles the world to the divine in Jesus Christ. These are objective
propositional claims to truth, even though they cannot be established in a
tradition-independent way.

Nor do I think that experiential/expressivist views are just expressions of
inner feelings, without any reference to objective reality. For Schleiermacher,
the main supposed target of the phrase 'experiential/expressivist', and his
spiritual successors, experience is not some sort of subjective feeling-state. It
is precisely the proper mode of access to the unique objectivity of God.

Experience is experience of the objective reality of God. The point of an experiential approach is to stress that religious beliefs are ultimately founded on experience. Such experience may be objective and historical (as in the life, death and resurrection of Jesus), or inward and personal. But experience does give rise to claims about an objective reality, to which a sort of experience that is not publicly repeatable, measurable and predictable, but is nonetheless capable of being veridical, is the most appropriate form of access. Of course our description of such experiences is shaped by our concepts and tradition, as can be clearly seen by comparing the differing descriptions of experiences in different religious traditions. Yet those concepts themselves resulted from reflection upon a cumulative set of experiences, grouped around a central paradigm. They do not just float in abstract conceptual space, without any basis in experience, even if they sometimes (as in some dicussions about the Trinity) develop what can seem like over-elaborate logical intricacies that have almost, but not quite, lost touch with experience altogether.

The contention that doctrines are best described as grammatical rules descriptive of a linguistic system given by the Bible, or by conciliar definitions, threatens to make them seem purely conventional definitions. It is true that statements like 'Speak of God as three' or 'Do not speak of God as three' are parts of wider conceptual schemes, like that of Christianity or Islam, in which they are embedded. But to imply that they are just rules for how Christians or Muslims ought to speak might imply that they do not refer to objective reality at all.

It can be helpful to see how such statements have developed gradually over many years, as parts of wider conceptual schemes that have grown and changed in an organic way. I agree that such conceptual schemes provide a general way of interpreting reality which enables us to see the world in which we live in a distinctive way. These perhaps are the main points Lindbeck wishes to emphasise. But speaking of them as grammatical (syntactical) rules underplays their semantic content, their intention to refer in some way to objective reality. The statement that 'God is three' is not just a recommendation of a way to use the word 'God'. It claims God is really threefold in being, and it is ultimately based on the experience of Jesus as the act and image of God, of the Spirit as the dynamic presence of God within the heart, and of the transcendent reality of God as the objective source of all reality.

Statements of Christian doctrine are not just cultural/linguistic rules. They always seek to refer to objective reality, and that implies that they should always be open to insights into that reality that derive from sources outside the Christian tradition itself, narrowly construed.

As I have stressed throughout this book, Christian doctrines are constantly being re-thought, and they can be seen as developments in ways of talking. But such developments occur in response to the problems and challenges of particular cultures. They result from reflections on how the basic Christian experiences of God in Jesus Christ and the church are to relate coherently to new historical situations. This is rarely simply a capitulation to culture, but it is equally rarely the construction of a language uninformed by culture. The re-thinking of doctrine arises from creative interaction with wider views of the world and its history. It arises from a continued concern for objective truth, and for a fuller understanding of truth that can only come with greater knowledge given by science, reflective thought and informed critical enquiry. In any case there is not just one church community, and the churches do not as such speak a different language from the rest of the world they live in. What we need to know is why certain 'grammatical rules' (like 'Speak of God in a threefold way') should be accepted. That requires a return to the sources of belief in history, personal experience and reflection on them.

Lindbeck claims that the Bible has its own conceptual universe, its own 'internal world', with its own criteria of rationality and intelligibility. 'A scriptural world is thus able to absorb the universe' (*The Nature of Doctrine*, p. 366). Christians must interpret their lives and the universe in terms of the biblical narrative. We can set aside critical questions about the Bible, just taking the narrative itself as our guide, a unitary narrative that describes God and his actions and gives Christians the language for interpreting the whole of their experience.

But the Bible does not just present one unitary narrative. It is a complex mixture of alleged 'words' of God, a history of Israel interpreted as a series of divine acts of liberation and judgment, reflections on divine providence (some of them very sceptical), songs, proverbs, stories, letters and cryptic prophecies of future events.

There is no single narrative in all this. There are many voices in the Bible, though of course Christians construct a 'grand narrative' or a number of such narratives from the text in the light of their beliefs about Jesus, narratives that are not acceptable, for instance, to Jews.

The Christian narrative is just one among many possible narrative strands in the Bible. Even then, it stands in need of the sort of doctrinal integration the church gave it, or imposed upon it, over the first few centuries. The synoptic narrative of the kingdom in Jerusalem had to be replaced by the cosmic narrative of the incarnation. The narrative of six-day creation now has to be re-interpreted by all those who accept the findings of evolution. And I have shown how throughout its history the Christian faith has been re-thought, precisely by openness to new insights provided by the culture of the time.

In view of this, it seems that Lindbeck's postulate of a 'biblical narrative' that provides a 'scriptural world' is false to the diverse nature of the biblical documents and to the continually revised metaphysics of Christian faith. More worrying, however, is the apparent renunciation of the idea of objective truth. If there is an objective truth, then we would hope that science, religion and philosophy would all ultimately be able to agree. At the present time, disagreements reflect our very limited ability to grasp truth, but they do not cast doubt on the importance of the search for truth. Belief in absolute truth does not entail a belief that we have direct access to such truth. In fact it ought to lead us to doubt that we possess the total truth, since we are so ignorant and prejudiced. Yet it protects us from the thought that truth is merely relative, that all is a matter of opinion, and so it does not really matter what we believe. Insofar as it leads to a renunciation of the idea of absolute truth, post-modern thought is a fickle friend, for it quickly leads to the belief that Christian faith is just an option for those who like that sort of thing.

THE THEOLOGY OF KARL BARTH

From the Christian point of view, a secular culture like that of the West in the twenty-first century does need to be challenged in many respects. But that challenge is not best made by the assertion that Christian language is just different, and must be accepted without any justification, or by a reiteration of a largely obsolete biblical or medieval worldview. The modern worldview must be encountered and then transformed. In our world, that means meeting the challenge of secularisation head on.

Despite his rejection of liberal German theology, one of the most important theologians of the twentieth century, Karl Barth, in fact absorbed most of the lessons of liberalism. He accepted critical views of the Bible, but simply did not see the need to refer to them in his positive exposition of biblical narratives. There is a need, however, to make acceptance of critical scholarship more open and apparent. For it is important to say that some biblical views – about the legitimacy of genocide or stoning to death, for example – are just mistaken, and reflect the limited opinions of specific writers, rather than the dictates of God.

Barth also accepted a radically revised view of God, derived largely from Hegel, as involving the divine nature in time and history, but did not clearly acknowledge his debt to philosophical thought. He gave the impression that his views owed nothing to philosophers, and this again led some of his followers to think that theology should owe nothing to philosophy.

Barth accepted the pluralist view that various competing worldviews can be equally rational or justifiable to their respective adherents, but made the invalid inference that no reasons can be given for accepting a particular revelation. He was right to think that the giving of reasons is very largely an 'internal' matter of exhibiting the coherence and integration of your own scheme of beliefs. But he was mistaken in denying that there could be a common basis of human knowledge and experience to which your belief-scheme needs to be related, with varying degrees of plausibility. All of us speak from a specific viewpoint, but we have the best chance of approaching truth when we take fully into account the viewpoints of others on what is, after all, the same reality.

Barth's apparently decisive 'no' to natural theology, to relating Christianity to a scientific or philosophical worldview, to a global dialogue of religions, is not after all so decisive. Regrettably, it has seemed so to some of his followers. Christians do need to affirm the priority of God and to have confidence that God's revelation in Jesus Christ has the power to illuminate every area of human thought and activity. But this is best done by openness to and engagement with, not rejection of, all the diverse aspects of modern global culture. That requires, not a view that rejects liberalism, but a more careful analysis of the positive values of liberalism, and of how liberalism is an instrumental but vital part of a contemporary commitment to Christian orthodoxy. Liberalism taken on its own may have the consequence of total scepticism or even relativism. But orthodox Christian belief in the priority of the personal, the reality of the embodiment of the eternal in time, and the final fulfilment and reconciliation of persons in God is best articulated by a

liberal commitment to freedom of belief, the acceptance of informed critical enquiry in the sciences and in history, and the freely chosen creative
expression of personal values. Only when those beliefs and values are taken
together can we see the outlines of a truly liberal Christian faith.

THE RISE OF NON-WESTERN CHRISTIANITY

The greatest challenge to Western secular culture comes, not from purely
intellectual arguments, but from a perceived link between elite liberal culture and political domination and oppression. With the collapse of old
imperialisms has come the danger of a new science-based secular imperialism that relegates religious faith to being a matter of private opinion and
that seeks to export a materialistic capitalism to the whole world, threaten-
ing to subordinate the third world permanently to multinational, Western-
based, economic interests. The vast majority of the earth's population
belongs to the economically developing world, emerging from the colonial
era into a world in which they are still structurally disadvantaged economically, politically and socially.

As the developing nations escaped from colonial control, Christian
churches sometimes became very conservative and traditional, often allying
themselves with repressive ruling elites. These tendencies have been
strongly influenced by the dominant Western culture, especially with the
Western counter-cultural conservative views represented by American fundamentalist interpretations of the Bible or by forms of biblical literalism
that reflect pre-critical European missionary beliefs.

A second, more positive strategy is seen in attempts to integrate more
closely with indigenous cultures (as Christianity did in Europe). Latin
American, Asian and Indian theologies are well developed, and they show a
concern to free Christianity from entanglement with 'Western' dominating
culture. Sometimes a clash of cultures seems dominant, especially in
strongly Islamic societies. But there is a central teaching in most religious
views that tolerance and peace are a proper goal of religious life. Insofar as
religious beliefs can be disentangled from the politics of resentment and
hatred, and a truly liberal commitment to freedom of belief and the acceptance of informed criticism can be established, there are many positive
possibilities for greater religious understanding and co-operation. The next

great development for Christian belief may come when the great religious cultures of the world are able to see themselves as diverse yet related paths of knowing and relating to a supreme reality or state of wisdom, compassion and bliss. If the social and economic barriers to justice and full acceptance of cultural diversity can be overcome, forms of culturally located religious life may develop that remain true to their own past while being re-thought in a much more positive relationship to diverse cultures and differing spiritual paths. In what is sometimes called the 'third world', many attempts at such cultural indigenisation are beginning to flourish.

A third and much more evident phenomenon is the amazingly rapid growth of Pentecostal movements throughout the world. These movements centre on an intense experience of the Spirit, manifesting in forms of spiritual possession very like those recorded in the New Testament as experienced by the disciples on the day of Pentecost. At the heart of these movements is the experience of a transforming activity of the Holy Spirit, undercutting all church hierarchies and dogmatic systems of theology and leading to the establishment of independent Christian fellowships of believers. Although these movements are very Bible based, they tend not to conform to the theologies of classical Protestantism and not to be interested in the long-standing theological disputes that still dominate much European Christianity. The theology of the Pentecostal movement is yet to be constructed. But it is possible that it will focus much more on the importance of personal experience than on acceptance of rigidly defined authoritarian beliefs. To that extent, there is the possibility that Pentecostalism may yet have an energy and creativity that will lead to a re-thinking of traditional beliefs in the light of a primarily experiential understanding of Christian revelation. The intellectual link with Schleiermacher and the liberal tradition may be unexpected, and it is far from being assured, but it is one of the more interesting intellectual possibilities for the future of Christian belief.

RELIGIOUS LIBERALISM AND POLITICS

It is, nevertheless, a fourth theological response from the third world that has most fully developed a distinctive twentieth-century re-thinking of Christian belief. This is the response of the theology of liberation. It seeks to challenge the dominant elites of the world, which in the twentieth century were largely Christian, in the name of social justice and of Christian concern for 'the poor'.

Liberation theology is sometimes opposed to liberalism, as the ideology of the underprivileged verses the ideology of the bourgeoisie. But it is better seen as an extension of the basic principles of liberalism to all persons without exception.

Some liberals did argue that the gospel has nothing to do with the affairs of the world and that, as Harnack put it, the concern of Christian faith is solely with 'God and the soul, the soul and God' (Harnack, *What is Christianity?*, lecture 7). Such a faith might well leave the structures of society untouched, left to be sorted out in accordance with their own, non-religious, principles. It is no accident that Harnack came from a Lutheran tradition that tended to separate religion quite sharply from political life. This is not necessarily part of a liberal view of Christian faith at all. But, since it was associated with some German liberal theologians, it is sometimes seen as a sixth strand of historic liberalism, a strand of individualism, that sees the freedom of the autonomous individual as of great, perhaps supreme, importance. This strand has been important in subsequent social, economic and political life. In those realms it has tended to oppose centralised social control and restrictions on individual economic freedom. Then it notoriously faces the paradox that the unrestricted freedom of some will negate the freedom of many. If we are concerned with the freedom of all to realise their unique gifts and capacities, we will have to have a much more positive view of the role of societies in making possible and extending the realms of possible activity open to individuals. All humans can be truly free only when they co-operate in societies that make many worthwhile exercises of freedom possible. In this sense liberalism is actually in conflict with radical individualism. But it may still oppose the authority of custom and tradition over individuals, who are encouraged to make their own free choices. In religion, it may encourage freedom from hierarchical authority and tradition.

Yet, if such liberalism is to gain a secure foothold, it requires freedom of belief, expression and critical enquiry, and therefore it requires the existence of a certain sort of free, secure and self-confident society. It is incompatible with a society that imposes one set of beliefs on all, that imposes censorship on thought and speech or that allows the freedom of some to impede the freedom of all. In other words, liberalism does have a political agenda. It is not just, as Harnack said, 'inwardness and individualism' (lecture 1). Even Harnack saw that Christian faith is concerned with the 'realised dominion of the good' (lecture 8), with belief in divine providence, and with the destiny of all to be children of God. These thoughts point to the necessity of developing some providential view of human history, and some idea of the sort of society within which humans can live as members of one common family in love. Since persons live in history and in societies, their freedom and independence cannot, or ought not to be, merely inward and individual. It can only exist in a society that nourishes liberty, fraternity and the sort of relationships that are essential to personal flourishing and to interpersonal love. Individual persons can only flourish in community, and so liberalism has to be concerned with the sort of community that best enables such flourishing.

In theory liberal thought should apply to all persons without exception, and its association with bourgeois lifestyles is thus a practical shortcoming, not a theoretical necessity. Liberalism asks that all should have freedom of thought and access to informed criticism. It asks that all created persons should have the capacity to develop their God-given capacities in freedom. If that is only possible in a society in which all have enough to eat and are not oppressed by a privileged class or a tyrannical dictator, then theological liberalism requires a liberal society that values freedom, and that seeks to provide some sort of equality of opportunity for personal flourishing, and protection against the arbitrary whims of government.

Marxists object to this sort of liberalism on the ground that it does not recognise the existence of a class war between rich and poor, or see that revolution is needed if oppression of the poor is to be ended. Liberal Christians have indeed traditionally sought a common good in which all could share harmoniously, and have opposed the use of violence to attain political or religious ends. Marxist commitment to conflict, violence and revolution are tendencies that Christians cannot share. Yet Marxism can be seen as a deviant form of prophetic religion. Anyone who believes in a creator God will be disposed to hope that the world will progress towards greater justice, and will probably acknowledge that it will have to do so through dialectical struggle, a continued struggle against selfishness and egoism, which perpetually takes new forms and disguises. But when God, and especially the notion of a God who suffers with the poor, is taken away, there may no longer be moral limits on the use of violence to achieve such goals. That is, sadly, what happened to Marxism, ironically turning it into one of the great repressive political systems of history.

Yet Marx did say things of great importance to twentieth-century theologians. He stressed that persons can only be free in relationship, so that they cannot be considered as isolated inward units. You cannot be free to hear a symphony if there is no orchestra or system of training in music – both social facts. He stressed that the material conditions of existence must be changed if personal values of creative freedom are to be expressed properly. He saw the necessity for a 'vanguard' of the final classless society, which could lead the way towards a better future for the poor and oppressed.

In all these respects, Marx contributed to a re-thinking of the sort of theological liberalism that held aloof from political life and remained content with an inward liberty, largely for those who could take external liberty for granted. Theologians of liberation do not renounce liberalism, understood as a search for the creative freedom of persons in community. They renounce liberalism only as a theology of pure inwardness in a world where huge numbers of people starve and die because of social oppression or indifference. Liberation theologians have to find their way between a Marxist-Leninist commitment to the violent overthrow of repressive social structures and a supine acceptance of social injustice. But they see that salvation or liberation involves social and political freedom, not just an inner spiritual freedom.

That was, after all, true of Hebrew thought, for which any talk of individual salvation hardly makes sense. It is the people, the community, who are to be liberated from their political oppressors, and that is God's will. Israel's liberation from her enemies is a political liberation, where the people will have self-government, peace will be preserved and the rules of social justice will be implemented.

What has complicated the issue for Christianity is that Jesus seemed to renounce violent or overtly political action, in going to his death without protest. That has given rise to the impression that Christian faith has no social or political agenda, but is just concerned with inner feelings or otherworldly hopes – that is certainly how Marx saw it, and he despised what he saw.

It must be remembered, however, that Jesus lived in a country under military dictatorship, which was just about to be destroyed and eliminated. He preached to Jews who had in Torah a code of social justice, and Jesus, according to Matthew, preached that Torah should be obeyed with the whole heart.

Jesus renounced any Messianic role as one who would overthrow Rome by some sort of revolution, but he lived in anticipation of the coming of a kingdom of justice. He called people to live by the laws of justice. Any attempt at violent revolution would have failed – as it did just a few years later. It seems fairly clear that his message was to seek justice – 'blessed are those who hunger and thirst for righteousness, for they shall be filled' (Matt. 5:6), but to renounce violence as a path to justice – 'love your enemies and pray for those who persecute you' (Matt. 5:44). It is simply untrue that Jesus' gospel had nothing to do with the affairs of the world. His reported words show that he longed for justice, but was not prepared to kill for it. There are other, harder, ways, and the cross gives the clue to what they are – not supine acceptance of fate, but active self-sacrifice for the sake of true human liberation.

THE CHURCH AND LIBERATION THEOLOGY

The kingdom did not come. But what replaced expectation of an imminent end of the world was the calling and obligation of the church to continue Jesus' role of making the material world a true sacrament of the divine will. As Jesus in his own body made the material a sacrament of the divine, so the church as the body of Christ has the vocation of making the physical and social world in which humans live transparent to the divine presence and purpose. That means actively changing the world, and changing it so that it is liberated from estrangement and despair to become a channel of forgiveness, reconciliation and love.

Possibly Harnack was unable to see this because he was blind to the Jewishness of Jesus, to the social teaching of Torah and to a sacramental view of the church as an imperfect but genuine continuation of the incarnation, as called to foreshadow the kingdom. But if the church is to be the body of Christ, it must forgive, reconcile, heal, feed the hungry and care for the outcast just as Jesus did. If the church is to prefigure the kingdom, it must seek to embody in the world a society committed to the rule of the divine law of love. The church has a social and political role, to seek justice, but by sacrifice and reconciliation, not by hatred and violence. This may be what Jesus meant when he said, 'I have not come to bring peace but a sword' (Matt. 10:34) – not a sword that he would wield in anger, but a sword wielded by others that would pierce his heart, and the hearts of his followers.

This historical vocation of the church was compromised by its collusion with state power. For liberation theologians, it is important to disentangle the church from such collusion and to recall it to a vocational role of being the servant of the divine will, which is to show unlimited love, and to show special concern for those who are disadvantaged or outcast. Some medieval views of the church saw it as the Ark of Salvation, in which a few could be saved from the terror of judgment to come that would fall on the outside world. For the theology of liberation this has been replaced by a recognition that what distinguishes the church is a call to serve the world in love and to proclaim both in word and deed union with God's love for all, not just for its own members – 'The church ... is interested in one thing only – to carry on the work of Christ ... to save and not to judge, to serve and not to be served' (*Gaudium et Spes*, Vatican II, 1965, para. 3).

To serve the world entails caring for the true good and flourishing of all. If the church preaches liberation from sin, then it must also proclaim liberation from social conditions that derive from or that exacerbate sin. Any social structure that encourages greed, hatred or the frustration of the abilities and opportunities of whole classes of people must be opposed by the church. The liberation theologians saw that most human societies stand condemned by this criterion. Racial, sexual and religious discrimination are in opposition to the divine will for the flourishing of the created gifts of all finite persons, not for a privileged class, race or sex. If racial groups have been enslaved and oppressed, as they have, and if women have been regarded as an inferior sex, as they have, liberation theologians call for action, especially within the churches themselves, that will redress such gross injustices. Black theology and feminist theology are just two twentieth-century movements that express a new sense of the social relevance and calling of the Christian gospel – though they both sometimes despair of the churches ever really having the will to break with their past social and elitist alliances. The gospel calls for a preferential option for the poor, not because God only loves the poor, but because they are the ones who are oppressed or ignored by society. The rich may need pastoral care, but they need no liberation from conditions that prevent them from creatively realising their own potentialities.

MARXISM AND LIBERATION THEOLOGY

Such an interest by the church in social and political life at once involved it in the greatest political upheaval of the twentieth century, the spread of revolutionary Marxism across the globe. Marx was no lover of religion, seeing it as a bulwark of conservative and reactionary social forces. He saw human history as a dialectical process of social and economic conflict that would culminate in the final revolution of the proletariat against exploitative capitalism, and the establishment of a classless society in which all would be free to fulfil their own capacities. Marxism is 'materialist', in that it takes the facts of economic existence – 'the modes of production and exchange' – as the real driving forces of history. Beliefs and moral values are by-products of these forces, and there is no such thing as absolute truth. 'Truth' is what is accepted by the dominant class of society. Marxism is 'dialectical', in that it does not see society as harmoniously striving towards the common good. Class struggle is an inevitable factor in history, and the oppressed classes must continually overthrow their oppressors, until at last, when the proletariat rule, there is no one left to overthrow. So Marxist-Leninism teaches that violence is essential to accomplish the final liberation of the poor. Talk of love and tolerance is a defensive mechanism of the rich to prevent social revolution taking place.

Marxism is a genuine post-Enlightenment or post-liberal philosophy. It is born from Enlightenment concerns for equality and liberty, for a historical and scientific approach to human thought and human nature, and for an ultimately optimistic view of how human action can change the world for the better. Yet it sees its parent, the Enlightenment, as mired in a self-deceiving ideology that lives in luxury by repressing the desires and ambitions of a huge underclass, which is regarded as not enlightened or capable of civilised behaviour. Marxism teaches that ideas and beliefs are only a scum on the surface of the will to power. It penetrates the deceit that there are some absolute truths known to a privileged few, whom others should just obey, and sees that it is rhetoric and power that will survive in the struggle for existence. It no longer claims to have 'the true' view. It only claims to have the view that is historically destined to win. It will out-narrate and out-fight the opposition and usher in a new age in which the oppressed workers are at last liberated from the chains that bind them.

The *Instruction on Certain Aspects of the Theology of Liberation*, issued by Cardinal Ratzinger in 1984, places the Catholic Church, at least, firmly in opposition to all such post-liberal views. Truth is not just a by-product of economic struggle. Conflict is not essential to society. Violence is not a justifiable means to a moral goal. History will not inevitably end in a wholly classless and just society, unless human hearts are first changed to love the Good. Religion is not essentially a justification for social oppression and inequality. On all these points the *Instruction* seems to be right.

Yet liberation theologians like Gustavo Gutierrez, the Peruvian theologian who significantly influenced the Medellin meeting of Catholic bishops in 1968 to declare a 'preferential option for the poor' and who wrote *A Theology of Liberation* in 1971, have rarely, if ever, agreed with such points in any case.

Gutierrez unequivocally believes that a morally demanding God is the creator of all things, and what God demands is a search for truth, reconciliation through love, and a turning of the heart to God as the beginning of human liberation. It is precisely because this God was incarnate in one who suffered and died for the sake of the poor that the church is commanded to opt for the poor and to seek justice for all. Gutierrez speaks of a 'mystical dimension' as well as a 'prophetic dimension' in the role of the church. The church must both teach the contemplation of the God who is perfect beauty and also seek to change history so that it can become a channel of God's beauty to all who inhabit the earth.

Inner liberation, the liberation of the heart from hatred to love the God who is unlimited love, may sometimes be the only thing open to a person who is oppressed by political forces. But such liberation is unreal unless it seeks, where possible, to mediate God's love to the world in practical and material ways.

Jurgen Moltmann, one of the founding fathers of liberation theology, says that 'the church represents the future of the whole of reality and so mediates this eschatological future to the world' (*The Church in the Power of the Spirit*, SCM, 1977, p. 196).

This means that the church must work, as it always has done, for liberation from hatred, greed and ignorance in the individual. But it also means that the church must work for liberation from oppressive conditions in the economic realm, from anything that has been socially imposed and so is socially removable, anything that frustrates the flourishing of created beings.

Marxism may be accused of a Utopian belief that economic change will of itself bring about a happy and just society. Liberation theology is not committed to that view. It is aware that happiness and justice, in the sense of genuine concern for the flourishing of all created beings, can in the end only spring from hearts converted to God and filled with God's love. Yet, in commanding that we love all created beings, God wills that we genuinely care for them, and that means removing conditions that impede their flourishing. The church not only proclaims that the kingdom has drawn near. It proclaims that we are to be co-workers in making the kingdom visible – as Moltmann puts it, in making God's future present. This is not Utopian, because it gives no guarantee that the just society will result from our efforts. That is in God's hands, but the responsibility for working towards it is in ours.

So a major twentieth century re-thinking of Christian faith is a realisation that the role of the church in the world is not to provide a secure path to heaven for a few who will escape the general doom of the world. It is to work, through acts of charity and reconciliation, for the liberation of every human being, and even, so far as it is possible, for the liberation of all created things, from all that frustrates the fulfilment of their God-created capacities. There is no guarantee that our efforts will realise such an ideal, but there is an absolute divine command to try. The church exists not for its own sake or even for the sake of its members. It exists for the sake of the world and its liberation. Any dispassionate oberver might say that a good place to begin the search for liberation might be with the church itself.

Chapter 13

A Truth that Lies Ahead

There is one self-existent source of the universe, having the nature of consciousness and intelligence. It is the most perfect possible being, since it actualises in itself and enjoys states of supreme, consciously recognised value. All things emanate from it, by a combination of necessity and intelligent will. It seeks to maximise value among created beings, and wills to unite them to itself in conscious knowledge and love. This being is God, who expresses the divine nature in a particular human life and is present in all human lives to unite them to the divine. But the consummation of God's rule, of the kingdom, is beyond ('at the end of') historical time. Christ will then appear in glory, as the finite embodiment of the infinite divine, who took human form in Jesus. At the end of cosmic time all evil will be destroyed and love alone will rule, in a cosmos renewed by and fully reconciled to God. Then Christ will return the kingdom to God, and God will be all in all (1 Cor. 15:24, 28).

THE PLURALITY OF CHRISTIANITY

This has not been a history of Christianity, though it may occasionally have seemed like it. It has been an attempt to select a number of critical points in Christian history at which the understanding of Christian faith has clearly and definitively changed. The point has been to ask whether there is an unchanging core of Christian belief, what the limits are to the Christian faith's capacity for change, and what an appropriate Christian statement of faith might look like in today's even more rapidly changing world.

One result has been to see that attempts to describe a 'kernel' of Christian faith, and separate it from a changeable 'husk', all seem to have differed from one another. There is no question that Christian faith is centred on the person of Jesus, that the New Testament contains the only reliable accounts of Jesus we have and that the many churches throughout the world take Jesus as their focal point in the worship of God. Christianity lives by the faith that the Jesus of the Gospels is the Son of God and that he is in some sense a present focus of worship and devotion.

Already, however, there are different interpretations of what exactly 'Son of God' means, of the sense in which Jesus is alive, and of the way in which it is proper to 'worship' him. The diversity of the four Gospels, and the ways in which they present Jesus, builds such diversity into the faith in a central way. This suggests that the model of one changeless identical core is not an adequate model for Christian faith. What we have is a central personal reality, manifested in the history of a particular person but also experienced in various ways in the churches, a personal reality that is taken as a disclosure of the character and purpose of God. From the beginning there have been many personal perspectives on it, and it transcends any one of those perspectives. The reason there is not one unchanging core is that no perspective will ever exhaust the personal reality of Christ, and there will always be new perspectives, as Christ is seen from new historical contexts. The mystery of Christ transcends every human, biblical and ecclesial perspective.

There is, however, a set of concepts that has been used from the first to present such perspectives. They include the concepts of God, of the kingdom of God, of the Messiah, God's chosen king, of sin and forgiveness, of the cross and sacrificial suffering, of judgment and exclusion from God, of resurrection and eternal life. This conceptual framework is not a rigid structure. It is flexible and adjustable in many ways, though not infinitely so. It is not tightly defined, and consists partly of metaphors (like 'Gehenna') or symbols (like 'Messiah') whose precise reference is not fixed.

Christians of all ages approach the central mystery of the person of Christ from a personal perspective that uses the symbolic framework of the Bible in a distinctive way that has arisen out of their own historical situation. In what follows I present my own personal assessment of the way in which we can interpret the history of Christian thought. It is certainly not meant to be a dogmatic assertion of final truth – that would contradict the main thesis of the whole book – but I have tried to assimilate the findings of the best modern scholarship and use them to provide one way in which the Christian past can be positively incorporated into a contemporary state-ment of Christian belief for today.

REVISIONS OF BELIEF IN THE NEW TESTAMENT

I have discussed six periods in history in which Christian faith has under-gone a major and revolutionary change of perspective.

The first major changes occurred at the very time the New Testament documents were written, and the New Testament shows these changes in process of taking place. In the synoptic Gospels the mission and teaching of Jesus are said to be concerned with the immanent restoration, within a gen-eration, of the twelve tribes in Jerusalem, living in strict obedience to Torah and under the rule of Jesus, who is to return with angels in glory to judge liv-ing and dead, eliminate all evil and usher in a new Messianic age.

But in the Gospel of John and in some New Testament letters a very dif-ferent perspective is given. Jesus is presented as the incarnate Wisdom of God, who gives eternal life to the whole world by faith in him as the disclosure of God. The teaching of the kingdom of God is largely spiritualised, so that it no longer deals with straightforward historical and political events. It speaks symbolically of a spiritual community in relation to God. The Hebrew 'Messiah', suggestive of a political liberator of Israel, is replaced by the Greek equivalent 'Christ', taken to refer to the suffering servant who redeems the world by love, by the sacrifice of the cross and the victory of resurrection.

Embryonic doctrines of the divinity of Jesus, the Trinity and the Eucharist were developed in the Gospel of John in a way most unlikely to have been taught by Jesus himself. Yet they can be seen to be implicit in Jesus' life and teaching, and especially in the facts of his death and resurrection.

For the survival of Christian faith it was essential that this change took place. As a Jewish Messianic sect it soon died out, and no remnants of it are left in Rabbinic Judaism. But as a gentile faith in incarnation and resurrec-tion it came to dominate the Mediterranean world for many years.

What can we say of Jesus himself? All we can safely say is that the New Testament presents some ways in which Jesus was seen by his followers.

A Truth that Lies Ahead   209

It seems likely that his teaching was such that it allowed a diversity of interpretations (some of which were excluded from the canon of the New Testament). He lived in a Jewish context, and it seems likely that he shared some of the Messianic hopes of his contemporaries. But if he was a great spiritual teacher, such teachers often give hidden or spiritual meanings to conventional religious expectations. His teachings adopted the forms and expectations of Messianic Judaism, but carried a spiritual depth that could outlive the destruction of those specific expectations.

Any assessment of Jesus will be made in view of the presuppositions and background beliefs of the assessor. If you believe there is a God, and that the Christian path is one that relates you to God in an authentic way, you will be disposed to view Jesus as a great spiritual teacher and as one who has rightly become an object of devotion, an appropriate image of God for us. That means it will be unlikely that you will view Jesus as a charlatan or as a failed apocalyptic prophet (though Albert Schweitzer came near to believing the latter). You will look for a spiritual depth in his teaching, not for false hopes of political liberation.

Present experience of the risen Lord, and belief that such experience relates you truly to the Supreme Good, will dispose you to accept the foundational experiences of the apostolic church, experiences of the risen Christ and of the Spirit, as genuine works of God. Then, if the resurrection accounts are taken as testimonies to authentic visions of a risen Lord (whatever precise form such visions took), they can reasonably be taken as vindications of Jesus' unique role as revealer of God and origin of a new path of spiritual union with God mediated by the Spirit in the church. So, even if Jesus' teachings were clothed in the imagery of an imminent restoration of the twelve tribes in Jerusalem, and a kingdom in which Torah would be truly obeyed, their inner meaning would outlast that imagery.

The imagery, taken in a spiritual sense, represents the community of the new covenant in the Spirit, in which the divine love is to rule in the hearts of men and women. It also represents the ultimate victory of the divine love, though that may be beyond the boundaries ('at the end') of historical time.

Such an account suggests several important insights into the biblical witness to Christ. First, the facts about the historical Jesus cannot be established with theoretical certainty. Our assessment of the recorded facts will depend upon our prior commitment to faith in God and the authenticity of the Christian way, or our lack of such commitment. Jesus can only be discerned as Lord by the eye of faith. Such discernment cannot be established by neutral historical study.

Second, the New Testament accounts include restricted accounts of Jesus' mission, which need to be expanded and corrected by subsequent reflection. Accounts of Jesus' imminent return in glory, to re-unite the tribes of Israel under the twelve apostles in Jerusalem in a nation obedient to Torah, express a restricted view of what it is for Jesus to be God's Messiah. We cannot pretend such accounts do not exist in the New Testament, or that they are of no significance, as some German liberal theologians did. We cannot pretend that somehow they are still true, as some twenty-first-century fundamentalists do. They are present, and history has decisively falsified them. This leads us to see Christian faith as a continual re-thinking of what it is that God revealed in Jesus, and how we are to interpret it for our own time.

Third, it is reasonable to think that John and Paul were right in re-interpreting the gospel as a gospel of the incarnation of God in time for the sake of universal human salvation. Jesus the Messiah was not a political liberator. He was the Saviour of the world by his own supreme self-sacrifice. This was not some sort of alien Hellenistic imposition on a primitive Hebrew gospel of moral renewal. It was a spiritual re-interpretation of the gospel of God's coming kingdom to signify the rule of the divine love in the lives of men and women, a love that had been fully realised in the person of Jesus and was now to spread through the whole world. But what that love implied, and what forms it was to take in the world, had to be worked out through trial and error over a long history of repeated failures of understanding, which never completely obliterated the gospel of the grace of God, given to forgive human failures and renew human lives in the image of Christ, who is the human image of God.

The German Patristics scholar Adolf von Harnack was right in seeing a major change between the teaching of Jesus and the teaching of the church a generation or two later. However, that change can be seen already taking place within the New Testament itself, and it was not a change from a simple moral teaching to a complicated Hellenistic philosophy. Jesus' teaching called for the reform of Israel, in preparation for the imminent coming of God's kingdom with power, and he was seen as having a crucial role in that kingdom as God's chosen Messiah. The teaching of John that Jesus is the incarnate Word who brings eternal life to the whole world is a universalising and spiritualising of Jesus' teaching, made in the light of the resurrection and of new life in the Spirit within the church. The teaching of Paul that Jesus' death on the cross manifests limitless divine love for the salvation of all, and prefigures the apotheosis of the cosmos, sets Jesus' teaching in its wider cosmic context (as the cosmos was then believed to be).

The changes are real and radical – nothing could be more radical than the rejection of Torah, the transformation of the idea of Messiah into the idea of a universal Saviour, and the creation of a universal church out of a Jewish sect. But they are natural, even inevitable, developments of what was present in the person, the teaching and the life, death and resurrection of Jesus.

Knowledge of these early radical developments in Christian faith has important implications for how the faith should be seen today. First, the Bible is not a complete set of doctrines that we, generations later, just have to accept as they stand. The Bible presents a diverse set of largely undeveloped reflections on the person and work of Jesus, and those reflections sometimes include very one-sided, restricted or even mistaken appreciations of what belief in Jesus as Lord implies.

Second, Christian revelation is not divine dictation. It is a set of differing perceptions of God's self-disclosure and liberating action in the life and in the events surrounding the life of Jesus of Nazareth.

Third, the church is not the guardian of an unchanging faith, passed down from Jesus to the apostles and preserved in purity ever since. It is a community, or a set of communities, of diverse, developing perspectives, each bearing the marks, some good and some bad, of its own historical context. The task of the church today is to continue this creative process of re-thinking Christian faith in a responsible way.

THE CREATION OF THE CREEDS

Such a creative re-thinking was undertaken by the early theologians of the orthodox tradition, and was encapsulated in the declarations of the first seven ecumenical councils of the church. Christian faith was re-fashioned as a way of union with the divine through sharing in the sacramental life of the church, seen as the mediator of the divine Spirit.

This re-fashioning is a natural development from the original belief that Jesus has a unique access to the infinite reality of God, that he is a channel of divine wisdom and power and the mediator of the Spirit to a new covenant community. But it has moved some distance in thought and understanding beyond the beliefs of first-generation Christians.

There are good reasons for thinking that the orthodox formulations of doctrine are not inerrant, final or exhaustive. On the contrary, a study of how they came to be formulated suggests that doctrinal reflection has always been diverse, creative and open to influences from the best available patterns of thought and understanding in the culture of the day. Regrettably, such study also shows how intolerance and repression and a tendency to authoritarian discipline have often marked church institutions.

Knowledge of early Christian doctrine is important for Christian understanding, and should not be dismissed as simply alien to the original gospel. Yet we might learn from such knowledge both to avoid the intolerance that often marked early Christian belief and to re-think doctrines anew in our own time and culture.

In that spirit, I have tentatively suggested that we might think of incarnation as an indivisible union and interpenetration of the infinite divine subject and a particular finite human subject of knowledge and action, and that this formulation may avoid some of the problems, while retaining the central intention, of saying that in Jesus two natures are united in one person, in a culture where such terms have changed their meaning considerably. I have also suggested that a fully incarnational theism may wish to allow for change and suffering in God in a way that Greek ideas of the divine did not permit.

THE MEDIEVAL LATIN CHURCH

In medieval Christianity there was a marked development in the doctrines of the Trinity, the atonement, Heaven, Hell and Purgatory. The thirteenth-century Western Church used the best thought of the time – the thought of Aristotle – to construct a vast cosmic drama of the fall and redemption of humanity. Humans were at the centre of the created world. When they disobeyed God the whole created order was corrupted and doomed to destruction. God in Jesus united a perfect human nature to the divine Word, and in that nature God suffered and died in order to restore fellowship with God to baptised and faithful believers. The church, through its sacramental order, saves from eternal destruction those who respond in faith, and prepares them to face with relative equanimity the terrible Day of Judgment, when many will be condemned to eternal torture but the faithful will obtain life in heaven with the saints, probably after a time in purgatory.

For this view, the church assumes crucial importance as the sole means of salvation, and the Bishop of Rome was sometimes seen as the supreme teacher and ruler of the whole world, political as well as religious. Error threatened eternal life and so had to be censored and repressed. The church was the guardian of inerrant truth and possessor of the keys of heaven. Its authority was, for many popes, God-given and absolute.

Whether or not these beliefs are accepted, it is obvious that they have developed a very long way from the New Testament world. None of the tortuous and still unresolved arguments about the nature of the Trinity is even mentioned in the New Testament. Anselm's explanation of the atonement is original with him and was drawn up in opposition to most previous interpretations of the atoning sacrifice of Jesus. The doctrine of Purgatory was not explicitly formulated until the twelfth century, and notions of Heaven and Hell were constructed by collecting and systematising a number of scattered, diverse, cryptic and almost certainly metaphorical texts in the New Testament. The idea of the church as exercising temporal rule is, it must be said, a surprising development from the reported refusal of Jesus to accept any political role.

My point is not to criticise these developments, but just to stress that they are developments. They point to a continuing process of creative and original re-thinking of Christian faith throughout the first millennium of its existence. It would be ironic if such a creative process was suddenly to congeal into a body of unalterable doctrines that prevented any subsequent creative thought. And in fact the documents of the Second Vatican Council of the 1960s manifest precisely such a further re-thinking, which retracted the exaggerated papal claims of the fourteenth century, established liberty of belief and religious practice, affirmed the possibility of the salvation of non-Christians and suggested revisions to the granting of indulgences.

In doctrinal matters the medieval church constructed a magnificent and moving (though in some respects terrifying) drama of cosmic fall and redemption. But from a modern perspective it also fell into the trap of literalising and ontologising a good deal of biblical metaphor. My suggestion is that a biblically based doctrine of the Trinity will be much more like John Macquarrie's idea of a primordial Father, an expressive Son and a unitive Spirit, three forms of the divine Being dynamically related to the world, than like a complex doctrine of inner relations between persons in the eternal nature of God. A biblically based doctrine of atonement will be much more sensitive to the range of diverse metaphors used to understand how Jesus' life, death and resurrection liberate humans from sin. And a biblically based doctrine of life beyond death needs to interpret New Testament imagery of Gehenna, outer darkness, Paradise, 'Abraham's bosom', prison and fire much more clearly in the light of Jesus' central teaching of the unlimited self-giving love of God, which will go to any lengths to save those who are lost. The Christian gospel is, after all, the good news that all creation can be renewed in the love of God, not the distinctly bad news that most people will go to Hell for ever.

THE PROTESTANT REFORMATION

It hardly needs argument that the Protestant Reformation initiated a major re-thinking of Christian faith, since it explicitly rejected, and was rejected by, the Catholic Church of the time. However, there is a widespread misunderstanding that Protestant groups are somehow returning to an imagined original unity and purity of the Christian faith, which had been lost in the Middle Ages. It is never possible simply to go back in time, and classical Protestants were wholly different from the first generation of Christians. The first Christians possessed no New Testament – they were still in process of compiling it. They had no standard doctrine of the Trinity, the atonement or the incarnation, as the Reformers had. And the very first Christians were much more Jewish in their practice than the Reformers were, and much more diverse in their beliefs.

So the Reformers were doing something new. They were rejecting a view of the church as a hierarchical organisation, under the Pope, instituted by Jesus, having supreme authority in faith and morals, and being the sole means of salvation from Hell. The classical Protestant writers believed in salvation by faith. But faith was not seen as acceptance of the authority of the church. It was personal trust in Christ, and the church is primarily the fellowship of those who have such trust.

Such faith does not require or entail that all your beliefs are correct. The right of dissent and liberty of conscience are essential to the very existence of Protestantism. There is no human authority to tell you what is true. Councils of the church can err, and have erred. Even interpreters of the Bible can err, and have erred, though they may still have true faith. It follows, of course, that Protestants can err, and we may state it as a fundamental Protestant rule that anyone can be mistaken.

It follows that I may be mistaken. By a simple induction from human experience, it seems probable that I *am* mistaken about some matters. So I must renounce all pretence to inerrancy and theoretical certainty in matters of religious belief.

Faith must now clearly become, as it has perhaps always really been, in Kierkegaard's phrase, a passionate commitment made in objective uncertainty. In the Christian case, it is commitment to the person of Christ as disclosing the highest form of goodness we know, and as mediating the power to transform lives to share to some degree in that goodness. It is saving faith, a personal commitment of trust that liberates from sin and freely gives a share in divine love.

For many Protestants, this idea of faith was tied to the idea that the Bible alone provides all that is necessary for saving belief. This sometimes led to dogmatic systems as inflexible as that of the Catholic Church from which Protestants sought release. For the Bible was sometimes thought to provide just one set of doctrines that were clear and consistent. Since the Bible was seen as the means by which alone Christ was known, interpretations of the Bible were given just the sort of inerrancy that Protestants should, if they were consistent, have denied to all human beliefs.

'Biblical Protestantism', in this sense, is a contradiction in terms. It is refuted by the existence of a vast number of divergent Protestant churches, which all disagree on what the Bible says. This shows that the Bible is interpreted in many different ways and that it is often interpreted with the aid of human beliefs that are not strictly in the Bible – like 'orthodox' belief in the Trinity and incarnation.

Any genuine biblical Protestantism would have to admit freedom of personal interpretation of the Bible and so would have to tolerate diversity of interpretation and understanding. It would have to deny to any human being the magisterial authority to issue the 'correct' interpretation of the Bible. In this sense Protestantism is essentially liberal. It permits and encourages dissent, freedom of conscience, and toleration of diversity. It insists on a fraternity and fellowship that includes those who disagree. It affirms that the one thing that matters is personal commitment to the person of Christ. All else is open to discussion and debate. This does not seem much like the Protestantism we commonly see. Yet it is what the Protestant Reformation essentially is and implies.

GERMAN LIBERAL CHRISTIANITY

The Enlightenment is the unexpected child of the Protestant Reformation. It carries the principle of informed critical enquiry to its conclusion, so that no religious authority, not even the Bible, is exempt from such enquiry. That does not mean that no authority can remain. But it does mean that all alleged authorities are called to give an account of themselves, to say why they should be accepted and what the limits of their authority are.

The model for many Enlightenment thinkers is the natural sciences, where the proper authorities are those who have mastered the practices of their science and who can appeal to repeatable observation and experiment in support of their claims.

In disciplines like history such an appeal is not obtainable. Authoritative historians must, however, have mastered the accepted techniques of critical research, and their appeal is to documentary evidence – though it is accepted that there is much room for diversity of interpretation in this field.

This is even more apparent in the social sciences, for example in disciplines like economics. Only a few people are competent economists, but even they often disagree very strongly, for they are concerned with the assessment and prediction of human behaviour, and there are very different views about that.

In philosophy matters are even worse (or better, depending on your point of view). Disagreement is virtually built into the discipline, since there is no way of neutrally deciding questions like what reality is ultimately like, or what moral principles we ought to adopt. There is still an area of knowledge and expertise, but there is no way of settling disputed questions that all accept.

When it comes to religious faith the requisite area of expertise is, broadly speaking, the ability to live and think in a way that shows especially intense or close knowledge of the ultimate religious object (for theists this is God). An appeal is ultimately made to experience in this area too, but if this experience is alleged to be experience of God, it will be especially difficult to describe, and it will by its nature be highly disputable whether it is genuine (those who think there is no God are bound to deny it).

In Christianity, Jesus is claimed to be one whose sinless life, supreme wisdom, and healing power showed him to have uniquely intimate knowledge of and relationship with God. The apostles have authority as first-hand witnesses to Jesus' life, death and resurrection. The New Testament has authority as a set of diverse meditations and reflections upon the apostolic witness. The tradition of the churches has authority as recording very diverse but continuing experiences of God through the risen Christ, and constantly re-interpreting those experiences in the light of their own culture and history. Such authority is greater than that of personal experience alone, because it covers a greater range of human cognition, it has been subject to continued theological criticism and intellectual enquiry and it includes the experiences of those much more closely united to God than most of us are.

The reason Christians should accept these authorities is that transforming apprehension of a supreme transcendent reality and value is the basis of religious faith. Such apprehension is fairly rare, it differs greatly in degree, and its specific character is the result of a long cumulative tradition of reflection and evaluation from which we have much to learn. For Christians, the prophets, sages and teachers of many faiths can be knowers of God (known under many names and forms) and mediators of such knowledge to others. But Jesus is believed to be the fullest possible instance of apprehension of God by humans, since he is the embodiment of God in a human person. Thus he becomes the definitive revelation of God, and for Christians the ultimate religious authority.

Yet Jesus is only known to us through the biblical witness, the traditions of the churches, and our own experience of God through Christ in our own faith community. In that sense, our grasp of divine revelation is indirect and very personal and partial. One of the most terrible mistakes in religion is to confuse our limited understanding of revelation with the objective revelation itself. Informed critical enquiry is necessary to guard against making that mistake. It will often disclose to us our own misunderstandings. Thereby it will disclose that honest error, whether on our part or that of others, is not culpable. But of course we should seek to avoid it.

Another mistake that has often been made in Christian history is to think that the authority of revelation has no limits. So whatever we read in a 'revealed' text like the Bible is bound to be true, whether it is about natural science or human history. We can escape this tendency if we keep a firm grip on the fact that religious authority is about experience and knowledge of God. It does not extend to ancient history or the origin or end of the universe. All historical statements in the Bible are subject to historical criticism. I have argued that enough is left to be the basis of a firm commitment to Jesus as the incarnation of God. But we must take Troeltsch's criteria of historical method – the principles of criticism, analogy and correlation – seriously, though I have also argued that we should not receive them uncritically. They will still often lead to a rather cautious and sometimes frankly agnostic account of events related in the Bible. They will lead us to see the Gospels as theological reflections on the life of Jesus, rather than as straightforward biographies. And they will lead us to accept quite a great diversity of interpretation of the biblical texts, and to stop attributing biblical quotations directly to Jesus, as used to be done in pre-critical days.

Where natural science and cosmology are concerned, the whole medieval narrative of the fall and redemption of the cosmos will have to be radically recast. Modern science provides the possibility of a new cosmic drama that brings out many elements of Christian faith in a new and exciting way. Christ can be envisaged, as John's prologue envisaged Christ, as the eternal Wisdom of God, the archetype of creation. The Holy Spirit is the dynamic power that drives the evolution of the cosmos towards its final goal of conscious union with the Supreme Good that is its ultimate source.

Humans are just a small part of a vast cosmos, which may generate millions of forms of intelligent life. Human estrangement from God is the result of generations of past decisions taken by our human ancestors which strengthened innate tendencies to lust and aggression at the expense of more altruistic tendencies towards care and co-operation. In this estranged world the cosmic archetype becomes incarnate, shaping a human mind and body to be an image and mediator of God's own action to liberate humans from sin and re-unite them to the divine life. The incarnation and the passion of Christ show that God enters into the sufferings of creation.

The resurrection shows that God is able to transform those sufferings and take human lives into the life of God. The experience of the Spirit at Pentecost shows that God continues to work within human lives to make them one with the divine.

The churches have the role of mediating the Spirit of Christ in the world, albeit in a flawed and imperfect way. The presence and work of the Spirit is not confined to the churches. Yet it is the churches' vocation to make the true character of the Spirit known, to make the divine love present in an estranged world and to incorporate all who will into the *koinonia*, the fellowship of the divine Spirit.

When this cosmos ends, all finite persons, whether human or not, will have had the opportunity in some way to begin to participate in the divine life. Then, almost certainly in another form of existence, beyond this cosmos, there will be a 'new creation', when all living things will find their completion in God.

This is the cosmic drama that modern cosmology and Christian faith can provide if they are taken together. It is a vision that the nineteenth-century German liberal theologians failed to provide, insofar as they saw Jesus just as a moral teacher and prophet of a just and equitable society in a foreseeable human future, and jettisoned the traditional doctrines of incarnation, Trinity and atonement.

The German 'liberals' are sometimes rather unfairly dismissed as having capitulated to the cultural norms of their own society, or as having collapsed doctrine into a sort of inner subjectivity and romantic emotionalism that had no defence against the horrors of National Socialism.

But theologians like Harnack had a strong belief in God, in the moral and providential order of the universe, and in a distinctive and challenging Christian morality. They saw God as the creator who made an absolute moral demand for universal love. They saw the Spirit as an empowering force making for higher righteousness. And they saw Jesus as foreshadowing the hope for the coming of the kingdom, a society in which evil would be eliminated and love would reign supreme.

Even Schleiermacher, who denied that religious faith was in itself, and by its essential nature, a form of moral commitment, was clear that the basic religious apprehension of 'the Infinite' properly and immediately gave rise to general metaphysical beliefs about the nature of the created universe (explicitly set out in his *Christian Faith*), and to distinctive forms of moral commitment.

The problem is that, while Christian faith does require a metaphysical foundation, theoretical speculation, especially in a culture that is sceptical of the arguments of traditional natural theology, seems an insecure basis for faith. It is natural, then, to see religious faith as more like moral commitment, but a commitment made in response to experience of transcendent value – a commitment that I have called 'transcendental personalism'. The German liberals were right in making this clear. They were wrong in seeming to reject the whole tradition of Christian doctrinal development and in failing to see that the incarnation and atoning death of Jesus are central to Christian faith.

Though they did not recognise the fact, their expositions of Christian faith could, with small verbal amendments, easily be utilised for an exposition of Judaism or Islam. These faiths too believe in God, providence, the demand for a just society, the infinite value of the human soul, and the importance of experience of God. That the 'liberal' account could hold of many religions might, of course, be considered a virtue, but it throws doubt on the claim that Protestant Christianity alone is the 'perfect' religion.

Christian faith does make a distinctive claim. It is that in Jesus the human and the divine were uniquely united. God entered into time and suffering, in order that through the Holy Spirit all humanity, and perhaps all creation, can be united to the Father 'in Christ'. This claim is ultimately founded on a liberating apprehension of the Supreme Good in the person of Jesus. But it carries major implications about the nature of the Good and its relation to the cosmos. The history of Christian doctrine is the history of how this has been worked out over many centuries, in many diverse contexts and through many changes of understanding.

GLOBAL CHRISTIANITY

The sixth re-thinking of Christian faith that I have considered is the twentieth-century globalisation of outlook that has transformed the earth into an interconnected social and economic totality for the first time. In the modern age there is no one philosophical system that could provide a coherent basis for (or against) faith. But as science has provided a vast perspective of cosmic evolution, and of the emergence of new properties through time, so theology has paid more attention to the importance of time and history and the emergence of novelty. Pre-modern views tended to look to the past as an authoritative and unchanging source of rational belief. The world was once perfect and has fallen away from God. Modern evolutionary views see the past as important but to be improved on and set in the perspective of a process of historical development.

Hegelian thought sees history as a progressive disclosure of the nature of the divine, and Christians have taken from this a re-thinking of God as dynamically and temporally related to history through incarnation and the activity of the Spirit, moving towards a future fulfilment, even though such fulfilment perhaps lies beyond historical time.

Process thought sees radical novelty and creativity in the world, and many Christian theologians have stressed the value of human novelty and creativity, and the way in which God may seek to persuade the world by love, share in its joys and sufferings and include the world in the divine Being in a transfigured form. Such a view strongly echoes much Patristic thought about the *kenosis* of God in creation, and the *theosis* of the world through the incarnation and in the unitive activity of the Spirit. But it speaks much more unequivocally about the entrance of God into time and the inclusion of the temporal in God. It stresses much more radically the freedom and creativity of creatures, and the extent to which they influence the future together with (or in opposition to) God.

Existentialists portrayed the human situation as one of despair and anguish, and sought ways of living authentically. Some Christians have used this portrayal to emphasise the heart of the gospel as the promise of personal liberation from spiritual death and participation in the Good.

Greater awareness and understanding of other worldviews and religious traditions led to a recognition of the plurality of human beliefs, the inappropriateness of building up monolithic stereotypes either of your own or of any one else's religion, and the importance of maintaining a distinctive Christian vision that would not exclude or repress others but would seek to make a positive contribution to the diversity-in-unity of global culture.

The conception of Christianity as a fluid and changing set of traditions, entering into a wider global kaleidoscope of beliefs, has been unsettling to many. So it is a marked feature of Christian faith in the modern world that many groups attempt to proclaim their form of Christianity as the 'one true faith', to exclude all who will not accept their view of it, and to erect clear barriers between themselves and all others.

If the central argument of this book is correct, such views can only flourish in ignorance of the history of Christian thought. But I have argued that it is possible to have a Christian faith that is both liberal and orthodox, in a fairly well-defined sense. It can be liberal in accepting the legitimacy of informed critical enquiry, in accepting freedom of religious belief and practice, in accepting a diversity of interpretations of Christian doctrine and in accepting that scientific and historical matters have their own proper canons of scholarly investigation. It will not, however, be liberal in the sense that it denies all the credal formulae of the undivided church, that it encourages people to follow whatever desires they wish or that it denies any possibility of divine action in history. It can be orthodox in accepting the legitimacy of the sort of conceptual developments of doctrine that the ecumenical councils of the church propagated, in accepting the main formulations of those councils as helpful amplifications of what is involved in accepting Jesus as Messiah, and in accepting that the Christian church should aim to be truly Catholic (i.e. universal), to be a fellowship, however precisely it is organised, that is inclusive of all who are engaged in a search for the truth of God as it is disclosed in and through Christ.

In the twentieth century, the idea of the church has changed, at least for many theologians, from the idea of an exclusive society of the saved to the idea of a fellowship called to serve the world, to proclaim and partially effect liberation from evil, both personally and socially. Personal liberation is always possible, by the forgiveness of Christ. But the call for social liberation, making space for the creative freedom of all persons in community without exception, so far as possible, is also a vocation of the church as the body of Christ and vanguard of the kingdom of God.

THE MYSTERY OF CHRIST

I have looked at some very different historical forms of Christianity. It is hard not to become aware that they are all limited by cultural bias and historical context. A clear grasp of the many changing forms of Christianity leads to awareness that forms of faith and belief have a historical placing, and that they continually change, as history continues to re-order human thought and understanding, in religion as in all areas of human knowledge and practice.

The churches will naturally wish to teach beliefs that provide an adequate human understanding of God. But if the members of the churches share in the general human condition of very limited knowledge and understanding, the churches will be best served by often making largely provisional suggestions about more adequate understandings of the mystery of God, a mystery that always remains beyond full human understanding. To say that many church pronouncements are provisional is not to say that one day they will be superseded. It is to say that we place no restrictions on the possibility of fuller future understanding. Seeing how many developments and re-formulations of faith have taken place in past history, it becomes reasonable to hope this process of enlarged understanding will continue, as human knowledge continues to grow and we slowly learn from some of our past mistakes. Christianity has been from its very first generation a revolutionary faith, re-thinking itself in many historical and cultural forms. Founded on a liberating experience of God as disclosed in the person of Jesus Christ, it has at its best been concerned to promote personal and social liberation from all that prevents human flourishing. It has been pluralist and creatively diverse in its interpretation of its own traditions and its openness to and engagement with non-Christian views and new knowledge of the world, welcoming of informed critical enquiry and yet fundamentally committed to an understanding of the world in the light of the existence of a God of self-giving, reconciling, unitive love.

This may seem an unduly rosy and optimistic view of Christian faith in a world where that faith is still divided into many quarrelsome and competing parts and where many of those parts sometimes seem still to be primarily concerned with making intolerant and exclusive (and conflicting) claims to 'unchanging' revealed truths. What I have sought to establish, however, is that an attentive and unbiased reading of the Bible and of the history of Christian thought will show Christianity to be essentially and from the very first generation diverse and constantly changing in response to new knowledge and understandings of the world. Moreover, a direction or tendency can be discerned in its historical developments, a tendency towards seeing the church as witness to and imperfect mediator of the self-giving and inclusive love of God that was manifested in Jesus. It is the bearer of a moral challenge and demand to care for the earth and for the poor and to bring all creation to its proper fulfilment by sharing in the life of God. And it is the keeper of the divine promise, founded on the resurrection of Jesus, that all evil will be overcome and all good will be held for ever in the mind and being of God. If these are indeed the truly fundamental Christian truths, the struggles, imperfections and abuses of Christian faith that sometimes dominate our attention will not prevail against the patient working of the Holy Spirit who 'will guide you into all the truth' (John 16:13). That guidance may be less evident or identifiable, and take much longer, than Christians may at first have thought. But it is a firm Christian hope, not a facile liberal optimism, that looks to a future in which truth and goodness will prevail.

In the world of the twenty-first century and beyond, this is a witness to the ultimate nature of reality and the ultimate destiny of human life which will become more, not less, important. For it is not a witness that claims possession of absolute truth and of the only way to Paradise. It is a witness to a truth that still lies ahead and partly veiled in mystery, and of a way to participate in the mystery of Christ now, because it has disclosed itself to us, however dimly and ambiguously, in and through the person of Jesus. What we shall see and know, when Christ is disclosed to us in the fulness of his being, is beyond all present imagining. But it will be something not less than we now partly discern and long to see more fully. It will be something infinitely more. 'For now we see in a mirror, dimly, but then we shall see face to face' (1 Cor. 13:12).

Notes

1. Albert Schweitzer, *The Quest of the Historical Jesus* (London, A. & C. Black, 1954 [1906]). An excellent modern treatment is: Gerd Theissen and Annette Merz, *The Historical Jesus*, trans. John Bowden (London, SCM, 1998). Also of interest: J.D. Crossan, *The Historical Jesus* (Edinburgh, T. & T. Clark, 1991); Gezer Vermes, *Jesus the Jew* (London, Collins, 1973). And a good general introduction: Martin Forward, *Jesus, a Short Biography* (Oxford, Oneworld, 1998).
2. C.H. Dodd, *The Parables of the Kingdom* (London, Collins, 1961).
3. Plato, *Timaeus*, trans. Desmond Lee (Harmondsworth, England, Penguin, 1965), main section 1, p. 42.
4. Nietszche, *The Anti-Christ*, trans. R. Hollingdale (Harmondsworth, England, Penguin, 1969), section 24.
5. Wolfhart Pannenberg, *Systematic Theology* (Edinburgh, T. & T. Clark, from 1991); Jurgen Moltmann, *The Trinity and the Kingdom of God* (London, SCM, 1981); David Brown, *The Divine Trinity* (London, Duckworth, 1985); Richard Swinburne, *The Christian God*, (Oxford, Clarendon Press, 1994), ch. 8; John Zizioulas, *Being as Communion* (London, Darton, Longman, Todd, 1985); St Augustine, *On the Trinity*, trans. E. Hill (New York, New City Press, 1991); Richard of St Victor, *De Trinitate*, ed. J. Ribaillier (Paris, Librairie Philosophique J. Vrin, 1958), book 2, ch. 14; Karl Barth, *Church Dogmatics* trans. G.T. Thomson (Edinburgh, T. & T. Clark, 1936), 1/1, ch. 2, part 1; Karl Rahner, *The Trinity*, trans. J. Doncel (New York, Herder & Herder, 1970); John Macquarrie, *Principles of Christian Theology* (London, SCM, 1966), ch. 9.
6. St Augustine, *On the Trinity*, book 13, ch. 4, p. 16.
7. For Gregory's view, see his *Great Catechism*, ch. 26.
8. For Aquinas's view, see Brian Davies, *The Thought of Thomas Aquinas* (Oxford, Clarendon Press, 1992), ch. 16, section 2.
9. For a sympathetic interpretation of Peter Abelard, see Paul Fiddes, *Past Event and Present Salvation* (London, Darton, Longman, Todd, 1989).
10. John Calvin, *Institutes of the Christian Religion*, trans. Henry Beveridge (Grand Rapids, Eerdmans, 1989), book 4, ch. 1, para. 9.
11. Luther's collected works, Weimar, 1883–, 51, p. 11.
12. trans. Lewis White Beck, in 'Kant on History', Bobbs-Merrill, 1963.
13. Immanuel Kant, *Groundwork to the Metaphysics of Ethics* [1785].

14. Immanuel Kant, *Critique of Practical Reason* [1788], part 1, book 2, ch. 2, sections 4–6.
15. John Stuart Mill, *On Liberty* [1859], ch. 2.
16. Joseph Butler, *Analogy of Religion*, preface.
17. Rudolf Bultmann, *Jesus Christ and Mythology* (London, SCM, 1958); Don Cupitt, *Taking Leave of God* (London, SCM, 1980).
18. David Friedrich Strauss, *Life of Jesus*, trans. George Eliot (London, 1973 [1835]).
19. On Natural Law, see Thomas Aquinas, *Summa Theologiae*, 1a2ae, question 94.
20. Ernst Troeltsch, *Historical and Dogmatic Method in Theology* (Tübingen, Germany, Gesammelte Schriften, 1913 [1898]).
21. These judgments can be found in lecture 13 of 'What Is Christianity?' a series of lectures given in 1900.
22. Ernst Troeltsch, *The Absoluteness of Christianity* (London, SCM, 1972).
23. For a good introduction to Hegel, see Stephen Houlgate, *An Introduction to Hegel* (Oxford, Blackwell, 2004).
24. See Karl Marx, *Selected Writings in Sociology and Social Philosophy*, ed. T.B. Bottomore and M. Rubel (Harmondsworth, England, Penguin, 1963).
25. David Hume, *A Treatise on Human Nature*, book 2, part 3, section 3.
26. Immanuel Kant, *The Metaphysic of Morals*, part 2 ('The Doctrine of Virtue'), esp. part 1, book 2; John Stuart Mill, *Utilitarianism* [1861], esp. ch. 2.
27. A good survey of twentieth-century theology is: David Ford and Rachel Muers (eds), *The Modern Theologians* (Oxford, Blackwell, 2005).
28. A good modern Thomist account is: Brian Davies, *The Thought of Thomas Aquinas* (Oxford, Clarendon Press, 1992).
29. Paul Tillich, *Systematic Theology*, esp. vol. 1 (London, Nisbet, 1968); John Macquarrie, *Principles of Christian Theology*, ch. 9; Karl Barth, *Church Dogmatics*, ed. G.W. Bromiley and T.F. Torrance (Edinburgh, T. & T. Clark, 1936), ii/i; Wolfhart Pannenberg (ed.), *Revelation as History* (New York, 1968).
30. A.N. Whitehead, *Process and Reality*, ed. D.R. Griffin and Donald Sherburne (New York, Macmillan, 1979), part 5, ch. 2.
31. Ian Barbour, *Religion and Science* (London, SCM, 1998); Arthur Peacocke, *Paths from Science towards God* (Oxford, Oneworld, 2001); Tillich, *Systematic Theology*, ch. 42.
32. Bultmann, *Jesus Christ and Mythology*.
33. John Hick, *An Interpretation of Religion* (London, Macmillan, 1989), ch. 14.
34. George Lindbeck, *The Nature of Doctrine* (London, Westminster/John Knox Press, 1984).

Index of Names

Abelard, Peter 90
Anselm 89–90, 95, 106, 213
Aquinas, Thomas 90, 106, 176–177
Aristotle 116
Athanasius 65
Augustine 75, 82, 106

Bach, J. S. 104
Barbour, Ian 179
Barth, Karl 75, 177, 179, 194–196
Basil of Caesarea 74
Bellarmine, Cardinal 92
Benedict XVI 84
Bentham, Jeremy 175
Blake, William 161
Boniface VIII 72
Brown, David 74
Bultmann, Rudolf 126, 177, 182
Buri, Fritz 126
Butler, Bishop 123, 138

Calvin, John 103, 106, 107, 108,
Cobb, John 178
Crossan, John Dominic 3
Cupitt, Don 126, 127

Dante 84
Darwin, Charles 117
Dodd, C. H. 15

Galileo 116
Gensfleisch, Johann 101
Gibbon, Edward 118
Gregory of Nazianzus 64
Gregory of Nyssa 89, 92, 95
Gregory Palamas 78
Gregory XVI 97, 123
Gutierrez, Gustavo 204

Harnack, Adolf von 66, 134–137, 143, 145,
    146, 147, 150, 198, 199, 201, 210, 219
Hartshorne, Charles 178
Hegel, G. W. F. 151–160, 177, 178
Hick, John 185
Hume, David 138, 171

Innocent III 73
Irenaeus 55

Justin Martyr 54

Kant, Immanuel 114, 115, 119, 121, 135,
    137, 139, 140, 150, 172–174
Kasermann, Ernst 3
Kierkegaard, Soren 215
Kung, Hans 185

LeGoff, Jacques 91
Leibniz 178
Lessing, Gotthold 133
Lindbeck, George 190, 193, 194
Luther, Martin 103, 104, 106, 107, 108, 111

MacIntyre, Alisdair 189
Macquarrie, John 75, 78, 177, 214
Marx, Karl 156, 203, 200
Mill, John Stuart 118, 172
Moltmann, Jurgen 74, 179, 204, 205

Nestorius 65
Newton, Isaac 116
Nietzsche, Friedrich 42, 138, 180

Pannenberg, Wolfhart 74, 177, 185
Peacocke, Arthur 179
Philo 21
Pius IX 98, 115

Plato 21, 98, 162
Pusey, Canon 118

Rahner, Karl 75, 80, 97, 185
Ratzinger, Cardinal 204
Reimarus, Hermann 133–134
Richard of St. Victor 75, 76
Ritschl, Albrecht 136, 143, 145, 147, 150

Sartre, Jean-Paul 181
Schleiermacher, Friedrich 160–168, 185,
    191, 219
Schweitzer, Albert 3, 26, 144, 209
Strauss, David Friedrich 134

Swinburne, Richard 74, 75

Tertullian 57, 58, 63
Tillich, Paul 95, 177, 179, 181–183
Troeltsch, Ernst 142, 143, 145, 147, 150,
    151, 218

Vermes, Gezer 3
Vincent of Lerins 96

Weiss, Johannes 3
Whitehead, A. N. 178, 179

Zizioulas, John 74

Subject Index

Absolute Dependence 162–163
Apostolic succession (and Paul) 34, 35
Atonement, theories of 89–91
    as participation 95
Authority and revelation 121–123, 216–218
Autonomy of ethics 134–140
Autonomy, principle of 173

Barth and liberal theology 194–196
Bible as the source of doctrine 101–102,
    105, 106, 112
Bible, inspiration of 50–53, 109–111, 120,
    211
Biblical worldview 14, 193, 194
Buddhism 183, 184

Central truths of Christianity 53, 131
Chalcedon, Council of 56, 57, 63, 64
Chinese religions 184
Christ as cosmic archetype 129–130
Christian revelation as personal and
    pluralist 29–32
Constantinople, Third Council of 61
Council of Jerusalem 35, 36
Creation 130
Critical belief and certainty 120, 121–124,
    145, 209–210, 218
Critical history, principles of 118–121, 125,
    131–134, 142–145
Criticism, Principle of 114–116
Cultural Linguistic theory 190–193

Developing world, Christianity in the
    196–197
Development of doctrine 48, 49, 94–97
Dialectic of history 151–153
Diversity in doctrine 53–55, 66–69,
    104–107, 113, 123–124, 212, 220

Eastern Orthodox Churches 71–72
Ecumenical Councils 64–66
Empty tomb, Gospel accounts compared
    4–6
Enlightenment Project 189, 191
Enlightenment, the 188–190, 203, 216
Ethical rules of the Bible 137–140
Ethical teaching of Jesus 136
Evolution and faith 117, 128, 131, 140
Existentialist theology 180–182
Experience as the basis of faith 160–168,
    192
Experiences of Transcendence 166
Experiential-expressivism 190–192

Faith and correct belief 107–109
Faith and works 108
Faith as personal encounter 102–104, 164,
    167–168, 215
'Feeling' in Schleiermacher 162
Filioque ('and the Son') 73–75
Freedom and the goal of history 157–159
Freedom of belief 97–100, 105–106, 113,
    125, 215

Globalisation 170
Gnosticism 55
God and time (in Hegel) 155–156
God as Supreme Good 131
God, classical concept of 176–177
God, knowledge of 125–128
God, post-Hegelian concept of 177–180,
    212, 221
God, Process concept of 178–179, 221
Gospels, differing perspectives of 19,
    29–31, 207
Grace, universality of 42–46, 84, 85
Gutenberg Bible 101

Hegel, theological reactions to 154–155
Hell 41, 43, 84–89, 213
Heteronomy in ethics 139
Hinduism 184
Humanism 174–175
Humanity of Jesus 56–57, 60–61

Immutability of God 69–70
Imperialism and Christianity 170
Incarnation 60–63, 129, 130, 212
Indifferentism 122, 124
Individulism and liberalism 198–201
Indulgences 93
Inerrancy, Biblical 51, 109–111, 138, 139
Intolerance, causes of 66–69, 212
Islam 183

Jesus as two natures in one person 57–59
Jesus, Messianic status of 2, 3, 6, 7, 14
Jesus, minimal requirements for faith in 4,
      25–27, 51–52, 110, 132, 133
Jesus, worship of 59
John's Gospel and incarnational theology
      18–24, 27–29, 208
Judaism 183
Judgment, divine 39, 40, 43, 86, 87

Kingdom of God as a social ideal 201–202,
      204–205, 211, 219, 222
Kingdom of God, New Testament revision
      of 9–11
Kingdom of God, Gospel conceptions of 8,
      9, 208
Kingdom of God, spiritual interpretation of
      11–14, 15–17, 208–211

Liberal Christian faith 115, 121, 124–126,
      133–135, 161, 172, 174–176, 186,
      195–196, 198–201, 222
Liberal theology
   (first strand: freedom of belief) 115
   (second strand: informed critical
      enquiry) 125
   (third strand: the 'German school') 133
   (fourth strand: the autonomy of ethics)
      135
   (fifth strand: experience as the ground of
      faith) 161
   (sixth strand: individualism) 198

Liberalism and Protestantism 111–113,
      123, 216
Liberalism, crisis of 171–173, 188
Liberalism, German 144–151, 161,
      219–220
Liberation theology 197–205
Liberation theology, instruction on 204
Logos 20, 21, 55

Marxism 199, 200, 203, 205
Merit 91
Metaphysics 176
Miracles 117, 119, 132, 143, 144
Mirari Vos 97, 122
Moral decision-making 36, 37
Mythology 182

Natural Law in ethics 140–142
Natural Science and religion 116–118, 125,
      128–131, 218–219
Nicene Creed 64

Omnipotence of Jesus 57–58
Omniscience of Jesus 56–58
Original sin 47, 82–84
Orthodoxy 54, 64, 212, 222

Panentheism 179
Papal authority, growth of 72–73
Parables of Jesus 84, 87, 88
Parousia ('second coming') of Jesus 38, 39,
      46, 53, 130–131
Paul's re-thinking of the Gospel 33, 34
Pentecostalism 197
Platonism in Christianity 69–70
Pluralism (diversity of belief) 104–107,
      113, 123–124, 132, 133, 206–208,
      215
Pluralistic hypothesis 185
Post-modernism 187–194
Preferential option for the poor 202, 204
Propositional views of doctrine 190, 191
Protestant Rule, the 106, 215
Protestantism and the church 102–104,
      108, 214
Purgatory 88, 91–94, 213

Quest for the historical Jesus 3, 24–27, 30,
      51–52, 208–209

Realised eschatology 15
Reason (in Hegel) 159–160
Redemption (in Schleiermacher) 163–165
Religion as 'myth' 126–127
Religion, a global view 182–186, 221
Resurrection bodies 130, 144
Retributive punishment 40–42, 85, 86
Revelation in Islam 31
Romans, Paul's letter to the 43, 44

Sacrifice of the Mass 91, 94
Salvation by faith 103, 215
Secularism 188, 189
Syllabus of Errors 98, 115

Tentativeness in theology 80–81,
    222–224

the Mass and the Reformers 103–104
Theosis – the unity of all things in Christ
    47–49
Torah, renunciation of 36–38
Transcendental Personalism 172–176
Trent, Council of 112
Trinity as God-in-relation-to-us 75–80
Trinity, social interpretations of 74–75
Trinity, the 21, 24, 57
Trinity, in Hegel 153

Unam Sanctam 2, 72

Varieties of Christianity 1, 2
Vatican II 99, 124, 213

World Council of Churches 183